Mass Communication Research Methods

Mass Communication Research Methods

Anders Hansen
Simon Cottle
Ralph Negrine
Chris Newbold

First published 1998 by
MACMILLAN PRESS LTD
Houndmills, Basingstoke, Hampshire RG21 6XS
and London
Companies and representatives
throughout the world

ISBN 0–333–61709–6 hardcover
ISBN 0–333–61710–X paperback

A catalogue record for this book is available from the British Library.

10 9 8 7 6 5 4 3 2 1
07 06 05 04 03 02 01 00 99 98

Copy-edited and typeset by Povey–Edmondson
Tavistock and Rochdale, England

Printed in Hong Kong

Contents

List of Figures and Tables

Figures

Tables

Acknowledgements

Our grateful thanks are due to Catherine Gray, Senior Editor at Macmillan, for her patience and guidance throughout the process of writing this book.

We would also like to express our grateful thanks to Rashid Siddiqui, Information Librarian, Leicester University Library for his valuable help with information sources listed in the Appendix of this book, and to Mark Maynard, Senior Computer Officer, University of Leicester, for his helpful comments on our description of Internet sources in the Appendix. Needless to say, any errors are entirely our responsibility.

We wish to thank Aspen Institute for permission to use extracts from R. Homet, *Politics, Cultures and Communications* in Chapter 4. We are grateful to Sage Publications for permission to use material from K. Siune and W. Treutschler (eds), *Dynamics of media politics*, and J. Blumler, J. McLeod and K. Rosengren (eds), *Comparatively speaking: communication and culture across space and time*, in Chapter 4 and for permission to reproduce Figure 4.1 from W. Dutton and T. Vedel, 'The dynamics of cable television in the US, Britain and France' in Blumler *et al.*

Grateful thanks are due to the following for kind permission to use their copyright material: Crispen Rodwell, Pacemaker and *Daily Mirror* for Image 8.1; *The Guardian* for Images 8.2 and 8.5; *Daily Mirror* for Image 8.3.

We are grateful to SPSS for permission to use SPSS Screen Images © SPSS Inc. in Figures 11.1 to 11.15. SPSS is a registered trademark. Neither Chapter 11 or any other part of this book is sponsored or approved by SPSS, and any errors are in no way the responsibility of SPSS.

A. H.
S. C.
R. N.
C. N.

1

Mass Communication Research Methods: Introduction

1.1 Introduction

The aim of this book is to provide an introduction to key research methods and approaches in the study of media and mass communication processes. We have selected methods which we believe to be the most coherent, appropriate and productive within an interdisciplinary, but nevertheless principally sociological, approach to the broad field of media and communication research.

The emphasis throughout this book is on the practical application, the 'how to', of methods and techniques of research. In general, each chapter seeks first to locate the individual method in its theoretical and historical contexts; this is then followed by a detailed discussion of its application and uses. This would consist, where appropriate, of examples drawn from both past and contemporary mass communications research, step-by-step guides, and examples of research instruments.

Although each chapter can be read separately and each provides a guide to a different research method, all chapters seek to emphasise two general and common points. The first is that good research usually benefits from the use of a combination of methods. In other words, researchers should not only consider which is the most appropriate method for the study of their chosen topic or problem but also what *combination* of research methods will produce a better and deeper understanding of it: survey research can often usefully be combined with, and enhanced by, focus group research; content analysis with audience surveys or group discussions; participant observation with content analysis; and so on. The aim should always be to choose those methods, or combinations of methods, which can light up the most angles and dimensions of what are invariably multidimensional and complex processes and phenomena.

The second point is a simple one, but it is one that is often overlooked. All research activities involve a number of key steps, which need careful consideration. Although often sequential, these are not rigid steps and there is always some flexibility depending on the nature of the problem to be researched. Nevertheless, they are steps which guide the researcher through the stages of research and alert him or her to the important elements of research work. In brief, and in general terms, the steps can be listed as follows:

- deciding on the area of research and defining the research problem, possibly in the form of questions or statements about relationships (hypotheses);
- reviewing the literature on the research topic in question;
- deciding on the most appropriate research method, or combination of methods, for the gathering of data;
- refining and reviewing the research problem;
- identification and selection (sampling) of research material or subjects, and development of research instruments, protocols, and parameters;
- piloting and 'fine-tuning' of instruments, protocols, approaches;
- collecting and analysing the data. Each method emphasises different procedures which may be specific to it. None the less, the data collected should be analysed in such a way as to reflect back on the initial research questions so as to provide a better understanding of the topic under investigation;
- writing up the research report. As indicated in several chapters, this is by no means an easy task. Consequently, enough time should be given over to this activity since it is at this point that researchers begin to pull together the many strands which make up a piece of work.

These steps are a general guide only but it is helpful to bear them in mind when designing, planning, costing and timetabling a research study.

1.2 The Structure of this Book

Following the Introductory section (Chapters 1 and 2), the core part of this book addresses research methods for each of the three main domains of communication processes: the domain of media organisations and media production; media content; and the domain of media consumption and media audiences. The final section (Chapter 11 and the Appendix) discusses data analysis and sources and resources for communication research.

In Chapter 2, 'Mass Communication Research: Asking The Right Questions', Professor James Halloran explores the important role of methods (no matter how conceived) in social scientific/mass communication research. He argues that methods are but means to an end and, important though they are, they are not an end in themselves, nor should they be used to define the end or the nature of the problem to be investigated. Yet they have often been so used, and this is one of the reasons why the research literature is replete with allegedly definitive quantitative statements about the trivial, the inconsequential and the plainly invalid.

Professor Halloran also considers the use of different methods to deal with different problems and issues, together with the distinction between 'hard' and 'soft' data, all within the framework of the debate on the nature of evidence and 'scientific nature' of social science. The claim that the quality and applicability of research results depends primarily on the nature of the questions asked in the first place is examined against this background, and in the light of what can be learned from theory (such as it is), research, and social/political concerns. The whole question of the compatibility between theoretical refinement, methodological rigour, and substantive concerns is discussed, as also is the autonomy and independence of the research exercise.

The method of participant observation, explored in Chapter 3 'Participant Observation: Researching News Production', has proved to be an invaluable tool for the investigation of media practices and media professionals working in the media production domain. Researchers deploying this method have provided rare insights into the bureaucratic and organisational arrangements of media production, including the routines of news processing, dependency upon institutional sources, the influence of corporate hierarchies and working cultural milieu and values of media practitioners.

These, and other, features of news production revealed through participant observation have provided, and continue to provide, a 'deeper' understanding of the complex forces and influences affecting news output. As such, these empirical findings and discussions often qualify the generalising claims of major theoretical approaches to the study of the mass media and provide the grounds for a more adequate, and sophisticated, appreciation of the media and the forces that shape them. This chapter provides a review of the major studies that have deployed the method in relation to news production, identifies the method's various strengths and considers its so-called 'methodological blindspots', before outlining the stages and sequence of a typical participant observation study. Drawing upon actual studies and experiences of researchers working in the field, the discussion also identifies potential difficulties encountered in participant observation research and suggests a number of practical solutions to these.

Chapter 4, 'Policy and Archival Research', focuses on those areas of research which rely more heavily on the use of secondary sources, sometimes combined with primary sources of information, in order to examine specific topics. For example, researchers may wish to explore the question of 'public service broadcasting', or the issue of 'deregulation'; or they may wish to explore the notion of 'the free press', or the significance of the declining trend in newspaper circulation. How one approaches these sorts of issues is the main focus of this chapter. It sets out how one begins to define the nature of the problem under investigation, and how one should proceed to seek and analyse relevant information. Using two case studies – the exploration of 'public service broadcasting', and the analysis of 'media policy' – it suggests how such topics should be researched, and what sources of information could be used to explore them in depth. Finally, the chapter also emphasises both the need for a broad theoretical framework to guide the research and the importance of employing a wide variety of sources and types of information (for example, audience data, interview material, survey analysis) to support it.

The technique of content analysis has been and continues to be one of the most frequently used methods in mass communication research. Chapter 5, 'Content Analysis', starts by locating this method in its historical context. It discusses some of the key strengths and weaknesses of the method, and its relationship to other types of data collection in communication research; and it examines longstanding debates about quantitative versus qualitative issues in the analysis of media content. The chapter provides a detailed outline of the key steps in content analysis, including sampling considerations, the construction and application of a coding frame, and the analysis and interpretation of the data generated. The various steps in content analysis are illustrated with examples from studies of both press and broadcast content. The different strategies required, and the different possibilities available, depending on the nature of the medium analysed are also discussed. Considerable attention is given to the need for combining strictly quantitative content analysis with more qualitative approaches to the analysis of textual material.

Chapters 6 and 7 introduce methodologies of narrative and genre analysis for the study of the moving image. Chapter 6 discusses tools for examining the meanings, myths and ideologies contained in moving image narratives. Through a discussion of major theories of narrative, it outlines key devices for narrative study. The concepts of narrative structure, equilibrium, role, function, binary oppositions, actants and alternative narratives are all discussed as viable methodological tools. The sections on narrative in this chapter are preceded by a discussion of the key technical and symbolic elements in moving image construction. This first section stresses the importance of a thorough knowledge of moving image construction to the researcher, for it is only through an understanding of this that he or she can begin to unpack the construction of meaning in texts. This first section of Chapter 6 inevitably also covers essential information for the study of genre discussed in Chapter 7.

Chapter 7 focuses on the concept of 'genre' and proceeds by outlining the main tools of genre analysis. Following a brief discussion of the notion of genre, the chapter discusses how to use the key concepts developed by people such as Christian Metz, Will Wright, and Thomas Schatz in terms of genre methodologies. In genre analysis, the central methods are divided into areas that we have called *principal elements* and *exchanges approaches*; these can be seen as being on the one hand classifying and categorising approaches, and on the other, ritual and ideological approaches. These areas are illustrated as methodologies through practical application to moving image content.

Chapter 8, 'Analysing Visuals: Still and Moving Images', reviews the state of the art in relation to visual analysis. Mass communication research has generally tended to pay insufficient attention to the visual dimension of media output. Language and linguistic properties of media content are all too often assumed to be the means by which media messages are communicated. A number of reasons account for this privileging of the verbal or written over the visual or imagistic and are outlined at the outset of this chapter.

Aiming to encourage researchers to attend to, and engage with, the visual dimensions of media content, the chapter identifies and outlines four analytical approaches to the study of media visuals. Focusing on studies of news visuals, it first discusses 'distortion analysis' and how access to the media production domain can provide researchers with an invaluable source of insight and evidence in the critical discussion of the selection and use of particular news images. How news images function symbolically to condense and help crystallise widespread social values, aspirations and fears is next discussed under 'symbolic analysis'. With the help of examples, the symbolic capacity of selected news images is examined.

The most developed method of visual analysis is, of course, 'semiotics', though even here studies of news visuals have only rarely made use of this powerful tool. The concepts and techniques of semiotics are first introduced, before they are demonstrated in a comparative analysis of press photographs, illustrating both *how* visuals can encourage and sustain certain meanings and how the technique can be deployed in applied analysis.

Finally the fourth visual approach, 'epistemological analysis', is outlined and again demonstrated in applied analysis. Developing upon the insights and approach of semiotics, epistemological analysis seeks to reveal the contribution of visuals to underwriting or 'guaranteeing' certain types of knowledge organised by media conventions and genres. This approach, though only recently formulated, has already been deployed to some effect and promises to help us discriminate between the differing appeals and knowledge claims of so-called 'serious' and tabloid forms of journalism. The chapter concludes by considering possible future lines of visual news analysis – lines of analysis that can also be applied to the mass media and its output more generally.

While the emphasis in critical audience research has in the last decade or so shifted towards the more qualitative approaches of group interviewing, participant observation, and audience ethnography, we argue in Chapter 9, 'Media Audiences: Survey Research', that the survey method continues to be of central importance in communication research. Its continued importance is sustained not simply as a tool for the regular monitoring of audience attitudes, opinion, and media-related behaviour *per se*, but perhaps equally significantly, as a method used in conjunction with observational methods, audience ethnographies and archival research. This chapter uses examples from selected survey-based studies as a way of highlighting: (1) when, and for what kinds of research questions, the survey method offers an appropriate approach; (2) its strengths and weaknesses compared with other approaches to the study of media audiences; and (3) the major types of survey research. It then proceeds to a detailed outline of the key steps involved in carrying out a survey, including sampling considerations, strategies for planning and managing the survey process, questionnaire design, direct interviewing versus self-completion questionnaires, interviewer training, coding of closed and open-ended questions, and analysis and interpretation of the data collected.

Whereas Chapter 9 looks at survey research which focuses on individual respondents, Chapter 10, 'Media Audiences: Focus Group Interviewing', reviews the 'place' and role of group interviewing as an alternative, and often complementary, approach to the study of media audiences. The particular advantages offered by this method over – for example – survey research are outlined, including its much greater potential for capturing the way in which audiences react to, construct meaning out of, negotiate, and make sense of television programmes and other media content. Likewise, the use of this method for gaining insights into the dynamics of people's media-use and media-related behaviour is discussed and compared with the often more 'frozen' picture obtained by other audience research methods. The chapter outlines the steps involved in selecting groups (that is, selection criteria and their relation to the aims of the research and the types of comparisons required), arranging and convening group interviews, preparing an interview structure or menu, strategies for coping with group-dynamics, and the use of visual material and other prompting for stimulating and focusing group discussion. It also discusses the logistics of recording of group interviews, of note-taking during group interviews, and of the subsequent ways of managing, analysing and interpreting the 'data' from group interviews.

Chapter 11, 'Computer-Assisted Handling and Analysis of Data', focuses broadly on computer-assisted handling and analysis of communication research data. In this chapter, we introduce (1) the analysis of quantitative data using SPSS, and (2) the computer-assisted management and analysis of 'qualitative' data. The chapter outlines the steps involved in preparing quantitative data – whether from a survey or a content analysis – for computer-analysis, and discusses the use of SPSS for the statistical examination of data. It further discusses the organisation, management, and analysis of 'qualitative' textual data, be they in the form of participant observation field-notes, interview transcripts, or electronic newspaper text. While seeking to avoid the detailed description of individual computer programs for these purposes, we introduce readers to the significant gains of flexibility, efficiency and reliability which computer-assisted handling of qualitative data offers over more traditional 'manual' or card-index based methods, and we outline some of the types of analysis which can be used productively in research on qualitative 'textual' data.

Finally, in the Appendix, readers will find an indicative guide to sources, resources and tools for media and communication research. This guide is only an indicative one since there are numerous sources and resources available nationally and internationally in a variety of print, audio-visual and electronic formats. A comprehensive listing of such sources is well beyond the scope of this book. Instead, the aim of this appendix is to provide the reader with 'starting points' for answering questions such as: 'Where can I find details on the circulation and readership of national newspapers?', 'Has the level of cinema admissions gone up or down in the last five years?', 'Who owns and controls the national newspapers?', 'Where does one get hold of television news from 1988?', 'What has been published in the last six years about the influence of alcohol advertising on young people?', 'What communications and media studies courses are offered at universities in the United Kingdom?' and so on. The appendix provides 'starting points' for searches in library print media, in electronic databases, and on the Internet.

2

Mass Communication Research: Asking the Right Questions

James D. Halloran*

2.1 Introduction

The other chapters in this book focus on various approaches to the generation, collection and analysis of data in mass communication research. This chapter is essentially of a different order. It addresses broader and perhaps more fundamental questions about the nature and validity of the data produced by the various methods discussed in detail in the other chapters. It recognises that these methods did not develop in a vacuum, and may reflect a range of interests – political, economic and intellectual. For example, in its early days mass communication research was heavily conditioned by market forces and the needs of the media. The possibility of methods – the means to an end – becoming an end in themselves and influencing, if not entirely determining, the questions to be asked in research will also be examined.

* James Halloran was Director, Centre for Mass Communication Research, University of Leicester, 1966–1991, and is currently Research Professor. He was President of the International Association for Mass Communication Research from 1972–1990, and is now Honorary Life President. He was consultant to the MacBride Commission and the Annan Committee, and has acted as consultant to UNESCO and the Council of Europe, and to many media and educational institutions. He is the author of numerous books and articles on the media and communication processes.

The questions that might or should be addressed in mass communication research will be studied against the background of research developments over the last thirty years, with particular reference to the emergence of a more holistic, processual, critical approach, which sought to remove the media from centre stage, and place them in a wider social context. The implications of these developments, for both questions and methods, will be discussed, with emphasis on the discontinuities and a lack of consensus in what is a multi-disciplinary field. How mature is a science, how reliable and valid are its methods, when research results can be produced in support of almost any contending position?

While recognising that there are other (non-social scientific) approaches to the study of the media and the communication process, the focus in this chapter will be on the social scientific approach, for this is at the heart of the other chapters. The question of whether or not the adoption of the 'scientific approach' is appropriate, or even possible, will be examined, together with the nature, possibilities and limitations of social science generally, and of mass communication research in particular. Should maturity through consensus be our ultimate goal, or should we recognise that the complexity of our subject matter calls for complementary perspectives, with all that this implies for both the questions asked, and the methods used?

There are implications too for the funding, commissioning, support and reception of research, particularly as they impinge on research independence and autonomy, and on policy and critical research. Can theoretical refinements, methodological rigour and substantive or social concerns be pursued at one and the same time? Are they compatible?

The essence of this chapter is that the various methods or techniques (surveys, interviews, participant observation, and so on) discussed in detail in the chapters which follow can only be adequately understood, appreciated and appropriately applied, if located within this wider framework.

2.2 Methods: a Means to an End

It would hardly be appropriate in discussing what questions should be asked in mass communication research to underplay the important role of methods in what is generally regarded as a social scientific activity. It must be stressed at the outset, however, that methods are but a means to an end and, important though they are, they are not an end in themselves, nor should they be used, as they have been, to determine the end or define the nature of the problems to be investigated.

Nevertheless, in social science (and here mass communication research is regarded as a branch of social science), if due attention is not given to methods, then we run the risk of finding ourselves in a free-for-all situation where anything goes. The danger is that knowledge is then reduced to mere perspectivalism. Can this be social science?

But what methods? There is nothing sacred or inviolate about any particular method. Whatever methods we advocate, they will not have been conceived, developed or applied in a cultural or political vacuum. It took a long time to appreciate – research contributing to this appreciation – that what appears on our screens and in print may be influenced by a wide range of historical, social, political, economic and cultural factors. Objectivity dies hard in journalism, but it dies even harder in the social sciences. There are still researchers who claim to be value free and objective – although over the last quarter of a century there has been a gradual realisation that research too, *the questions asked and the methods used*, may be subject to a wide range of extraneous influences.

If we cannot accept that any one approach is as good as another, then we have to take a stance, albeit a provisional one. We cannot afford to be dogmatic or exclusive and, whatever stance we take about research, we must recognise its limitations, its tentative nature, the various circumscriptions and the factors that impinge on the research process.

2.3 Social Science: Boundaries and Linkages

The overall orientation of this book is social scientific, so presumably this means something. It has been said that there are as many definitions of social science as there are social scientists. But as a starting point we shall settle for a fairly simple approach – one that encompasses the main characteristics of social science, although obviously this, in itself, represents a selective judgement.

Social science, which is generally regarded as including psychology, sociology, anthropology, economics and political science, consists of the *disciplined* and *systematic* study of society and its institutions, and of how and why people behave as they do, both as individuals and in groups within society. At a minimum it would appear that 'scientific' entails a systematic and disciplined method of acquiring knowledge and, what is more, that knowledge must be *verifiable knowledge*. This presents a problem at the outset. For society, its institutions and social relationships may not be susceptible to scientific study. Consequently, the methods of the natural sciences are not necessarily applicable to social phenomena.

We also need to recognise the humanistic affinity of social science (this is particularly true in mass communications), and its overlap with philosophy, law, geography and literary criticism. Several perspectives (for example, critical, theoretical, empirical and humanistic) may be detected in social science (Inkeles, 1966). Consequently, even among those who consider themselves social scientists we are likely to find many different approaches to the study of the media and communications. These approaches may range from those who strive to be scientific, adopting or adapting models from the natural sciences, to those on the other wing who, in studying the same subjects, rely more on imagination and insight, unfettered, as they see it, by scientific paraphernalia. Just to complicate matters, there are also those who attempt to blend the two approaches.

Although the focus in this book is on social science and social scientists, social scientists are not the only scholars with a contribution to make to a debate on communications and the media. This debate has been carried on by literary critics, social philosophers, moralists, artists and educators who, judging from their comments, often feel that the social scientists are so preoccupied with research techniques and methodological devices that their works lack immediate social relevance, and that they suffer further because they are unrelated to the general intellectual discussion of mass culture on the one hand, and its historical development on the other. The social scientists may reply to this by questioning the whole nature of the evidence produced by these writers, and by criticising what they consider to be the undisciplined nature of the generalisations, interpretations and speculations which abound in this field (Halloran, 1964).

This issue has been with us for some considerable time but, in recent years, with the burgeoning of cultural studies, it has re-emerged in new forms and taken on an added significance. Cultural studies covers a multitude of positions and manifests marked differences at many levels. James Carey, an outstanding scholar in this field and a founding father of cultural studies, maintains that it does not represent a homogeneous point of view; 'it is not a body of propositions or methods commanding universal assent from those who practice scholarship under its banner' (Carey, 1992).

Carey's wing of cultural studies shares with critical social scientists a faith in liberal democracy and in reformist measures to make society more just and open. Together with some schools of social science, it represents a revolt against the extreme scientific approach ('scientism'), and is interested 'in charting and explaining social conflict, in uncovering the meanings embedded in social practice, [and] in laying out the dimensions and politics of social struggle'. Surely this is social science, at least as it is interpreted here, so whether one should regard Carey and others like him as social scientists is not really relevant – it is the overall approach that matters. Carey is quick to remind us, however, that there are those working in cultural studies who are far removed from his approach. These tend to equate pretentious speculation and interpretation with theory, adopt a selective approach to the use of evidence, and appear to have abandoned, or perhaps have never even embraced or understood, a systematic approach to knowledge (Roach, 1993; Hughes, 1993).

But far more serious than this, according to Carey, is the failure of these writers to understand history, economics, organisations, power, social relationships and the nature of social reality in the complex contemporary society. In other words, their work reflects an ignorance of the social scientific perspective and an absence of intellectual analysis and political understanding. Moral and ideological posturing are no adequate substitute for an analysis and programme which recognises the economic, political and cultural contexts of social struggle. It is interesting that a renowned cultural scholar, such as Carey, draws attention to this problem, particularly in view of the increasing tendency to indiscriminately mix cultural studies and mass communication research.

2.4 Social Science: Not Everything Goes

So, even in our relatively inclusive approach, not everything goes. In searching for guidelines and criteria we could do worse than follow the advice of the sociologist John Rex (1978). He emphasised the need for systematic and accurate observation, a respect for evidence, careful examination and description, caution and the consideration of alternatives. He saw these qualities as the *sine qua non* of social scientific endeavour, and he rejected dogma, doctrinaire assertions, selectivity and the work of those who were either unable or unwilling to make the distinction between ideology and social science, and who often promoted the former in the shape of the latter.

However, it is important to stress that, because validation and disciplined, systematic study are given priority over assertion, this does not imply indifference to values and social concerns, nor should it prevent us from advocating and working towards preferred futures, and having our own specific aims and objectives. We need not accept a value vacuum and the accompanying political and educational paralysis. However, it is essential to recognise that others may have different preferences and objectives. To some it is the commitment, the social concern and the wish to use results to produce change that gives research not only its dynamic quality, but also its justification. As Alvin Gouldner maintained, the critical, moral component is a vital part of an endeavour which is essentially purposive, and in which social scientists might be likened to 'clinicians striving to further democratic potentialities' (1955, pp. 506–7). Ideally, the pursuit of theoretical refinement, methodological rigour and social objectives *need not* be incompatible but unfortunately, in practice, they often are.

We also need to draw attention to the limitations of social science. It is important to do this because some social scientists have created false expectations by suggesting that clear answers and successful formulae may be produced at short notice. In doing this they oversimplify by omitting that which does not fit into their neat schema, and this tends to lead to a failure to recognise what really amounts to the intrinsic unpredictability of the field. Social science can be sold short by selling too hard. As Andrew Schonfield has argued:

> In the social sciences it is rarely possible to pose questions and provide answers in the manner of some of the natural sciences, and it is a refusal to recognise this that has often led us up the wrong path. It is the nature of most of our work that it tends to produce useful ideas and an increasingly firm factual base, rather than clear-cut answers to major policy questions. We must try to tease out the relationships which have a crucial effect on policy and, in doing so, provide not so much widely applicable generalisations as a sound, informed basis for decision-making and, at the same time, cut down the area of reliance on guesswork and prejudice. (Schonfield, 1971)

If we design and carry out our research with this in mind – in other words, not attempting to do the impossible (establish unilinear, causal relationships), we might make more progress and be seen as more credible.

2.5 The Importance of Social and Historical Context

That research – the questions addressed, the methods used and the facilities and support made available – cannot be adequately explained or understood apart from the culture within which it developed and operates, becomes abundantly clear when we examine the short history of mass communication research. In its early days mass communication research, which at that time (that is, the 1950s) was very much a product of the USA, was heavily influenced by media requirements and commercial considerations. The main aim was to assess accurately how many and what kind of people read, listened, watched, and so on and how they regarded what they consumed. These requirements contributed to an oversimplification of the issues, as also did the application of interpretations of wartime experiences in relation to propaganda and psychological warfare. Social concern about the possible negative influences of the new media, as well as over-optimism and enthusiasm about its cultural and educational potential – the former invariably attracting more attention and funds – also helped to frame the questions that were asked in research.

To summarise, and risking oversimplification, we may say that, on the whole, at that time the research was fragmented, *ad hoc*, atheoretical and lacking in conceptual refinement. Hypotheses were rarely formulated or tested; the emphasis was on doing rather than on thinking in an administrative and commercial service research effort which was geared primarily to serving the system, either implicitly or explicitly, rather than to questioning it. Reliability prevailed over validity, and method over substance, in what was a narrow, media-centred, decontextualised, simplistic, psychological, individualistic orientation. Concepts such as 'social process', 'structure', 'power', 'organisation', 'control', 'culture', 'agenda-setting', 'legitimation', 'professional socialisation' had not been introduced, or allowed to make the simple causal equations more realistically complex. Rarely were attempts made to study the social meaning of the media in historical or sociological contexts. Moreover, the bulk of the research was unbalanced, tending to concentrate on one aspect of the process (effects and reactions) to the neglect of the factors that influenced what was produced (Halloran, 1981; Hardt, 1992).

It is possible that someone reviewing the situation today might evaluate in terms similar to those just outlined and, up to a point, this might be excused, for a great deal of what today passes for mass communication research still bears many of the aforementioned characteristics. But, to do so would miss something which is present today which was not present thirty years ago. Over the past quarter of a century there have been clearly discernible developments away from the mainstream, conventional, simplistic, service research referred to above, and it is these developments – steps towards asking the right questions – that will be illustrated in what follows.

In mass communication research as in any other social science, we must remember that no matter how sophisticated the methodology, the research can never be better than the questions that are asked in the first place. So, if the questions are inadequately formulated, the answers obtained from the research are not likely to be valid. Furthermore, if we ask irrelevant questions and then use what might be regarded as sophisticated methods, we may compound the error by giving spurious 'statistical certainty' to the findings. Unfortunately, so much in conventional mass communication research consisted of little more than 'statistically definitive statements' about the irrelevant, the inconsequential, the trivial and the purely invalid. This was primarily because there was little theoretical underpinning or conceptual refinement – short-term, useful answers were what was required. Yet, in our work, theory could be – should be – the most practical and economic thing at our disposal for, among other things, it determines the nature of the questions we ask.

In conventional research, problems were defined within narrow parameters. The implications of this were particularly misleading when approaches, which may have been appropriate to media and market, were applied to wider social questions. The research was too media-centred, so that the prevailing tendency was to ask what the media did to people. It would have been both more interesting and more valid if the question had been rephrased to ask what people, differentially located in society, therefore with different possibilities for control, access and participation, with different experiences and skills, different competencies and abilities, did with the media.

Crude ideas about the process of influence also prevailed at the time. These largely stemmed from the psychological orientation of so much of the early conventional research. This research seemed to assume that influence could be confined to changes in the attitudes and opinions expressed and *measured* at an individual level. But we now know that influence cannot be confined to disembodied attitudes, for it also operates at cultural and societal levels. Influence at these levels, however, is more difficult to measure than attitude change, and measurement is important – sometimes all-important – to those social scientists who, at times, even allow method (susceptibility to measurement) to determine the problem to be researched. For these it would appear to be more important to measure something that does not matter (with little or no theoretical or substantive significance), and to give statements of high probability about these than to give statements of low probability about issues that really do matter.

What do we mean by things that really do matter? These are the things that are important to the researcher, and they are defined from a value or theoretical position. We need to rid ourselves of the phoney objectivity which has characterised the positivistic research effort. Most of us believe that some things are more important than others and our task, as concerned social scientists, is to make this clear and then use our social science to address these selected issues in a systematic and disciplined manner.

As already indicated, social psychological approaches to the communication process tended to confine the notion of influence (not consistently defined) to something that could be measured at the individual level in terms of imitation or changes in values, attitudes and opinions. This approach is not only inadequate – it is misleading, and it has facilitated the formation of an entirely erroneous impression about the part played by the media in our society.

Imitation, modelling and attitude change need not be discarded, but there is much more to influence than such concepts and processes can possibly cover. We need to recognise that the media operate at several levels, although influence at these levels is not as susceptible to measurement as with attitudes and opinions – and this matters. The media operate at societal levels by creating a social ethos and climates of opinion. They may provide meanings, confer status by approving and disapproving, offer models for identification, define problems, suggest remedies, offer selected guidelines, and so on. They may effectively control the social and political dialogue by setting the agenda, ordering priorities, and inviting contributors to participate. This agenda-setting function is one of the most important that the media can perform, and research indicates that the overall implications of this – no matter how certain people may complain about the radical or provocative nature of certain programmes – is to legitimate and reinforce the status quo. We are all aware of those occasions where the media have appeared to perform a dramatic role in social or political change, but we need to remember that in most societies, most of the time, the media perform a maintenance and reinforcement function with regard to prevailing values and structures.

Of course, people select from what is provided, and these selections reflect, among other things, non-media experiences as well as the deep social divisions with regard to experience, opportunity, ability, and so on which exist in many societies. Nevertheless, one can only select from what is offered. The media, then, are certainly not without influence, but this influence is exercised in more complex ways, and at different levels from the simple, direct, unilinear–causal ways of popular thought and ill-conceived research. The questions we ask in research should reflect this complexity.

2.6 The Need for a Holistic Approach

Let it be emphasised that mass communication is a field of interest, *not a discipline*. It is a field which may be illuminated from several different disciplinary positions. The nature and complexity of the subject makes the adoption of complementary perspectives inevitable. Although this creates problems, particularly in theory-building, in no way should we subscribe to an opposing view that there is one position, one theory, one approach which is superior to all others, and which should guide our research, give meaning to our data by superimposition, and structure our interpretations and applications.

The methods employed in research should also reflect this plural standpoint. Quantitative and qualitative approaches are both valid – one should complement the other – and the hierarchical distinction between 'hard' and 'soft' data is not a valid one. Another important related point has to do with the twin methodological concerns of reliability and validity. Reliability has to do with replicability. Reliability is normally considered to be high if two or more researchers, addressing the same subject with the same methods, come up with the same, or very nearly the same results. Validity relates to the nature of our findings, and the degree to which these are a true reflection of what we formally state we are dealing with in declaring our aims and objectives. For example, do our findings relate to real behaviour, or are they artificial, being little more than artefacts of the research design? Both reliability and validity are important methodological considerations and need not be incompatible. Unfortunately, all too often in conventional, mainstream, communication research, reliability has been achieved at the cost of validity. The categorisations and classifications that facilitate reliability often make it difficult, if not impossible, to do justice to the richness and complexity of the subject matter – say of human relationships and social interactions.

Over the years there has been a growing appreciation that the whole communication process needs to be studied, and that includes those who provide (including their institutions) as well as the nature of what is provided, and those who receive what is provided. For example, the production of programmes in broadcasting fulfils functions for the institution, the broadcaster, the audience and society at large. This needs to be recognised and dealt with in research. Intentions, aims, purposes, policies, organisational frameworks, modes of operation, professional values, funding, general circumscriptions, external pressures and ideological considerations all need to be taken into account.

Ideally, the media should be seen not in isolation, but as one set of social institutions, interacting with other institutions within the wider social system. The failure to recognise the relevance of context and interaction between institutions has resulted in a neglect of the part played in the communication process by non-media institutions, and an underestimation of the importance of mediation, support factors, follow-up activities, and the like. The other side of this coin is the problem of media-centredness. The media do not work in isolation, but in and through a nexus of mediating factors. What any medium can do on its own is probably quite limited.

Let it be repeated that, simply stated, this means that we should not be asking what the media do to people, or what they could do to people, but what will people, variously located in society, with different experiences, opportunities, skills, competencies and needs make of what the media and other sources provide, and which are available to them? This is really at the heart of the problem, and if we fail to get this question right, our research will be worthless.

2.7 The Media Production Process

The point has already been made that mainly because of commercial and market demands and requirements, and because the communication process was not regarded as a social process, the research effort was unbalanced. Far more attention had been given to reception by the audience than to the production process, or to the operations of professional producers. It is essential that, in our work, we should question basic assumptions and policies, challenge professional mythologies and prevailing values, enquire about existing structures, external pressures, and *modus operandi* and, where appropriate, suggest alternatives.

Central to this concern is the need to study what is generally known as professional socialisation. New members are socialised into their profession, and this means that they have to take on a range of beliefs, values, basic assumptions and understandings as well as sets of occupational routines, in order to be accepted as qualified and successful. Much of this adoption and adaption goes on at unconscious or subconscious levels – hence the need to 'unpackage the professional unconscious' if we wish to know how they really operate. If the unpackaging does not occur, then we shall still have to contend with media mythologies which are often expressed as tautologies. For example, 'It's news because it's news, because it's news, and if you were a journalist instead of a remote social scientist you would know why it was news'. The application of independent criteria as to the definition of news in this, as in other areas of the profession, is not welcome because it challenges professional values and routines.

In this chapter we can only touch on this important aspect of communication research and the closely related issue of news values. It would be remiss, however, in emphasising the importance of asking the right questions, not to include a reference – albeit a very brief one – to news values.

Those engaged in media production, particularly in journalism, often refer to 'objectivity'. Research indicates that this is yet another media myth – one very closely related to those already exposed. Essentially, news entails a selective production process leading to the presentation of a version of reality which is governed by the aforementioned professional values and occupational routines. But these values and routines are not imbibed in a vacuum. They are assimilated in the course of professional socialisation; a process which itself reflects prevailing values about the role of the media in society and about the financial requirements necessary for the media to stay in business. News is not unrelated to the selling of time and space, and it is shaped within this context, not as part of a plot or deliberate bias (although this can and does happen at times), but as a result of a much more important factor, namely the unwitting bias inherent within the system (Halloran, Elliott and Murdock, 1970).

We may still judge news in terms of fairness or balance, but if one accepts that news is fashioned as indicated above, then it is no longer valid to refer to 'objectivity'. News might be seen as a commodity consisting of certain fixed ingredients put together in an ordered way and then processed, packaged and distributed within an established framework. This means that to start a debate, say on press freedom, from the commonly accepted dichotomy of free press and unfree press is also invalid, for it begs the main question, which has to do with degrees of freedom linked to the influence of a combination of extraneous factors which is likely to vary from country to country.

We may state our preference for one media system rather than another, but not in crude question-begging, dichotomous terms. There is no such thing as a completely free media system. In all systems news is influenced, in varying degrees, by a range of economic, political, cultural, professional and technical factors. The task of the researcher is to tease out the power of these various influences in different systems. Preferences may then be expressed from a value position, on the basis of evidence.

2.8 Complex Approaches for Complex Problems: 'Media and Violence' as Example

We started by looking at the state of mass communication research over a quarter of a century ago and suggested that, given its condition, it was not capable of asking the right questions about the nature of the communication process and the role of the media in society. Illustrations were then given of the development of some aspects of a more holistic, contextualised, sociological and indeed potentially critical approach which, given the standpoint adopted here, is considered to be more likely to lead to the right questions being asked.

To develop these points it would now be useful to take a major problem area (major if only because of the amount of research that has been carried out), namely the 'Media and Violence', and deal more concretely than hitherto with the definition of problems and the questions that ought to be addressed in research. But, *in principle*, what is written about this problem area may be applied, *mutatis mutandis*, to other areas within the general field of communications.

First, let us take the alleged relationship between the media and violence accepting that, as yet, there is no satisfactory evidence which establishes unilinear, causal links between screen portrayals and social behaviour, either in a positive (cathartic) or negative way. Taking this 'not proven' stance is not to absolve media communicators from their responsibilities, or to defend the gratuitous insertion of violence. A social scientist must ask, 'What do we know about the relationship between television on the one hand, and violence in society on the other?' It will be argued here that what we should ask stems from a totally different mode of thinking from that which has characterised so much of the research in this area in the past, with its emphasis on simple causality (Halloran, 1980 and 1990).

It follows from what was said earlier that the media/violence problem should be set in a wider, more holistic context than has been the custom. First, the nature of the expressed concern about violence might be examined. This concern is often expressed by grassroot moralists who tell us, with great certainty, what is wrong with the world, what has brought this about, and what ought to be done about it. The concern should not be ignored, but the grounds for it need to be investigated. There is evidence from research that some of those who are most vociferous in complaining about violence on the screen tend to be in favour of capital and corporal punishment, and against penal reform. On the whole, then, such people are not opposed to all forms of violence. They have highly selective definitions. These concerns must be seen in the wider setting of other relevant attitudes to violence, aggression and punishment in different contexts.

We might also note the wellnigh universal tendency to look for a fixed external point of evil – a scapegoat – a primary cause of a problem. In certain cases this may be television, but in other cases it could be Catholics or Protestants, Arabs or Jews, blacks or whites, capitalists or socialists. There is a tendency to over-simplify matters by having recourse to this fixed external point. Once it is identified we use it not only as a main causal factor, but also to absolve us from looking at our own possible involvement in the problem. Using the media in this way might enable one to play down the possibility that perhaps the most important contribution to violence could be rooted in economic and social conditions in relation to unemployment, deprivation and alienation. In this connection it is also important to note how the media might be under pressure – direct and indirect – to deal with social problems in such a way that attention is taken away from the root causes of violence and directed to law and order solutions.

It is also interesting to look at how technological developments in communications have been regarded throughout history. From Caxton and Gutenberg onwards, there has been a sort of Luddite, iconoclastic outburst every time a new piece of communication technology has been introduced. The innovation has been regarded as a major cause of whatever social problems happened to be causing concern at the time. It happened with the penny press, comics, films, television and videos, and no doubt we shall find something else in due course.

In addressing this alleged television violence relationship we must return to the question 'What is violence?' Violence is culturally and even sub-culturally defined, and definitions and interpretations change over time. There are quite a few people who have become prime ministers in different parts of the world who spent some of their lives in prison for being 'violent', as that was politically defined at the time. There have been (and still are) situations in which a specific act of behaviour by one group is called violent or terrorist; yet the same act of behaviour by another group may be regarded as 'the legitimate use of force in the national interest'. So, in this subject as in others, we do not have agreed, simple definitions of what is violent behaviour. We do not have a clear understanding of the definition and evaluation of what people do – for we surround acts of behaviour with cultural, ideological and political connotations and interpretations. For example, so many of the things that our educational and historical books, reflecting the received wisdom of society, would have us believe are good and praiseworthy – things to be cherished as part of our national heritage – were in so many instances achieved by what were regarded as violent acts at the time. What is now regarded negatively as 'terrorism' or 'aggression' is defined selectively, and the selective definitions differ according to political and ideological standpoints. The reporting of the Gulf War, the Falklands War and the various interventions by the USA in Latin America is replete with examples of this.

The main point is not that one definition is better, or more acceptable, than another, but that we need to be more conceptually precise, both with regard to the stimulus and the response, in examining the implications of media violence. We need to avoid simplifying the whole process into a crude analysis of what television portrays, and then try to ascertain if children copy or change their attitudes, or have increased their aggressive drives because of the portrayals. I am not suggesting that some sort of imitation could not possibly take place, but that imitation, say by one or two people, is really peripheral to what we ought to be investigating in the media–violence relationship.

The first task, as suggested earlier, should be to take the media away from the centre of the stage. We should not always start by asking questions about the media – what do the media do? – in some direct, linear, causal fashion. Our main concern is surely *violence in society*. This is much more relevant, much more crucial than violence on television. So, let our analysis start at the beginning, with violence in society.

Violence in society has been studied by criminologists, psychiatrists, sociologists, psychologists and others, although many mass communication researchers seem unaware of this. Several explanations have been offered about the aetiology of violence, and some would say there was no need for us to call on television as an additional causal factor. There were many other social forces that contributed to violence in society long before television existed, and many of these forces – some of them reinforced – are still with us. If we take the most thorough and comprehensive report on violence in society that has ever been produced, namely the report by the Kerner Commission after the riots in the USA at the end of the 1960s (National Advisory Commission on Civil Disorders, 1968) television, or the media, did not figure prominently in the list of contributory factors. However, the report, reflecting other research, had a great deal to say about poverty, overcrowding, unemployment, alienation, feelings of helplessness, relative deprivation, and frustration. These factors may be related to both collective and individual violence – again, an important distinction to make.

So, if we want to look at the media and their possible contribution to violence in society, we should examine how they might be related to some of the known and well-established contributory factors just mentioned. We might ask, therefore, to what degree does television contribute to unrealistic expectations, to feelings of deprivation and to the frustration and aggression which might stem from these? This could be a far more tenable and potentially productive hypothesis about the role of the media in society in relation to violence than any of the simple imitation models which are so frequently used. If we are looking for a useful lead into the alleged relationship between the media and violence in society, we might start with advertising and its possible contribution to the creation of unrealistic expectations. We might scrutinise the portrayals of what Thorsten Veblen referred to as 'the ostentatious display of conspicuous consumption', not just in advertising, but through the general portrayal of affluent lifestyles and the emphasis on material prosperity in the media more generally. Granted the levels of unemployment in many societies, these displays could exacerbate the situation. These are the lines of enquiry we might usefully follow – the right questions we might ask – but the powers that be are not likely to welcome this.

It is also worth noting that some research has suggested that the most significant outcome of showing violence on the screen may not be imitation, increased aggression, or even desensitization, but an increase in fear and apprehension. Portrayals of violence could make people more fearful of their environment, which then comes to be seen as more violent than it really is, and that this may lead people to be more willing to accept law and order 'solutions' to the problems of society, as distinct from 'solutions' which tackle the basic social causes. Work on riots in Britain, particularly racial riots, provides indications along these lines. These relate to the way the media deal with problems within the previously mentioned conventional frameworks on news values, that is, stressing the superficial events, incidents, conflicts, for example, rather than the root causes. Implicitly – sometimes explicitly – solutions are formulated and applied accordingly (Hansen and Murdock, 1985; Schlesinger, Murdock and Elliott, 1983).

These points are made here not to prove a point about the roots of violence, but to illustrate the sort of questions that might be asked in research about the role of the media in society, as distinct from those which have usually been asked, and which will still continue to be asked unless we adopt these more realistic sociological perspectives and definitions. The basic principle is widely applicable.

Despite all this, however, we need to remember that the conventional research (the research which still asks the wrong questions, and which is still very much with us), although regarded as superficial and invalid from this point of view, is not necessarily rendered sterile because of this. It is of use – perhaps great practical use to those who benefit from current media operations and the maintenance of the *status quo*. Moreover, its 'scientific purity and neutrality' is used in counter-attacks against the approach advocated here, which is often accused of being politicized – as if all research was not politicized in one way or other. Granted the state of mass communication research, it is not difficult for media managers and policy-makers to find social scientists who will attack or defend virtually any position.

2.9 Research and Policy

Research of the kind advocated here calls for a study of the total communication process. But the total communication process, including the ownership, control, organisation and operations of media institutions cannot be studied adequately unless the media institutions agree to co-operate. This kind of comprehensive research may require the media institutions or communication industries to provide access and facilities, not to mention financial support. It may also depend on the policies and interests of grant-giving bodies.

Media practitioners and policy-makers, although stating that they welcome research, tend to be selective in their reactions to research results. They prefer researchers to deal with problems that have been identified and defined by the media, and rarely agree to 'external' definitions from independent research which suggest that there may be other problems that are more important, both to society and to communication. Why should they welcome research which might challenge their basic values, or question their well-established professional ways of doing things? It is as well to remember that the two groups (researchers and those who work in the media/communication industries, and policy-makers) may have few, if any, common points of reference.

However, we need to recognise that if cooperation has been lacking on vital issues – and it has – then this need not be entirely the fault of those working in the media and the communication industries. While we may consider that research is essential in order to provide the base for informed policy-making, it would be unwise for researchers to think this view is widely shared, and more shortsighted still to create false expectations by claiming that successful formulae and clear answers can be produced at short notice. As previously emphasised, it does research no good at all if it claims too much, and promises more than it is able to deliver. Researchers might also learn to present their findings in a more comprehensible form.

When we deal with policy research, or policy-orientated research, we must recognise that we are also confronted with other problems about the nature of social science, for it may be that social science should never accept an exclusively therapeutic or problem-solving role. If both the aims and instruments of research are controlled, as they could be, how can there be the autonomy and independence of enquiry which some would claim is the *sine qua non* of any truly scientific endeavour? When we make research recommendations, plan strategies of intervention, and seek greater involvement, can we avoid the clash between policy interests on the one hand, and the requirements of social scientific enquiry on the other? Or, more fundamentally, is there an agreement about the basic requirements of social scientific enquiry? Irving Horowitz argued, many years ago, that where policy needs rule the critical effort would be the exception rather than the rule, and deterioration in the quality of social science would be inevitable. Are we sufficiently aware of this danger when we make our proposals? (Horowitz, 1968).

In fact, Horowitz maintained that the realities of the situation were such that the utility of the social sciences to policy-making bodies depended on the maintenance of some degree of separation between policy-making and social science. It is important in this connection to make a distinction between policy research and policy-orientated research – the former serving the policy-makers on their terms, the latter addressing the same policy issues (or at least including such issues on the research agenda), but addressing them externally and independently, and with a view, where appropriate, to question and challenge, and propose alternatives with regard to both means and ends.

Relationships between social science and policy differ from country to country and from time to time. The pattern may vary from complete servitude to genuine critical independence, but there is more than a suspicion that independence and purity are usually inversely related to power, status and influence in decision-making. In this sort of situation there is almost bound to be considerable confusion and uncertainty about the role of social science with regard to policy. Stay outside, valuing independence, and risk being ignored and opposed. Go inside, and serve rather than challenge.

If our main aim, as social scientists, is to contribute to making society a better place to live in, then it must be realised that this can be done by transcending rather than by accepting political and sociological consensus. We do not have to be over-concerned with the restitution of normative patterns, nor need we fall into the trap of examining the costs of dissensus and ignoring the price we pay for consensus. As mentioned earlier, we may address ourselves to social problems without necessarily identifying ourselves with the values of the establishment (Horowitz, 1968). This is policy-orientated research. But, as we have seen, there is usually a price to pay for this.

The agencies, trusts and councils which fund research (we should never forget that research costs money) have their own special interests and priorities and these, not surprisingly, lead to certain types of research being favoured and to certain questions being more likely to be addressed than others. Moreover, on occasion attempts have been made to stifle publications if the research results did not fit the preconceived ideas or needs of the sponsors. Two examples of this are provided in the recently published history of the International Institute of Communication, previously the International Broadcast Institute (Halloran, 1994).

Publishers also have their policies and interests and, in addition, they have commercial considerations to take into account. All of these play an important part, not only in disseminating the results of research, but in conferring status and the seal of approval. In social science the link between status and publications on the one hand, and 'quality' and usefulness on the other, is not always self-evident.

2.10 Conclusion: Towards Critical Eclecticism

Not all the obstacles to asking the right questions are external to the social sciences. So let us conclude by returning to some of the points raised earlier about the nature of social science and the approaches and attitudes of social scientists, noting that, in some cases, the internal conditions may be conducive to external opposition.

Let us assume that, as researchers, we are asking to be taken seriously about our work on the role of the media in society, claiming that we have a worthwhile contribution to make. But this might be questioned. How good is our past record? What have we contributed? It has been said that when we are not trivial we are contentious and dogmatic, and that we are rarely relevant. There is plenty of evidence to support this. We have to consider the possibility that, to the non-social scientist, we may not present a very convincing picture. The field is inhabited by scholars from different disciplines, with different values, aims and purposes, who seek to construct reality in their own ways. The complexity of our subject matter, and the embryonic stage of development of our subject, are among the factors that make this inevitable; in fact, ideally necessary. Nevertheless, it does not help matters when media practitioners and policy-makers know they can find a researcher to attack or defend virtually any position.

That the field of mass communication is multi-disciplinary is one of the main problems, and this is exacerbated by the fact that not only are there differences between the various 'disciplines' within the field, but that there are also differences and discontinuities within any given 'discipline'. There are even those who question whether it is appropriate to use the word 'discipline' with regard to *any* of the social sciences. Consensus is not the norm so, if consensus is regarded as a sign of maturity, then social science is far from being mature.

But, at this stage in the development of our field, should consensus be our main concern? It was argued earlier that social science should entail a disciplined and systematic study of society from the standpoints of the contributing disciplines. Fine, but we still seek an appropriate blend. Social reality – real life – is multi-faceted. Although not universally accepted, its adequate study requires various theories and approaches applied together, and no single approach is capable of providing more than the partial picture of social reality permitted by its own narrow perspectives and conceptual limitations. In this sense we should welcome eclecticism, not apologise for it. But, at the same time, we must recognise the implications of these conditions, and be prepared for the reactions of media practitioners and policy-makers to what they see as confusion and uncertainty.

Let us remind ourselves that social science is fundamentally different from the natural and physical sciences, among other things because of the differences, discontinuities and lack of consensus already mentioned. There are differences in the natural sciences, but they are not of the type which render constructive dialogue wellnigh impossible. Moreover, these differences and conflicts cannot be explained independently of the cultures in which the various models and concepts have been conceived, formulated and applied. This is what leads to confusion, a lack of certainty and low credibility, but it is no good pretending that things are otherwise. This is the nature of the beast (Halloran, 1991).

Having rightly rejected the absolutism of positivism and all its universalistic implications for research, we must be careful not to jump out of the frying pan into the fire. In rejecting a position there is no logical necessity to adopt wholeheartedly its mirror opposite. Yet some do this. The danger in this unthinking, knee-jerk reaction is that knowledge is reduced to mere perspectivalism – a riot of subjective visions – and a form of anarchy prevails. There are many examples today, inside and outside our particular field, which demonstrate the tyranny of the absolutism of non-absolutism, where anything goes and where systematic, disciplined research is dismissed. Useful research cannot thrive in such conditions which, incidentally, are also conducive to political and educational paralysis.

So, in our explorations, we have to navigate between Scylla and Charybdis in the hope of eventually reaching a safe port, although an added difficulty is that, as yet, we have not quite decided on our destination, or the port we wish to reach. The very nature of social science impinges once more – but choices have to be made and, in the end, we cannot dodge the issues of validity or values.

In our research we need to start with an acceptance of differences at all levels. But it is quite legitimate – in fact necessary – to proceed from this base and attempt to identify, establish, articulate and combine what, if anything, is common. As Paul Hirst (1993) argues, different ways of life may be related by ties of symmetric reciprocity, and we may eventually find common denominators or universals which reflect the nature and needs of every culture and sub-culture. At least this possibility should not be ruled out, but it has to be established in our research, not simply assumed, taken for granted, or dogmatically asserted.

The main message of this chapter is not pessimistic or defeatist. It is realistic, conscious of both the limitations and the potential of a research approach which, if pursued along the lines advocated by Andrew Schonfield and elaborated in these pages, is still, despite the shortcomings, the most effective mode of enquiry at our disposal. There are still many obstacles to overcome, but systematic, disciplined, fruitful studies can be carried out within an eclectic framework, and assessed accordingly. This is not an escape from rigour, but an acceptance of an approach (albeit as yet by no means a fully developed approach) which, with its complementary perspectives, is capable of doing justice to the complex set of relationships, structures and processes which characterise our field of study. It is a necessary prerequisite for asking the right questions.

2.11 Summary

- This book focuses on the methods used in the social scientific study of the mass media as social institutions and communication as a social process, taken together with other social institutions and processes within the wider social system.
- Social scientists are not the only scholars with a contribution to make to the debate on the media and the communication process. It is also the concern of literary critics, social philosophers, artists and educators, and even within social science (for example, psychology, sociology, economics, anthropology and political science) it is possible to identify empirical, theoretical, critical and humanistic perspectives.
- We are dealing with a field rather than a single discipline and this produces problems with regard to both theories and methods. In fact, it has been argued that in such circumstances it is well nigh impossible to develop theories, although these might be regarded as the *sine qua non* of scientific endeavour. Correspondingly, different methods, often with little in common, are not in short supply.
- To add to these field-specific problems we have those associated with social science in general. The borrowing of concepts and methods from the natural sciences, so it is argued, is not appropriate. The relationships and interactions are not susceptible to such treatment. There are, then, discontinuities and differences both within the specific communication field and within the wide social scientific arena, an understanding of which is essential in any discussion on research methods.
- While recognising this, the authors of this book adopt a general social scientific stance, which, despite its limitations, is still the best approach available. The emphasis is on a systematic and disciplined method of acquiring knowledge, which must be verifiable.
- The theories, concepts and methods in mass communication research were not conceived and were not applied and developed in a social or political vacuum. They were conditioned by external forces. The needs of the media and the market place dominated in the early days, and these taken together with a positivistic orientation led to a concentration on methods which produced accurate information on relatively simple and narrow phenomena (reading, listening, and so on). But these simple categorisations and classifications were not appropriate for the study of more complex social

relationships and interactions; attitudes and behaviour – yet they were often used in this way.

- A related question here has to do with the autonomy and independence of research; with serving or challenging; with policy or policy-orientated research; with questions asked and methods used. Both questions and methods have frequently been determined not so much by objective scientific criteria as by the policy requirements of funding and support bodies.
- Gradually over the last thirty years approaches have been developed which are capable of dealing with the richness and complexity of the total communication process. These, which *inter alia* removed the media from centre stage and placed them within the wider social system, were more sociological, contextual, holistic, and processual. The whole process could now be studied, that is, what is produced, the various factors governing its production, how it is received and the factors influencing the reception, and the implications of this. This called for new methods although the old ones were by no means discarded.
- These developments were accompanied by the emergence of a more critical thrust which questioned and challenged existing systems and prevailing practices rather than simply serving the systems and seeking to make them more efficient. But there was a downside to this progress which, so it has been argued, took the shape of 'ideological hijacking'. This is where anything goes, where there are no criteria, and where any one view of method is as good or bad as any other. There is no developed, systematic study and no respect for evidence. This is conducive to 'a mere perspectivalism' and to 'plural subjectivism masquerading as knowledge'.
- So although the social scientific approach adopted here is very inclusive, it is not totally so, there being no room for mere perspectivalism. The complexity of our subject matter demands an eclectic approach (ideally a *critical* eclectic approach) embracing complementary perspectives. This does not solve our problems, particularly with regard to theory-building, and it can still lead to a situation where research results can be found to support virtually any viewpoint on any given issue. But in the circumstances, granted the nature of our field and the embryonic stage in our development, it is the only valid starting point. Ideally it should provide a base from which we may pursue theoretical refinement, methodological rigour and social concern, the assumption being that they are not necessarily incompatible. From there we might also explore the

possibility of eventually finding common denominators or universals which could cater for the requirements of all relevant situations and conditions. Admittedly this does imply an optimism, a leaning towards 'maturity only through consensus' whereas increasingly there are those who see dissensus not only as inevitable but as desirable. Whatever the case these are the parameters within which any useful discussion on specific research techniques and methods must be located.

References

Carey, J. W. (1992). Political correctness and cultural studies. *Journal Of Communication*, **42**(2), 56–72.

Gouldner, A. W. (1955) 'Metaphysical Pathos and the Theory of Bureaucracy' *American Political Science Review*, **49**, pp. 506–7.

Halloran, J. D. (1964) *The Effects of Mass Communication* (Leicester University Press).

Halloran, J. D. (1980) 'Mass Communication: Symptom or Cause of Violence?', in G. C. Wilhoit and H. de Boch (eds) *Mass Communication Year Book*, vol 1, pp. 432–49 (London: Sage Publications).

Halloran, J. D. (1981) 'The Context of Mass Communication Research', in E. McAnany, J. Schnitman, and N. Janus (eds) *Communication and Social Structure: Critical Studies in Mass Media Research*, pp. 21–57 (New York: Praeger).

Halloran, J. D. (1990) 'Mass Media and Violence', in R. Bluglass and P. Bowden (eds.) *Principles and Practice of Forensic Psychiatry*, pp. 571–5 (Edinburgh: Churchill Livingstone).

Halloran, J. D. (1991) 'Mass Communication Research – Obstacles to Progress', *InterMedia*, **19**(4–5), 23.

Halloran, J. D. (1994) 'How "Making the News" Made the News', in R. Winsbury and S. Fazal (eds) *Vision and Hindsight*, pp. 153–9 (London: John Libbey).

Halloran, J. D, P. Elliott and G. Murdock (1970) *Demonstrations and Communication: A Case Study*. (Harmondsworth: Penguin).

Hansen, A., and G. Murdock (1985) 'Constructing the crowd: populist discourse and press presentation', in V. Mosco and J. Wasko (eds) *Popular culture and media events* vol. III, pp. 227–57 (Norwood, N.J.: Ablex).

Hardt, H. (1992) 'On Ignoring History: Mass Communication Research and the Critique of Society', in *Critical Communication Studies: Communication, History and Theory in America*, pp. 77–122 (London: Routledge).

Hirst, P. (1993) 'An Answer to Relativism', in J. Squires (ed.) *Principled Positions*, pp. 50–66 (London: Lawrence & Wishart).

Horowitz, I. L. (1968) *Professing Sociology* (Chicago: Aldine).

Hughes, R. (1993) *Culture of Complaint* (Oxford University Press).

Inkeles, A. (ed.) (1966) *Readings on Modern Sociology*, pp. 1–39 (Englewood Cliffs, N.J.: Prentice Hall).

National Advisory Commission on Civil Disorders (1968) *Report of the National Advisory Commission on Civil Disorders* [Commission Chairman Otto Kerner] (New York: Bantam).

Rex, J. (1978) 'British Sociology's Wars of Religion', *New Society*, 11 May, pp. 295–7.

Roach, C. (ed.) (1993) *Communication and Culture in War and Peace* (London: Sage).

Schlesinger, P., G. Murdock and P. Elliott (1983) *Televising 'Terrorism': political violence in popular culture* (London: Comedia).

Schonfield, A. (1971) Introduction to the Annual Report, Newsletter Special (London: Social Science Research Council).

3

Participant Observation: Researching News Production

3.1 Introduction

Participant observation can be one of the most exciting, challenging and, potentially, rewarding of all mass communication research methods.[1] *Exciting* because the method promises to provide, what remains, a rare look into the inner sanctum of media production, that privileged domain in which media professionals ply their trade, make their decisions and fashion their collective outpourings for consumption by the rest of us. Given the ease of access to media content, studies of media output are legion, but only a handful or so of studies have conducted detailed 'behind the scenes' research. These studies, as discussed below, have won important insights into the complex of constraints, pressures and forces that surround, select and shape media output. Entering a media production domain continues, therefore, to provide a sense of entering relatively unexplored territory. While past studies have provided general maps to this terrain, there is no shortage of new research trails to be pursued. Moreover, given the shifting nature of the media industry landscape, as much as changes in mass communication theory in recent years, findings from studies of only a few years ago may now be in need of up-dating and revision. The promise of finding out and theorising something new always remains a distinct possibility.

Also, it would be difficult for any social scientist not to be excited by the opportunity of studying a media production domain, and news production particularly. The romanticised image of news workers as independent watchdogs challenging government and powerful vested interests may say more about the profession's self-projected image than what remains for the most part a highly bureaucratic and less than critical professional practice. Even so, media professionals have privileged access to important decision-makers, centres of power and the latest social and political happenings. Unlike the vast majority of participant observation studies, then, studies of media professionals are not concerned directly with the 'underdogs' of society – the poor, the dispossessed and those labelled as deviant – but, unusually, with an elite group which itself has close links to other powerful groups and institutions. If professional groups and organisations are generally better equipped to resist surveillance from outsiders (always ironic in the context of journalism with its much vaunted claim of 'the public's right to know'), once access has been gained this same professional and organisational power can become a fascinating subject for study in its own right. How journalists and the news media interact with other organised centres of professionalism and social and political power has long been observed by participant-observers to be a fundamental relationship of far-reaching importance, a relationship which the method of participant observation is eminently suited to reveal.

Participant observation can also be highly *challenging*. It demands much from the researcher, including a sustained and intensive period in the field and an ability to reflect upon and adapt one's ideas and behaviour throughout the research process. Strictly speaking participant observation is not a single method at all, but rather a methodological approach involving at least three different forms of data collection and associated skills. First, the researcher must learn to become a good observer; second, he or she must become skilled in talking with and interviewing his or her professional subjects; and, third, he or she must discover, retrieve and, on occasion, generate various forms of organisational documentation. On each count, issues of quantity or frequency can usefully be brought into play, though clearly participant observation draws more upon qualitative than quantitative modes of investigation and interpretation.

Whereas other research methods typically involve the design and deployment of a research instrument, whether a content analysis coding schedule, survey questionnaire or audience interview schedule, the participant observer becomes his or her own research instrument. She or he must physically place her or himself in a position from which to make observations (data collection) and is dependent upon the practical skills of writing-up field notes (recording data). How the participant observer responds to the unfamiliar professional environment and negotiates relationships in the field can also become the object of self-reflection and reflexivity. Reflection on one's own intellectual and emotional responses can provide important insights into the norms and, often unspoken, rules, customs and values informing the professional practices of those observed; it can also throw into sharp relief those of the researcher. This can prove to be a disorientating experience: as the researcher struggles to interpret and understand the working milieu of his or her professional subjects, so he or she is also forced to reflect on personal value positions, theoretical commitments and assumptions. Field relationships can also be a source of further discomfort and are likely to be renegotiated throughout the research experience. If all good research should involve reflexivity, participant observation by its very nature demands it.

This is partly why the method can prove so *rewarding*. Through striving to arrive at a deep understanding of a working milieu, organisational culture and professional practice different from one's own, the participant observer will also have to clarify, firm-up and possibly adjust his or her own theoretical preconceptions. Rewarding also, because participant observation literally rewards the researcher's efforts with unforeseen and fortuitous events, contingencies and new avenues of investigation. Whereas other mass communication researchers set out, rightly, with a focused set of questions, participant observers remain relatively open to *in situ* developments and impromptu lines of inquiry. This is not to suggest, however, that the method can be deployed in a theoretically innocent way. Prior reading, the development of background issues, and the identification of basic areas of research interest inform participant observation as much as any other research strategy. Data rarely simply present themselves, but must be won with the help of a theoretically informed and selective process aiming for valid interpretations and findings of possible wider generalisability.[2] That said, if the researcher can respond flexibly to opportunities when presented, unforeseen lines of inquiry can be pursued, new findings secured and, following a period of conceptual and theoretical labour, revised understanding may result. As with all good social science, the method of participant observation can develop our thinking in ways not anticipated and even challenge a priori theoretical commitments.

Participant observation can indeed, therefore, prove to be an exciting and challenging experience which, if conducted with commitment and reflexivity, will reward the researcher with improved understanding of his or her chosen group of professionals and their production domain. Often such understanding represents an explanatory gain in so far as we are now better equipped to understand exactly why media output assumes the forms that it does.

With the intention of providing a user-friendly and essentially practical introduction to the method of participant observation, this chapter now seeks to do three things. First, it briefly reviews a number of participant observation studies, identifying principal lines of inquiry and findings. Second, it provides a defence of the method, identifying a number of strengths before considering a source of possible weakness, its so-called 'methodological blindspot'. Third, and finally, it outlines step-by-step the typical sequence and stages to a participant observation study. With reference to actual participant studies this last discussion addresses possible difficulties encountered at each stage of research and provides possible solutions.

3.2 News Participant Observation Studies: a Brief Review

A wide range of social science literature concerned with the general field and methodology of ethnography now exists. This ranges from relatively straightforward introductions (Burgess, 1993; Fielding, 1993), to more detailed field manuals (Burgess, 1982; Lofland and Lofland 1984; Bernard, 1994) as well as more theoretical discussions of basic ethnographic principles and practice (Hammersley and Atkinson, 1986; Hammersley, 1992). These are all worth consulting, but obviously do not provide detailed discussion of media-related studies. Two recent discussions which review the sociology of news literature and situate production-based studies within the wider field of media theory may be found useful, though neither directly addresses issues of participant observation (Schudson, 1991; Cottle, 1993a).

In overview terms, it is possible to group news production studies into three overlapping phases: (1) formative studies of news processes; (2) substantive ethnographies; and (3) focused production-based studies.

3.2.1 Formative Studies of News Processes

These represent the first wave of significant journalist and newsmaking studies. Often failing to engage in a full production study of journalists and news-making, they none the less singled out aspects of the news process for detailed attention, whether the gatekeeping selections of news editors (White, (1950) 1964);[3] the reasons for journalist conformity to a news policy, both in relation to press newsrooms (Breed, 1955), and press and TV newsrooms compared (Warner, 1971); the effects of collective journalist expectancies upon reporting behaviour (Lang and Lang, 1953); the strategic use of 'objectivity' by journalists as a means of warding off criticism (Tuchman, 1972); the journalistic reliance upon typifications in routinizing the unexpected nature of news (Tuchman, 1973); or the role of organisational policies in conflict avoidance between reporters and their superiors (Sigelman, 1973).

These early studies, all worth reading to this day, pointed to the explanatory potential of attending to aspects of the news production process and becoming familiar with the journalist's working environment. Other studies did likewise, though these relied mainly on professional interview testimonies and retrospective accounts of media production and organisational factors. Thus early studies of specialist correspondents (Tunstall, 1971), crime reporters (Chibnall, 1977), the institution of the British Broadcasting Corporation (BBC) (Burns, 1977), and political programme makers (Tracey, 1978), all made numerous references to the determining influences of organisational contexts and production practices – as recounted by the professionals themselves. A seminal study of a particular news event, documenting journalist reporting practices based on interviews and observations of both TV and press newsrooms also proved influential with its discussion of how news values and a journalistic expectancy or 'inferential framework' came to structure the reporting of a major anti-Vietnam war demonstration (Halloran, Elliott and Murdock, 1970). These early studies, then, indicated something of the insights that could be won from attending to professional practices and the news production domain.

3.2.2 Substantive Ethnographies

Across the 1970s and 1980s a number of studies developed further this interest in the organisational, bureaucratic and professional nature of news production and news processing (Epstein, 1973; Altheide, 1974; Tuchman, 1978; Schlesinger, (1978) 1987; Golding and Elliott, 1979; Gans, (1979) 1980; Fishman, 1980; Gitlin, 1980; Ericson, Baranek and Chan, 1987; Soloski, 1989). This second wave of studies truly deserves the anthropological label of 'ethnography'. Based on extensive and intensive periods of newsroom observations and interviews, sometimes conducted across many years and different news outlets, researchers became fully conversant with news-making processes. How news was subject to temporal routines, how newsroom layouts were organised spatially, and how news-processing was organised in relation to a newsroom division of labour and corporate hierarchy all became basic building blocks to understanding. Indeed it is this organisational character of news production that has remained a consistent theme across these studies and provides a key to understanding news and its ideological limitations: 'The organisational imperatives of network news, and the logics that proceed from these demands, irresistibly shape the picture of society in consistent directions' (Epstein, 1973, p. 265); 'The routines of production have definite consequences in structuring news. The doings of the world are tamed to meet the needs of a production system in many respects bureaucratically organised' (Schlesinger, 1987, p. 47); 'It is the organisation of news, not events in the world, that creates news' (Ericson, Baranek and Chan, 1987, p. 345).

Researchers also observed the professional pursuit of deep-seated news values and the operation of a journalistic culture and milieu sustaining of colleague relationships, journalist professionalism and news policies. Indeed participant observers of journalism continue to draw attention to the organisational function that both professionalism and news policies can play:

> Both news professionalism and news policy are used to minimise conflict within the news organisation. Like a game, professional norms and news policies are rules that everyone has learnt to play by; only rarely are these rules made explicit, and only rarely are the rules called into question'. (Soloski, 1989, p. 218).

On occasions researchers became so deeply immersed in the professional culture of their subjects, some even admit to temporarily 'going native'. This further reference to the anthropological literature and the phenomenon first recounted by anthropologists of losing their sense of cultural identity when immersed in the culture of their host society, again indicates the extent and depth of researcher involvement in the world of journalism. These studies in the sociology of news represent a substantive literature, rich in empirical detail and theorisation of the mechanics of news production. They also drew attention to a wider field of interaction however. Gaye Tuchman, for example, argues that her study:

> emphasises the ways in which professionalism and decisions flowing from professionalism are a result of organisational needs. It explores the processes by which news is socially constructed, how occurrences in the everyday world are rendered into stories occupying time and space in the world called news. This theoretical task makes the book not only an empirical study in the sociologies of mass communication, organisations, and occupations and professions, but also an applied study in the sociology of knowledge. (Tuchman, 1978, p. 2)

While others may demur from Tuchman's social constructionist approach, studies of news production have generally sought to examine the relationship between news centres and the wider society. A wider society, that is, which is also in large measure institutionally organised and structured in dominance. Here a key finding of most studies concerns the way in which news producers and news production generally depend upon a few institutions of organised power for routine news copy. Bureaucratically expedient and serving journalist claims to objectivity via accessed authoritative (and authority) comment, news organisations access, as a matter of routine, official spokespeople and the views of the powerful (Hall, Critcher, Jefferson, Clarke and Robertson, 1986). Whether the media serve as 'primary' or 'secondary definers', or perhaps as something else, is currently a moot point. But what is apparently clear from the studies above is the heavy dependence of bureaucratically organised news institutions upon other, resource-rich, knowledge-disseminating institutions. The obverse obtains: resource-poor, unorganised knowledge sources will find it relatively hard to secure favourable routine news entry (Gitlin 1980). Taken together, these studies have produced an invaluable sociological record and analysis of news production and the forces constraining news output. In short, no would-be participant observer can fail to recognise their achievement. Even so, recent studies have developed new lines of interest.

3.2.3 Focused Production-based Studies

More recent studies, loosely termed here 'focused production-based studies', indicate that much remains to be gleaned from the method of participant observation. This is not surprising; as mass communication theory and media industries change, so past findings and new inquiries inevitably point to the continuing relevance of research. Recent American studies, for instance, all deploying participant observation, have pointed to the impacts of the 'competitive ethos' of news making on news output (Ehrlich, 1995), the market-driven nature of local news (McManus 1994), and the role of the subcultural milieu of specialist war correspondents (Pedelty, 1995). More generally three theoretical developments now look set to inform future research in this area and can be grouped around concerns of media-centrism, media differentiation and notions of the 'public sphere'.

Whereas substantive ethnographies focused more or less exclusively upon media-source relationships from the journalists' point of view and their working domain, recent studies have sought to realign theoretical sights in a less media-centric way and explore the operation of major source institutions and their news interventions (Ericson, Baranek and Chan, 1989; Schlesinger 1990; Schlesinger, Tumber and Murdock, 1991; Schlesinger and Tumber, 1994). This opens up a whole new vista on the play of institutionalised social power and the circulation of knowledge claims within the public arena, and necessarily corrects previous tendencies to privilege media organisations and actors. Work has only begun in this area but already important insights have been secured at the interface between news sources and news organisations. It can be anticipated that participant observation, in contrast to the interview method, will shortly be fully deployed in a major news source organisation. The value of participant observation has also recently been demonstrated in a study of a further media-related, but hitherto neglected, domain (a major oversight of mass communication research), that of a professional journalist training school (Parry, 1990).

Increased recognition that the news media may not be quite the 'dominant ideology disseminating monolith' once presumed, points to increased interest in news differentiation. If all news outlets are bureaucratically organised and heavily reliant upon certain new sources, how are we to account for evident differences of news output, both within and between broadcasting and press output? Here observations of news workers and news processes can be carried out with an interest not so much in the general production of news, but rather the production of a differentiated news product. A recent participant observation study of the distinctive, popular, but relatively neglected, UK regional TV news form aimed to do just that (Cottle, 1993b). Relatedly, past findings concerning organisational reliance upon key news sources may also need to be qualified in the light of discerned differences of hierarchies of news actor access, particularly in relation to populist TV news and press forms (Cottle, 1993c) as well as across news subject areas, whether crime or the environment, for example. Detailed participant observations of how journalists process text also continues to promise insights which could not be achieved by any other method (Van Dijk, 1988, pp. 95–137; Bell, 1991; Cottle, 1991; Jacobs, 1996).

Recent research into the media informed by ideas of the 'public sphere' has sensitised many to the contested nature of public discourse and the facilitating or constraining impact of media forms on accessed voices (Elliott, Murdock and Schlesinger, 1986; Cottle, 1993b; Livingstone and Lunt, 1994). Participant observation of programme design and production will, no doubt, in future throw considerable light on considerations of choice of programme form and their impact on mediated public contestation and debate. A recent discussion highlighting production considerations influencing choice of different news formats, each differentially enabling or disabling opportunities for news access and discursive participation, is perhaps a case in point (Cottle, 1995). Though none of these may be 'substantive ethnographies' in the sense described above, each points to new and promising departure points for further participant observation inquiry. In short, access permitting, the field is wide open.

3.3 Participant Observation: Strengths and Methodological Blindspots

From the discussion so far a number of strengths of the method have already become apparent. These can now be formalised and added to as follows.[4] The method of participant observation:

(1) records and makes the invisible visible
(2) counters the 'problem of inference'
(3) improves upon other methods through triangulation
(4) qualifies or corrects speculative theoretical claims
(5) reminds us of the contingent nature of cultural production
(6) provides evidence for the dynamic as well as embedded nature of cultural production.

3.3.1 Records and Make the Invisible Visible

Participant observation is the only method by which the normally invisible realm of media production can be recorded and made available for wider consideration. Published insider accounts and interview testimonies may be of interest, but these remain dependent upon insider viewpoints and values. As such, though they may be rich in anecdotes and tell us about professional value judgements and perspectives, the fact remains that media practitioners immersed in their professional outlook and working ethos may be poorly placed to articulate and reflect upon the taken-for-granted assumptions or wider systems of constraints routinely informing media work and output.

3.3.2 Counters the 'Problem of Inference'

Participant observation goes behind the scenes of media output to help reveal the complex of forces, constraints and conventions that inform the shape, selections and silences of media output. Too often critics of the media have made the illicit leap from a critical reading of media content to inferences about motivations or explanations accounting for this output. In such accounts, ideas of agency and intentionality, even conspiracy, are likely to be forefronted, though these may be far from accurate explanations. Participant observation studies continue to provide empirical findings of direct relevance to explanations about media output. They can also analyse unused and edited news material and observe editorial processes consigning such material to the newsroom waste bin. This is potentially revealing, but out of bounds to the cultural critic dependent upon published or transmitted news.

3.3.3 Improves Upon Other Methods Through Triangulation

As stated above, participant observation typically deploys a number of methods including observation, talk and interviews, and attending to documentary sources. Though each on its own may be considered to have its weaknesses, together they provide a solid source of evidence and findings which can be triangulated. That is, claims and accounts produced from one source can be contrasted to those from another. Consistencies can be recognised and interpreted, discrepancies or differences can be pursued further, but all in pursuit of deeper, more valid, interpretations. Triangulation can be carried out in a variety of ways – across time, space, personnel, settings, organisations, methods, and researchers. But one only needs to consider the discrepancy between, say, a local TV journalist's claim in interview to support community news access as a matter of course, and newsroom observations of that same journalist routinely relying on only institutional sources, as well as perhaps a quantitative breakdown of newsroom documents detailing accessed spokespersons, to appreciate the value of triangulation. When presented with such evidence, the journalist may well proceed to provide a more meaningful account of community access and those possible practical or professional reasons for the discrepancy between stated aims, newsroom observations and documented outcome. This can prompt, in turn, further multi-pronged inquiries until the researcher is confident that a realistic understanding and interpretation of the situation has been achieved.

3.3.4 Qualifies or Corrects Speculative Theoretical Claims

Media theory has never been short of ambitious theoretical approaches. While improved understanding can only proceed within the guiding framework of theory, theories should never be allowed to remain at a speculative level only: they must be encouraged to engage with sources of evidence. Participant observation of news organisations provides a rich source of evidence which can usefully be put to a wide range of theoretical approaches, including instrumental conspiracy theories, social compositional approaches, political economy and cultural studies perspectives. These, and other approaches, frequently claim to have identified the mechanisms accounting for partisan or discerned ideological forms of media output. On each count, findings from the studies reviewed have tended to contradict or at least qualify some of the more blanket statements advanced by each.

3.3.5 Reminds Us of the Contingent Nature of Cultural Production

Related to the above, it is sometimes easy to become so immersed within the guiding framework of a theoretical approach that the world can assume the form of an aesthetically pleasing, but empirically distorted, theoretical object. Both the 'billiard ball smoothness' of some ideological analyses of cultural processes criticised by Paul

Willis, or the arid and mechanical apparatuses termed the 'orrery of errors' associated with Althusserian Marxism by E.P. Thompson, both some time ago, usefully remind us that processes of cultural production and consumption are likely to be less clean, less tidy, more happenstance, more leaky than theorists sometimes acknowledge. Attending to both the routine and the contingent nature of media production, in all its complexity, dents the idea that cultural production is a smooth running operation and points to the 'mediatedness' of cultural processes.

3.3.6 Provides Evidence for the Dynamic as Well as Embedded Nature of Cultural Production

It is also the case that media production is not hermetically sealed from the rest of society and its dynamics of change. Cultural production must constantly respond to wider forces of change – whether political, commercial, technological, cultural. Participant observation studies have identified a number of these pressures for change in action, and observed how past corporate 'settlements' of programme design, production and output have become unsettled. Once again, such studies draw attention, simultaneously, both to the embedded industrial nature of cultural production, as well as its responsiveness to forces of change.

3.4 The Methodological Blindspot Reconsidered

All methods have their weaknesses, all have blindspots. Participant observation, of course, is no exception. None the less, and for reasons already indicated, the weakness of this particular method may be less damaging than sometimes claimed. The criticism often takes two forms.

First, that the focus of attention on the immediate organisational vicinity of news production is likely to privilege precisely those organisational considerations of production and, in consequence, will be insufficiently sensitive towards, or aware of, those wider but impacting extra-organisational forces – those of commercialism and the marketplace say, or the surrounding cultural repertoire of discourses and values reproduced by journalists and programme-makers.

This criticism could, possibly, be on target if participant observation studies were conducted through the theoretically innocent prism of naive empiricism. Almost without exception, however, the studies reviewed escape this charge. Most have devoted considerable attention to the interaction between media production and wider society, even if deliberately focusing upon internal organisational and professional arrangements. If the immediate production domain is the principal object of investigation, how and to what extent and with what impact wider commercial forces or surrounding cultural typifications, for example, inform the operations of the media organisation have not, for the most part, been lost from view. A recent study of regional television news, for example, was acutely aware of, and observed at close quarters, the intensified commercial, technological and political pressures bearing down upon a particular media organisation and how this then resulted in corporate restructuring and affected programme design, production and output (Cottle, 1993b). Far from bracketing off such wider pressures and forces, production studies can throw them into sharp relief at that very point where they impact the most.

Second, it has been argued that 'the ethnographic approach has a methodological blindspot that tends to obscure the way in which managerial pressures are brought to bear on journalists' (Curran, 1990, p. 144). This is, perhaps, a more damaging criticism since, as Curran has suggested, 'it is difficult to gain regular access as a participant observer to senior levels of management' and 'managerial controls are rarely exercised with continuous force' (Curran, 1989, p. 132). In response, difficulties there may be, but senior decision-making as well as variations in editorial and corporate control do not necessarily escape the participant observer's net. A number of studies have stepped outside the newsroom and deliberately sought to gauge the informing impact and control exercised from higher up the corporate line of command (Burns, 1977; Schlesinger, 1987; Cottle, 1993b). Cross-referenced interviews at comparable levels of management seniority as well as with those above and below (further forms of triangulation), and all informed by observations of programme production and change, can provide considerable insight into corporate and editorial lines of command and control. Schlesinger's research, for example, provides an exemplary study of how a participant observer was able to recover and interpret the formal and informal channels of control at the BBC, arguing:

> The command structure does not usually perform its work of editorial control through obvious routine intervention at the production level. Rather, in general it works according to a system of retrospective review, as a result of which guidance is referred downwards and becomes part of the taken for granted assumptions of those working in the newsrooms . . . a commitment to the BBC's Weltanschauung is central to the mediation of control. (Schlesinger, 1987, p. 162)

Clearly, senior management intervention and editorial involvement is recoverable through participant observation. In summary, while participant observers must never assume their observations will necessarily capture the shifting, and largely invisible, play of corporate power and editorial control, the involvement of surrounding cultural typifications or the relentless pressure of the marketplace, there are good grounds for suggesting that the method, if applied to various corporate levels, departments and professional strata and drawing upon as many sources of data as one can muster, will leave the approach with at least one eye fully open.

3.5 Participant Observation: Sequence and Stages of Research

The discussion so far has, we hope, introduced the method of participant observation. A review of studies has indicated the variety of inquiries pursued to date and some of their principal findings. The method's strengths as well as possible principal weakness have also been considered. But what about the method itself? How, exactly, should you go about putting the method into practice and what do you need to consider when operationalising it? This last part of the discussion provides a step-by-step approach to the method and its typical research sequence. But first a health warning.

The problem with published research studies is that they read as eminently logical, perfectly executed, and with everything in its place. The reality of the research process, however, typically falls far short of the image found in the published (polished) report. Participant observation, perhaps more than most other methods, as indicated earlier, is destined to be reflexive, open to the contingencies of the field experience and therefore less than strictly linear in its execution or predictable in its findings. The health warning now over, it is also the case, however, that 'good' participant observation depends upon a series of sequenced research stages, each of which forms an indispensable part of the ethnographic research process. Six analytically distinct (but in practice typically overlapping) stages to participant observation can now be discussed in turn, under the following headings:

(1) Design
(2) Access
(3) Field relationships
(4) Collecting and recording data
(5) Analysing data
(6) Write-up.

3.5.1 Design

With all academic research, researchers need to have at least some idea of what they are about, why they are about it, how they intend to go about it, what they hope to achieve by it and what they intend to do with it once they have achieved it. Participant observation studies are no exception. It is only on the basis of answers to these fundamental questions that a research design can begin to take shape. Whether carried out by an undergraduate or postgraduate student, a salaried or a commissioned researcher, research will take place within inevitable confines, principally those of time and resources. You may be able to do little to increase either quantitatively; prior reading, reflection and the development of a broad area of theoretically informed interest or, better, the formulation of a research problem, may enhance qualitatively what can be achieved in relation to each. As the review of studies has indicated, much interesting work has already been carried out, so it would be foolhardy to ignore this considerable body of insight; there is little value in setting out to rediscover the wheel. On the other hand, you should not assume that all the interesting work has been done. As published findings settle into orthodoxies so, at the very least, it is possible to pursue one or more of these with a view to going deeper or wider than previous studies may have done, arriving at a new, probably refined, perhaps revised or, even, rejected, conclusion. In all events, you will have made an important contribution to the field and moved the debate on.

At a more ambitious level, you may have identified a relatively unexplored or new set of theoretical concerns for investigation, in which case your study will be embarking on an original trail. Even here, however, the value of your study will depend, in large measure, on its discerned improvement over existing knowledge and theoretical frameworks. It is necessary, therefore, to become familiar with extant literature, if only to engage with it before moving on to new research pastures. At a preliminary level the research design should seek to formulate general areas of interest and recognise that your research will, inevitably, be confined by time and resources. This is probably the most important stage of any research programme; much that follows will depend on informed and clear thinking at this stage. It should be seen as a period of considerable intellectual labour and granted sufficient time within the overall research period. All the studies reviewed above have set out informed by prior reading and the identification of general areas of research interest.

The research design can be seen as a kind of map, identifying the route you intend to take, the approximate time allowed to travel between a number of milestones along the way, and the final point of destination. Of course, there are potentially limitless journeys and different destinations. It is as well to remember that you cannot travel to them all, no matter how interesting they may be. It is better to arrive decisively at one destination with a good record of where you have been, than set out on a number of poorly documented or confused false-starts. In the case of participant observation the research design should aim to incorporate all six stages discussed here, filling in as much detail as you can about each. Of course, some of the detail will only become apparent at later stages of research, but even at the outset it is important to try to predict and plan as far as possible the research process, including anticipated problems and, importantly, the amount of time you intend to devote to each stage.

There are no set times for conducting participant observation, nor guidelines on what or how many media should be studied. All depends, of course, on the overall research aims and, no doubt, limitations of time, resources and conditions of access. That said, Gans, for example, chose to study two TV news programmes, and two major weekly magazines and did this in two phases, having visited each over several months between 1965 and 1969, followed up by a second phase in 1975 which involved a further month of visits and interviews and finally last-minute interviews in 1978 before writing-up (Gans, 1980, p. xii). Tuchman also drew upon a lengthy period of investigations conducted over a ten-year period, involving observation and interviews at a TV station, newspaper office, central city press room and interviews with involved participants in, and reporters of, the women's movement (Tuchman, 1978, pp. 9–12). Ericson, Baranek and Chan pursued a team approach to field-work between 1982 and 1983 which comprised 200 researcher days in the field or a total of 2 500 hours, including the preparation of field notes; they spent 101 days with a newspaper over a nine-month period, and eighty-six days with a TV station over a seven-month period (Ericson, Baranek and Chan, 1987, p. 86). Clearly, participant observation can be extremely time-consuming. Less ambitious, but none the less important, studies confined to one medium and organisation, and with a manageable and focused set of production-based inquiries, could achieve a great deal in a relatively concentrated short period of time. The old maxim applies: cut one's cloth according to one's means.

3.5.2 Access

One of the first hurdles, and potential stumbling blocks, to any participant observation study is access. Without access the study is a non-starter. The literature includes accounts of difficulties and partial refusals, as well as limitations placed upon would-be observers. A few observers, however, have managed to avoid all such problems because they are already *in situ*. This raises the question of the exact status of the 'participant-observer'.

A few studies have been conducted by former, novice or paid *in - situ* reporters and journalists (Breed, 1955; Murphy, 1976; Fishman, 1980; Soloski, 1989). Soloski, for example, worked as a copy-editor on a news desk with the specific purpose of studying its news organisation. These *participant*-observers, though avoiding usual problems of access and undoubtedly securing an intimate vantage point on news processes, may also have been constrained by having to carry out a job of work and thus being less mobile or flexible in what they could pursue. On the other hand, *observer*-participants who remain outsiders to the group studied may lose something of that insider knowledge, but are likely to have more autonomy in their movements and ability to follow-up new avenues of interest. In practice, as time goes by and as the researcher becomes acquainted with the field setting and manages to forge useful relationships with his or her professional subjects, it is not unknown for the researcher to be afforded a sort of 'honorary insider' status, to the extent that confidences will be shared, and even requests to carry out certain professional tasks will be made (cf. Ericson, Baranek and Chan, 1987, pp. 90–1). In these circumstances, the strict distinction between participant-observer and observer-participant becomes less clear, and in any event is likely to change in line with the changing nature of field relationships throughout the research process.

Assuming that most researchers do not already have an established journalistic role, access must be gained. This can be easier said than done, though it is probably a great deal easier now than in the past. Some time ago Philip Schlesinger recounted how the BBC reluctantly granted him access and some of the lengths he had to go to in order to secure it, but how 'ITN (Independent Television News) has kept its doors firmly locked' (Schlesinger, 1980, pp. 341–4). Fortunately, in the 1990s there is now perhaps a less mistrustful or paranoid response to researchers' requests. Even so, a few general principles obtain. Do your homework, find out who's who in the organisation and consider carefully whom you need to approach first. Provide sufficient information about your proposed research in a non-threatening matter, and suggest a provisional meeting where you will be more than happy to explain your intentions and the value of the research. The 'friend of a friend' approach often proves useful. That is, if you have contacts, it generally helps to use them. Family, friends, relatives, colleagues, past researchers in the field, and acquaintances of all of them, can prove instrumental in paving the way to gaining access. Always be sensitive to the demands that you are placing upon an organisation, be courteous, and remain cool in the face of unwarranted refusal. If you do not succeed at first, rethink your strategy, and try and try again.

Finally, a word of warning. As a condition of access, never give an undertaking not to publish material that your host organisation thinks unacceptable. The cautionary tale of Tom Burns' study of the BBC is still worth recounting:

> It was quickly made clear to me that their sole interest in the report was in preventing its publication. In this they were able to rely, as they were entitled to do, on the undertaking I had given not to publish anything based on the study without the consent (which did not necessarily mean the approval) of the Corporation. (Burns, 1977, p. xiv).

3.5.3 Field relationships

An important key to successful participant observation is the forming of useful field relationships; it can also, on occasion, be one of the most difficult things to do. Having successfully gained access, it is imperative that you get off on the right foot, introducing yourself to all interested parties and reassuring them that you are not out to murder professional reputations and pillage newsrooms in pursuit of publishing trophies and academic kudos. You may find, for example, that your entry into the newsroom if agreed at a more senior level, is not entirely welcomed on the ground. You are also likely to come across a prevalent journalist mythology that all researchers of news and journalism hold the conviction that news is 'biased' and are out to pin the blame on them personally. In the past some researchers may have done little to disabuse journalists of this view, so you may find it difficult to shake off, and may have to deal with a good deal of mistrust. With time, however, and as familiarity grows between you and your subjects, newsroom relationships will depend less on generalised myths, and more on your personal conduct and interactions.

Part of this process is a two-way street: as you invite journalists to respond to you in a more meaningful way, so you may have to adjust any preconceptions you may have about journalists. One researcher, for example, first entered a newsroom with a sense of trepidation, wondering if he could really mine the depths of this imposing milieu of high-powered professionalism. Perhaps clutching for reassurance, he struggled to hold on to what differentiated him from those around him: his academic reading of mass communication theory. Imagine his surprise on talking to two newsroom reporters to find that they had both recently completed postgraduate study in communications.

One way of ingratiating yourself into the newsroom in a relatively painless way is by first carrying out a number of basic but informative tasks. It is often useful, for example, to familiarise yourself with the basic organisation of the newsroom, who sits where, and their respective responsibilities. As you draw your spatial and personnel map, so you can introduce yourself to the individuals concerned, 'break the ice' and gain basic nuts and bolts information. A similar exercise can be carried out over the first few days or weeks observing and recording the various newsroom rhythms and temporal processes. Such information is likely to be indispensable later, and provides you and your subjects with a relatively easy lead-in to your period of participant observation.

Clearly, the success of the enterprise depends on forming useful and informative relationships, but what should the role or projected stance of the researcher be? And how have journalists responded to researchers? Past researchers have noted how this can vary on a number of factors. It has been suggested, for example, that whereas such prominent and experienced academics as Tom Burns, Herbert Gans or Richard Ericson may have been at ease with their senior media counterparts, young postgraduate researchers, as Philip Schlesinger and Gaye Tuchman then were, may have enjoyed less defensiveness on the part of newsroom workers (Tuchman, 1991, p. 86).[5] Interestingly, Schlesinger notes how journalists were often curious at first and even flattered that 'respectable' academic interest should be directed at their work. This later gave way to a more sceptical attitude informed, he says, by surrounding public controversies about the news and a recently published news study (Schlesinger, 1980, pp. 352–3). He also relates how his personal style was self-effacing and how he took care not to proclaim commitments or convictions (p. 353). Though this was fostered, in part, in response to the prevailing personal style of the BBC, his host organisation, it probably remains general sound advice.

Continuing acceptance within the newsroom and the willingness of professionals to volunteer information and insights depends on finding an acceptable 'front' or newsroom role. This may have to be renegotiated throughout the research period. Perhaps a stance of respectful humility and naïvety, appropriate at the beginning of the research process, may later change to that of a deeply interested and informed inquirer. The nearer the presented 'self' to that of your actual state of mind and feelings, the better, so long as it is the most appropriate (and ethical) stance for eliciting responses from others. Self-reflection and reflexivity, as always, are called for. As social actors we all tend to be practised in the skills of 'front-management', and it is important to be sensitive to the various cues presented from others in interaction and, as occasion demands, adjust and renegotiate relationships.

Lastly, for some the sudden immersion into what can appear a strange environment where everyone apart from you is an insider and has a role, can be anxiety-inducing. It is as well to remember that feelings of isolation and difference are a product of the enterprise on which you are embarked and not a sign of personal inadequacy.

Having a temporary retreat (if only periodic trips to the toilet) from where you can reflect, write up brief notes and plan your next period of observation, is generally recognised to be important. If your front-managed role is at variance with your normal public demeanour, this may also be a place of timely retreat. Interestingly, however, and as discussed below, exiting the field can also generate feelings of discomfort, as the researcher now struggles to find a renewed critical distance.

3.5.4 Collecting and Recording Data

The three techniques of data collection involved in participant observation – observation, talk and interviews, scrutiny of documents – all generate a mass of details, information and general impressions that need to be collected and recorded. Without adequate recording of the field experience in all its aspects, later stages of the research process will be seriously impaired. Take observations first. Observers can become practised in observing settings, scenes and interactions. The problem comes in knowing exactly what to record and what not to. Part of the solution may lie in directing your observation to certain phenomena and occurrences and not others. For example, as suggested above, a useful thing to begin with is the basic spatial, temporal and hierarchical infrastructure of the newsroom. Having documented these in detail in your field log, you may then want to pursue particular lines of interest, or follow particular activities or personnel in a more detailed way, always allowing for the contingent, the unexpected or the simply 'interesting' (even if you do not quite know why it is 'interesting' at this stage).

As a rule of thumb, fieldnotes should aim principally to record, not comment or rush to make wider interpretations or theoretical connections. They should be written-up from basic observation notes and memory prompts, and within a day or so at the latest if memory drop-out is to be avoided. They should record basic data for subsequent reflection, ordering and analysis. Good description of settings, scenes, people, events and interactions may prove invaluable later. However, as this labour of recording takes place, so you will undoubtedly be stimulated to make more critical comments, see connections between your data and findings and arguments from other studies, and raise a number of questions and issues for future reference and possible development. These should also be jotted down as prompts for further thought and later analysis. A wide margin or separate space on each page of your field log for such conceptual or analytical thoughts is a useful way of encouraging this formative process of reflection.

Talk, impromptu conversations and structured and semi-structured interviews can quickly generate an avalanche of data. (For a more detailed discussion of conducting interviews, see Chapter 10 in this volume). An immediate response to the newsroom setting may be to grab the tape recorder and press 'RECORD'. This needs to be considered carefully, however. A tape recorder accepted by those present in one setting, may be felt to be intrusive and affect what is said in another. Tape recorders can capture hundreds of hours of talk and sounds, but who is going to translate all this and make sense of it? It can take an average typist anything up to three hours to transcribe one hour of taped talk, more if the quality of the recording is poor. The use of a small pocket-size tape recorder is ideal for recording newsroom morning conferences and weekly forward planning conferences; these relatively short meetings of assembled journalists provide a rich source of dense journalistic comment and verbalised decision-making. The pressurised nature of the occasion – decisions have to be made fast – minimises the possible effects of either the researcher's presence or that of the (inconspicuous) tape recorder. These recorded exchanges provide some of the most insightful professional exchanges, revealing journalistic values and judgements in action (Cottle, 1993b, pp. 74–6). The tape recorder can also be used for formal and impromptu interviews, generating many hours of material for transcription and later analysis. However, when overhearing journalist newsroom talk and participating in informal conversation, it is clear that others may feel the tape recorder to be intrusive and, in some sense, a betrayal of the informal nature of the relationship entered into. Judgements have to be made with a view to fostering long-term relationships. 'Record and run', or 'smash and grab' raids are of little use in serious participant observation study where a sense of trust needs to be cultivated for long-term gains.

Newsrooms, news organisations and news sources all generate a wealth of documentation – both hard copy and, increasingly, on computer disk. The researcher is likely to want to gain access to this and secure copies of selected documents. Newsrooms are bombarded daily with press releases through the post and by fax; they typically monitor press agencies' reports via computer systems, and have access to computerised archival records and picture libraries; they monitor daily other news outlets including rival news organisations, whether press, TV or radio; they monitor official listings such as court lists; they put together portfolios of press clippings and other documentation related to past and present news stories – especially running stories; they generate their own news copy and various edited versions of the same, often stored on a centralised computer system; they produce running orders, meeting agendas, prospect lists, and circulate memoranda; they make and transmit or publish news documents, whether TV and radio broadcasts or newspapers; journalists also scribble notes to themselves and each other. Even the simplest document can be a source of insight and evidence. A memo, for example, which simply told all newsroom journalists to wear their contact bleepers before the Handsworth Carnival in case of trouble, is suggestive, with other sources of evidence, of a journalistic 'trouble' frame in operation (Cottle, 1993b, p. 86). With the advent of photocopiers and, if fortunate, granted access to computerised news related material and a print-out system, the researcher is able to collect and/or record a vast amount of relevant documentation. He or she may also generate his or her own newsroom-related documentation: for example, a quantitative analysis of incoming news sources (Ericson, Baranek and Chan, 1987, pp. 182–3).

Clearly, participant observation will rapidly generate reams of data for later analysis. If this data is to be easily retrievable, an appropriate system of storage, ordering and indexing needs to be considered.

3.5.5 Analysing Data

As stated at the outset, the analytical stages of the research sequence do not, and should not, be seen as chronologically separate. For example, you will undoubtedly have been stimulated to think about your collected data while in the process of collecting and recording it. Indeed, you probably began to order your material even before it was collected in so far as you deliberately directed your observations, conversations and interviews and retrieval of certain documents in particular ways and directions. The process of data analysis, then, is a protracted part of the research process. However, having collected your tome of field notes, transcripts and countless sources of documentation (which may well run to many hundreds of pages), it is now the time to begin to sort through what there is and identify the material which will be shaped into your final presentation. At this point it usually helps to put some space between you and the field setting. This is more than a symbolic act indicating that you have reached an important stage in the progress of your research. It may also prove necessary to regain a sense of critical distance, both literal and figurative, on your field experience and the deep appreciation of a professional milieu. Schlesinger describes this necessary adjustment as a time of 'disengagement', in contrast to the equally necessary process of 'captivation' earlier, and maintains:

> integral to this process was the gradual reassertion of the primacy of sociological concerns. The main effort of simply decoding a journalistic setting was in the past; it was now possible to address the material I had gathered more theoretically. (Schlesinger 1980, p. 355)

Part of the process of analysis, then, requires you to read and re-read your notes and documents, and begin to identify cognate or related material, develop ideas about a number of core themes or areas of interest, and begin to order your material accordingly. A first step in this process might be to produce an index of all your material based on extant news study indexes and self-generated concepts, themes and issues. These may prompt the development of possible covering themes or concerns. You may also find it useful at this point to re-read relevant studies to see how your material relates to or departs from previous findings. You should endeavour to work up from your material, however, rather than simply selecting one or two instances which may appear to confirm or contradict established findings and arguments. In short, this stage of the research process may be experienced as the most stressful, confronted as you are with an inert pile of field notes, thoughts from prior reading and your recent struggle to get a theoretical hold on both your material and recent experience. This, undoubtedly, is a time of sweat and perseverance.

To make the task more manageable you may want to make multiple copies of your field notes and physically allocate selected material to a number of relevant piles (or shoe boxes).[6] It is then easier to see what you have. Your material may warrant the formulation of concepts or ideal-types as a means of describing important differences. For example, in one study of a regional TV newsroom, and contrary to the idea found in the literature of general newsroom consensus and conformity, it was found that there was a strong difference of opinion and professional approach. This appeared to cohere around what, for descriptive purposes, could be termed the old-guard of 'news magazine entertainers' and the new breed of 'news programme informers' with both influencing the distinctive populist nature of the current news programme (Cottle, 1993b, pp. 37–68). Building such forms of conceptualisation up from your data, even at this relatively simple level, helps to get a purchase on your material, organise it and begin to engage with wider findings from media research and issues of media theory. Ideally this process continues until you have identified a number of themes, each supported by a wide range of relevant field evidence and documentation which, in turn, may support revised or new forms of conceptualisation and ordering, and possibly relate to identified positions and debates of media theory. You should also be considering how these broad themes or areas relate theoretically to each other and how they could provide a general framework for the overall argument and written presentation. Writing by now will probably have already begun with provisional chapter length discussions of selected themed material or case studies.

It is perhaps worth restating once more that this stage of formal analysis is not intellectually separate from everything that has gone before, even though it can be discussed separately. Remember, in so far as the research design initially identified broad areas of concern, later followed up in the field study itself and recorded in fieldnotes with accompanying analytical and conceptual prompts, so this stage is unlikely to be bereft of ideas. The opposite, in fact, is more likely, with the main problem now one of identifying which of your many ideas and sources of accompanying data, evidence and conceptualisation will form the core discussions, and which will play a more subsidiary role.

3.5.6 Write-up

The process of final write-up is intimately related to the stage of analysis. In fact the two are almost entirely inseparable to the extent that the process of writing is a continuation of the analytical process. As every writer knows, it is only when you put pen to paper that you discover what you do not know and are forced to revisit sources and struggle with the organisation of thoughts. Do not underestimate the amount of time realistically needed to carry out formal analysis and writing-up, both are a time of considerable intellectual labour and will consume many weeks and months of your waking thoughts. As first and second draft chapters are won, so the shape and organisation of your overall presentation should also begin to be constructed.

There is no right or wrong way to write up your material, but it may help to consult related published studies and see how they have managed it. You may also want to give serious thought to the prose style adopted and the 'voice' or 'register' in which it is written; whether, for example, you write in the first-person replete with personal accounts and reflections, or perhaps in the seemingly more detached tones of an impartial observer, dispassionately portraying the scene as you found it. Ultimately, there is more at stake here than convention; how you present your claims to knowledge and understanding is likely to relate to where you stand in relation to the positivist–realist–interpretivist continuum that informs social science practice and epistemology.

How you organise your material is also theoretically meaningful. As already indicated, when discussing how fieldnotes and documents can usefully be separated and allocated to themed piles, your material is unlikely to remain at a descriptive or chronological level, simply narrating the 'story' of what you did and saw, etcetera. Indeed, it is likely to be poor ethnography if it does this. Rather, both the organisation of your material and write-up will seek to reinforce the shape and form of your analysis. So, for example, the presentation may follow the principal themes now organised into chapters, or it could present a series of case studies each developing a particular argument. Perhaps it could follow the temporal flow of news-processing through stages of story assigning, reporting and editing. There again, it could work its material inwards from wider extra-organisational pressures to corporate structures down to newsroom routines to final news story-processing, or reverse the direction of analysis and presentation outwards from the newsroom to wider society. Decisions on how to organise and present your participant observation study can only be decided by you in the light of what does justice to your material, analysis and general informing theoretical framework.

Most book length studies typically opt for a combined form of presentation from the above. Schlesinger, for example, provides a historical chapter, a chapter outlining basic news processing, three newsroom-related themed chapters, a chapter which widens its sights to the level of the corporation, a case study chapter and a conclusion (Schlesinger, 1987). Ericson, Baranek and Chan adopt a more straightforward approach, with introductory theoretical and methodological chapters, followed by chapters on the news institution, the news process and a conclusion (Ericson, Baranek and Chan, 1987). Tuchman, for her part, presents her study through two chapters concerned with the basic spatial and temporal structures of news organisations, followed by a more detailed examination of journalist professionalism, and chapters on news facticity and one on narrative. These are followed by a detailed case study, wider discussion of news in contemporary capitalism, and theoretical discussion of news as a form of social knowledge (Tuchman, 1978). Each of these presentations works in its own right, and each manages to construct an organised sequence of interrelated chapter discussions. Analysis and presentation appear to be mutually reinforcing. What none of them do, is descend to the level of a descriptive narrative of the participation observation field experience. This is not surprising because the field experience, though indispensable, is only the means to an end, not the end itself. The end, of course, is the developed analysis and formulation of improved understanding and theorisation of news, news-making processes and the relation between news and wider society. Participant observation remains eminently suited to this important task.

3.6 Summary

- Studies of media organisations and production provide findings and insights simply not available by other means. These findings provide a basis from which differing theoretical approaches to the mass media – whether conspiracy theories, social compositional accounts, studies in political economy or cultural studies approaches – can be appraised and their (often) generalising claims qualified.
- The 'method' most often used in studies of media organisations and production is that of participant observation. This involves a number of differing methods and skills, including observation, interviewing, documentary collection and generation.
- Participant observation can prove to be a highly exciting, challenging and rewarding method. The researcher must adapt his or her theoretical and methodological approach as well as personal stance in the field as the research proceeds. This calls for reflexivity, opportunism and, in terms of the methods used, creative eclecticism.
- Given the nature of the research opportunity and the contingencies of the field experience, the researcher must be open to the possibilities of the unexpected, the fortuitous as well as his or her

own preconceptions and blunders. Naïve empiricism as well as rigid theoreticism are to be avoided.

- The method has provided rich insights into and improved understanding of a number of media institutions and professional domains. Studies of news production have proved particularly illuminating across the years, developing from 'formative' to 'substantive' and, most recently, 'focused' studies of news professionals and their production practices.
- Like all methods, participant observation has its weaknesses. Its so-called 'methodological blindspots' may be less debilitating than sometimes thought, however. When informed by prior theoretical reading and reflection, the danger of naïve empiricism can be avoided, and the wider influences of the marketplace, commerce, and culture upon the production domain and practices, for example, can be observed. Relatedly, if the researcher occasionally steps outside the immediate production domain and researches the surrounding institutional context, hierarchy and decision-making, the method can also accommodate the influence of wider corporate culture, context and forces of change.
- Participant observation has a number of strengths. The method: (1) records and makes the invisible visible; (2) counters the 'problem of inference'; (3) improves upon other methods through triangulation; (4) qualifies or corrects speculative theoretical claims; (5) reminds us of the contingent nature of cultural production; and (6) provides evidence for the dynamic as well as embedded nature of cultural production.
- Six typical overlapping stages to participant observation research can be identified: (1) theoretical and practical design; (2) access; (3) field relationships; (4) collecting and recording data; (5) analysing data; (6) write-up. Though in practice each stage is likely to overlap and interpenetrate, the researcher is well-advised to reflect upon each and to reflect critically upon the skills required and difficulties that will need to be negotiated and managed as the research proceeds.

References

Altheide, D. L. (1974) *Creating Reality* (Beverley Hills and London: Sage).
Bell, A. (1991) *The Language of News Media* (Oxford: Basil Blackwell).
Bernard, H. R. (1994) *Research Methods in Anthropology*, 2nd edn (London: Sage).

Breed, W. (1955) 'Social Control in the Newsroom', *Social Forces*, **33**(4), 326–35.
Burgess, R. G. (1993) *Research Methods* (Walton-on-Thames: Thomas Nelson).
Burgess, R. G. (ed.) (1982) *Field Research: A Sourcebook and Field Manual* (London: Allen & Unwin).
Burns, T. (1977) *The BBC: Public Institution and Private World* (Basingstoke: Macmillan).
Chibnall, S. (1977) *Law and Order News – An Analysis of Crime Reporting in the British Press* (London: Tavistock).
Cottle, S. (1991) 'Reporting the Rushdie Affair: A Case Study in the Orchestration of Public Opinion', *Race and Class*, **32**(4), 45–64.
Cottle, S. (1993a) 'Behind the Headlines: The Sociology of News', in M. O'Donnell (ed.) *New Introductory Reader in Sociology* (Walton-on-Thames: Nelson).
Cottle, S. (1993b) *TV News, Urban Conflict and the Inner City* (Leicester University Press).
Cottle, S. (1993c) 'Mediating the environment: modalities of TV news', in A. Hansen (ed.) *The Mass Media and Environmental Issues* (pp. 107–33) (Leicester University Press).
Cottle, S. (1995) 'The Production of News Formats: Determinants of Mediated Public Contestation', *Media, Culture & Society,* **17**(2), 275–91.
Curran, J. (1989) 'Culturalist Perspectives of News Organisations: A Reappraisal and a Case Study', in M. Ferguson (ed.) *Public Communication* (London: Sage Publications).
Curran, J. (1990) 'The New Revisionism in Mass Communication Research: A Reappraisal', *European Journal of Communication*, **5**, 135–64.
Ehrlich, M. C. (1995) 'The Competitive Ethos of Television News', *Critical Studies in Mass Communication*, **12**, 196–212.
Elliott, P., G. Murdock, P. Schlesinger (1986) ' "Terrorism" and the State: A Case Study of the Discourses of Television', in R. Collins, J. Curran, N. Garnham, P. Scannell, P. Schlesinger, and C. Sparks (eds) *Media, Culture and Society – A Critical Reader* (London: Sage Publications).
Epstein, E. J. (1973) *News From Nowhere: Television and the News* (New York: Random House).
Ericson, R. V., P. M. Baranek, J. B. L. Chan (1987) *Visualizing Deviance: A Study of News Organisation* (Milton Keynes: Open University Press).
Ericson, R. V., P. M. Baranek, J. B. L. Chan (1989) *Negotiating Control: A Study of News Sources* (Milton Keynes: Open University Press).
Fielding, N. (1993) 'Ethnography', in N. Gilbert (ed.) *Researching Social Life* (London: Sage Publications).
Fishman, M. (1980) *Manufacturing the News* (Austin and London: University of Texas Press).
Gans, H. (1980) *Deciding What's News* London: Constable. [First pub. 1979, New York: Vintage].
Gitlin, T. (1980) *The Whole World is Watching* (University of California Press).
Golding, P., and P. Elliott (1979) *Making the News* (London: Longman).

Hall, S., C. Critcher, T. Jefferson, J. Clarke, B. Roberts (1986) *Policing the Crisis* (Basingstoke: Macmillan [first pub. 1978]).
Halloran, J. D., P. Elliott, G. Murdock (1970) *Demonstrations and Communication: A Case Study* (Harmonsworth: Penguin).
Hammersley, M. (1992) *What's Wrong with Ethnography?* (London: Routledge).
Hammersley, M. and P. Atkinson (1986) *Ethnography: Principles in Practice* (London: Tavistock).
Jacobs, R. N. (1996) 'Producing the News, Producing the Crisis: Narrativity, Television and News Work', *Media, Culture and Society*, **18**(3), 373–97.
Lang, K. and G. E. Lang (1953) 'The Unique Perspective of Television and its Effects: A Pilot Study', *American Sociological Review*, **18**, 168–83.
Livingstone, S. and P. Lunt (1994) *Talk on Television: Audience Participation And Public Debate* (London: Routledge).
Lofland, J. and L. H. Lofland (1984) *Analysing Social Settings* (Belmont, Calif.: Wadsworth).
McManus, J. H. (1994) *Market-Driven Journalism* (London: Sage).
Murphy, D. (1976) *The Silent Watchdog: The Press in Local Politics* (London: Constable).
Parry, O. (1990) 'Fitting in with the Setting: A Problem for Adjustment for both Student and Researcher', *Sociology*, **24**(3), 417–30.
Pedelty, M.(1995) *War Stories* (London: Routledge).
Schlesinger, P. (1980) 'Between Sociology and Journalism', in H. Christian (ed.), *The sociology of journalism and the press* (University of Keele).
Schlesinger, P. (1987) *Putting 'Reality' Together* (London: Methuen [first publ. by Constable in 1978]).
Schlesinger, P. (1990) 'Rethinking the Sociology of Journalism: Source Strategies and the Limits of Media Centrism' in M. Ferguson (ed.) *Public Communication* (London: Sage).
Schlesinger, P., H. Tumber and G. Murdock (1991) 'The Media Politics of Crime and Criminal Justice', *British Journal of Sociology*, **42**, 397–420.
Schlesinger, P. and H. Tumber (1994) *Reporting Crime* (Oxford: Clarendon Press).
Schudson, M. (1991) 'The Sociology of News Production Revisited', in J. Curran and M. Gurevitch (eds) *Mass Media and Society* (London: Arnold [first published as 'The Sociology of News Production', in *Media, Culture & Society* (1989) **11**, 263–82]).
Sigelman, L. (1973) 'Reporting the News: An Organizational Analysis', *American Journal of Sociology*, **79**, 132–51.
Soloski, J. (1989) 'News Reporting and Professionalism: Some Constraints on the Reporting of News', *Media Culture & Society*, **11**, 207–28.
Tracey, M. (1978) *The Production of Political Television* (London: Routledge & Kegan Paul).
Tuchman, G. (1972) 'Objectivity as Strategic Ritual: An Examination of Newsmen's notions of Objectivity', *American Journal of Sociology*, **77**, 660–79.
Tuchman, G. (1973) 'Making News by Doing work: Routinizing the Unexpected', *American Journal of Sociology*, **79**(1), 110–31.

Tuchman, G. (1978) *Making News: A Study in the Construction of Reality* (New York: Free Press).
Tuchman, G. (1991) 'Qualitative Methods in the Study of News', in K. B. Jensen and N. W. Jankowski (eds) *A Handbook of Qualitative Methodologies for Mass Communication Research* (London: Routledge).
Tunstall, J. (1971) *Journalists at Work* (London: Constable).
Van Dijk, T. (1988) *News as Discourse* (Hillsdale, NJ: Lawrence Erlbaum).
Warner, M. (1971) 'Organizational Context and Control of Policy in the Television Newsroom: a Participant Observation Study', *British Journal of Sociology*, **22**, 283–94.
White, D. M. (1964) 'The "Gatekeeper": A Case Study in the Selection of News', in L. A. Dexter & D. M. White (eds) *People, Society and Mass Communication* (New York: Free Press [first publ. in *Journalism Quarterly* (1950) **27**(4), 383–90).

Notes

1. 'Participant observation' is also often referred to as 'ethnography'. Strictly speaking, participant observation is the principal method deployed in ethnographic study, that is, the detailed and in-depth study of human groups and societies, their milieux, culture and practices. However, 'ethnography' can also make use of other methods, for example, 'life-histories'. That said, the two terms are often used interchangeably.
2. For a more informed discussion of the general philosophical issues surrounding participant observation, and in particular its philosophical 'realist' variant, the position broadly informing this discussion, see Martin Hammersley's excellent 'Ethnography and Realism' in Hammersley, 1992.
3. For the purposes of this chapter and its historical review the original publication date of earlier studies has been included (in brackets) followed immediately, where applicable, by the publication date of the later edition actually referred to in this discussion. Full publication details of both editions are found in the bibliography at the end of this chapter.
4. This part of the discussion is indebted to and adds to Schlesinger's discussion of the method's value (Schlesinger, 1980, pp. 363–6).
5. Field relationships may also be informed, of course, by considerations of class, gender, ethnicity and various other dimensions of social identity as well as age and status. The reflexive participant observer can thus also be sensitised to possible newsroom norms and practices on the basis of his or her own newsroom experiences.
6. You may here want to explore the possibility of transferring or in-putting directly fieldnotes into an available computer software package for text indexing, ordering and retrieval (see Chapter 11). Alternatively, you may still prefer to arrange and manipulate your data by hand.

4

Policy and Archival Research

4.1 Communication Policies

Not all researchers who pursue their own specific interests in the field of mass communication will necessarily be confronted with the need to undertake wholly original field work. There are many areas of inquiry which do not leave themselves open to some of the other sorts of research methods outlined in this book, research methods such as surveys and content analysis.

To take some contemporary examples, researchers who wish to explore:

- the introduction of pop music radio stations in Britain
- the evolution of governmental approaches towards cable television and satellite broadcasting
- or the changing rules regarding the ownership of the British print and broadcast media

will not find it particularly rewarding to rely solely on some of the other methods described in this book. A survey in the form of a questionnaire to media companies may be of some use, but it is unlikely that a brief and limited excursion into this field will produce sufficient data to be of great use in a more detailed study of any of the above topics. Similarly, an analysis of media content on any of the above topics would be of limited use, since it would only highlight *public* comment rather than the deeper level of historical evolution, policy debate, lobbying, policy formulation, and the like.

Nevertheless, these examples, and there are countless others, are crucial for our understanding of the evolution of the media industries across time, as well as in different settings. They require not only sensitive historical and contemporary analyses rather than a mere narrative recitation of events, but also a contextualisation of the emergence of ideas, technologies and policies.

One way of approaching this sort of work is to consider the areas under investigation as part of broader changes in the structure and organisation of communication systems; as part of contemporary concern with *communication policies*.

4.2 What is 'Communication Policy' and 'Communication Policy Analysis'?

Broadly defined, communication policy analysis seeks to examine the ways in which policies in the field of communication are generated and implemented, as well as their repercussions or implications for the field of communication as a whole. This is, admittedly, a broad definition but it permits us to include all media – as commonly understood – and also the newer forms of *tele*communication which, in their own way, are beginning to blur the distinctions between the traditional definitions of communication media. Where, for example, would we place video-on-demand which is made possible via telephone networks? Similarly, what are the implications for the print industry if news/information can be down-loaded to individual computerised households via a phone line?

The blurring of distinctions in the field of communication is one outcome of technological change and it underpins much of what can be described as 'communication policy' research and analysis. Nevertheless, it is important to see this phrase only as a useful and handy description of a concern about the management of change across communication and *tele*communication sectors. Equal weight, in other words, should be attached to the field of inquiry – communication – and the focus of attention – policy. Just as 'communication' confronts us with questions about what is within the boundaries of this field, so too does the term 'policy'. 'Policy analysis' is often taken to imply an exploration of a coherent package of ideas and strategies which are designed to deal with a particular area – education, energy, media, for example. But this view arises from a simplistic interpretation of what constitutes policy, certainly as it is applied in the field of communication. Several reasons come to mind as to why this should be so. These include:

- Policy is very often not made up of a coherent set of statements, nor very often a comprehensive, well thought out set of statements.

- Sometimes policies are not visible or set down. Inaction is a policy; an absence of a policy is therefore a positive decision in favour of non-intervention in media industries.
- Policies can often have unintended consequences, and these may be critical for certain media.
- Policies are often incremental and may be contradictory in as much as they will deal with some sectors but not with others. Thus, print policy may differ from broadcast policy, so creating anomalies – as was formerly the case with the restrictions on broadcast reporting of terrorist spokespersons, the Broadcasting Ban (which did not apply to the print media).
- Policies may be contradictory because the technology or medium which they are intended to legislate may span two, or more, government departmental concerns. Thus, in Britain we have recently (1993/4) seen moves by the Department of Trade and Industry to increase its interest in the BBC's affairs, an institution which falls within the remit of the Department of National Heritage. A similar tussle was experienced by the cable television industry a decade earlier (Negrine, 1985).

We therefore need to be aware of the complex forces that come into play when policies are being made. Furthermore, we need to exercise caution when trying to ascertain what a particular policy is: should we be looking for the policy in a single document, a series of documents, a speech by a minister, a paper from a ministry? Rather than relying on single documents, however, sometimes each of these will contain different clues to 'the' policy in question.

The task of determining what 'the' policy is, and therefore also how it came into being, is thus not a simple nor straightforward exercise. It requires searching various sources of information as well as looking into the relationships between interested parties, connections between events, and the context within which all this takes place. Moreover, since that contextualisation is nowadays increasingly of an international character, the task before the researcher gains added complexity.

Determining what combination of research methods is necessary in order to carry out 'communication policy research' will be the main focus of this chapter. That combination will be discussed in detail in the second part of this chapter. The first part of this chapter is devoted to the prior stage in the research process, namely, how to select and define the area of inquiry. This is a crucial part of any investigation; the clearer the aims of the research and the more thought that goes into the work at this stage, the easier it becomes to put the research process into motion. Without a clearly defined problem, and some thoughts about its resolution, the greater will be the difficulties in implementing the research process. Two examples will be used to illustrate the main issues here. The first will concentrate on the development of cable television, the second on the future of public broadcasting in Europe. The final section of this chapter will summarise the main stages involved in 'communication policy analysis'.

4.3 Selecting and Defining the Problem

The broad definition of the field offered above creates enormous problems of choice. Researchers confronted with the task of writing a report – of whatever length and for whatever purpose – will wonder, at least initially, about *how* to select a topic for research. The next question they will ask will usually raise an even more difficult problem of how to make it different of original enough to be of merit. As always, there are no easy answers, but there are some useful guidelines which ought to be considered. For this reason, it is perhaps worth while to treat separately the two questions posed above.

4.3.1 How to Select a Topic

This is an easy question to answer in as much as the field of communication is a very broad one indeed. From a media-centric point of view there are countless media which can be explored: television, radio, films, cable, satellite. Furthermore, each of these can be broken down even further into component parts. Radio, for example, can cover anything from the early days of radio under the BBC, through the competition offered by the Continental commercial services in the 1920s and 1930s, through to the radio pirates, the introduction of legal, commercial pop music stations, and so on up to the present day. Each of the other media identified above can be similarly broken down into more specific areas either in terms of chronology, or changes in policy regimes, restructuring, changes in ownership, and so on.

A different way of approaching this question is to focus on issues, whether local, national or international, which do not necessarily specify particular media. The study of 'public service broadcasting' would be one such issue; another could be the emergence of the European Union as a force in media regulation in the 1980s; yet another could be the question of community broadcasting. Each of these issues raises important questions concerning the generation of policies and the implementation of those policies. For example, the European Community's Directive ('Television without Frontiers') (1989) has implications for European broadcasting, for broadcasting within nation states, and so on.

But how does one ensure that the choice of topic is a 'sensible' one? There are two considerations here. The first is that the topic selected should be of interest to the researcher undertaking the research. This ensures both that one is prepared to devote long hours to exploring it and that one has some loosely worked ideas about the topic, that is, some loosely formed ideas about why one may want to pursue it, what it says about communication, what changes it heralds, and so on. The second consideration is perhaps more of a test of resolve. Once chosen, researchers should be able to defend their choice of topic when consulting with, for example, their colleagues or peers. In this respect, colleagues and peers can often act as mentors steering the researcher away from 'choppy seas and towards calmer waters'. But, at the same time, by defending or arguing in support of a particular choice a researcher will be putting together a case in support of their choice of topic as well as setting out points of relevance in respect of communication and policies. Researchers should not, therefore, be reluctant to announce, and defend, their choice of topic.

A very general rule would be, then, that researchers should perhaps only select an area for investigation if it is one that interests them and which has been tentatively discussed with others. It is possible, though not necessarily advisable, to proceed without prior discussions with others, but it is not recommended that researchers embark on a study of an area in which they have no interest whatsoever.

4.3.2 Originality

Having made a decision (of sorts) about the general area for investigation, how does one ensure that the work will be, at least in part, different and/or original? The answer to this varies according to the level – academic or professional – of the research. For example, at undergraduate level or taught postgraduate level, students are expected to produce work which as a minimum shows that:

- there has been an attempt to grapple with a difficult problem in an original way;
- the conceptualisation of the work is original;
- the student uses primary literature (for example, original sources), and does not simply rely on secondary sources;
- the student examines the problem from a number of different perspectives;
- the student perhaps undertakes a small piece of original research, for example, a small number of interviews or questionnaires, to round off the project;
- the student produces work which combines elements of the above.

It is *not* usually expected that undergraduate students should produce a piece of work that is wholly original from conception, through execution, to conclusion. Research work of this nature, and quality, is more of a requirement for postgraduate students. However, this should not be taken to mean that undergraduate students should not attempt to move beyond a mere recitation or repetition of something that has already been examined at length. Given the breadth of the field in question, and the numerous problem areas which can be identified, it should be possible for students to be imaginative, and quizzical, about the world which they inhabit.

At other academic levels, say, for post-doctoral work or work funded by outside agencies, the process of selecting an area of study and submitting research proposals inevitably requires the researcher not only to engage with the existing literature and research but to go one step beyond and put forward areas of work or even methods of work which develop and/or go beyond what is currently known. Such a process ensures that researchers are familiar with contemporary work and can begin to differentiate their own proposed work from the work of others.

But once the topic has been chosen, what next?

4.4 Defining the Problem

Choosing the topic of inquiry is the beginning of a long and treacherous road. Long because any good piece of work needs to go through many stages before it emerges as a satisfactory and complete project; treacherous because there are always difficulties which may halt the progress of the researcher. These difficulties may include insufficient information and bibliographic material on which to base the analysis, the lack of a clear idea of where the work is leading, a misunderstanding of the problem area, and so on. Many of these difficulties can be overcome if the researcher – with advice – can *properly define* the problem and, in the process, become aware of the problem areas.

Defining the problem should, therefore, be seen both as a part of the early development of the project and as a crucial stage in the process of research. Once defined, and defined properly, many difficulties can be avoided. On the one hand, a well-defined area of investigation immediately maps out the area by identifying not only what is within the boundaries of investigation but also what is outside those boundaries; on the other hand, it enables the researcher to focus his or her thinking precisely and so to clarify for himself or herself what the problem is. Ultimately, it gives a clear and focused direction to the work at hand – it suggests what reading ought to be done, how the work should be constructed, what other sources of information need to be explored, and so on.

It may be useful at this point to consider an example which would identify these stages. In principle, these stages can be made relevant to most areas of research relating to communication policies.

4.4.1 Example 1: Cable Television: a Case Study in the Development and Implementation of Policies in Respect of New Technologies

There are, broadly speaking, at least four main areas within the general topic of 'cable television' which could be said to fall under the umbrella term of 'communication policy research'. These are:

- the historical development of cable television in the UK and/or in any other country;
- the more contemporary, that is post-1975, development of cable television in the UK and/or in any other country;
- a comparative analysis of different paces of development of cable television, for example, in Britain compared with the USA, France, Germany, and so on;
- the impact of cable television – in conjunction with satellite television – on terrestrial television.

At the heart of each one of these areas of inquiry is some consideration of the nature and development of cable television. Where the principal differences would arise would be in the specific direction in which the research develops. Thus, different elements would be in the background or foreground, different time periods would be under investigation, and different sources of information would be sought. For instance, while the first example would focus primarily on the historical dimension, the last would look in detail at very contemporary issues and concerns.

But why should this topic area be of interest, and in what way is it part and parcel of 'communication policy research'? Apart from the obvious answer that cable television is here and is making a worldwide impact on communication structures, there are some other reasons which are worth considering. At one level, cable television can be treated as a new system of communication, a new technology, so that the study of cable television can become a study of the interconnections between technologies and societies. Why do some technologies develop rapidly and others not? What forces aid, or inhibit, such development? In the case of Britain, an historical analysis of the early years of communication by wire demonstrates the way in which the BBC under John Reith, its Director General, put pressure on the Post Office to control, and so inhibit, the rise of this new system of communication (Negrine, 1984). Such an analysis is therefore valuable in outlining the way in which technologies develop *within* societies, and so do not develop autonomously. A case study of satellite broadcasting, or telephony, would provide material for a comparative analysis or analyses.

At another level, the idea that technologies develop within societies points the way to an analysis of the diffusion of new technologies. Why did the VCR become so commonplace so rapidly? Why has cable television taken so much longer despite its promise? And why has the rate of growth of cable television been different across different countries? Such questions begin to touch on the ways in which cable television sits alongside other media – satellite television via a dish, terrestrial broadcasting, VCRs – and the possibility that these media may be competitors rather than simply allies. But, at the same time, it suggests that we have to have an understanding of the regulatory, economic and political forces which direct the speed, and the form, of development in different countries. For the researcher interested in the broad field of mass communication, all these questions are of great importance, and what, on the face of it, appears a dry and uninteresting topic area turns out to be of general social scientific interest.

So, having chosen the general topic of cable television, it then becomes necessary to specify what it is that the project will focus on. In this instance it will focus on a comparative analysis of the development of cable television in Britain, France and Germany (Dutton and Vedel, 1992; Vedel and Dutton, 1990; Schneider *et al.*, 1991) and, more precisely, on an examination of the reasons for different patterns of growth (Dutton and Vedel, 1992).

It is necessary, therefore, to establish a sequence of work, or perhaps even a checklist, which identifies the major issues and points which will have to be discussed. These include:

(1) the patterns of cable growth in the countries in question. What has been the rate, and pattern, of growth?
(2) how can that pattern of growth be explained? This would require a discussion of the background to cable policies in the countries in question; a discussion that takes in the cultural, historical, economic and political forces which are most likely to contribute to the generation of policies;
(3) are there similarities and differences which may need to be accounted for? What are these, and what accounts for them?

Implicit in this sequence of work is a sense of the analytical requirements of the project – what needs to be covered, if you like – and, equally importantly, what sorts of literature need to be collected, digested and discussed. A good literature search not only maps the area of work but establishes the foundations for the whole project. The process of searching a library for relevant material is made much easier by computerised catalogues; searching with the appropriate key words – in this case, cable television, broadcasting, television, communication policy, and some others – would generate an enormous amount of material. Following up cited references is another good way of extending the search. Other useful sources of information include: newspapers, particularly the *Financial Times*, *The Economist*, and certain other periodicals and journals such as *Screen Digest*, *Broadcast*, *Television Business International*, *Cable and Satellite Europe*. Some are indexed, others are not; some are easily available, others not. So a good search and a willingness to seek out the more unusual journals would easily repay the time invested. One other research method which can always be employed in work of this nature is to carry out interviews with certain key individuals whose understanding of the subject matter might prove helpful in interpreting events, documents, and the like. These could be regulators within the Independent Television Commission, civil servants in the relevant ministries, academics or journalists. Each can bring something different to the material and can help to make sense of it.

Getting hold of the material is a small, but important part, of the research process. Once the material has been collected, it has to be made sense of. A good example of the way such material can be explored can be found in Homet's (1979) writings on policy-making in Europe and the US. It is worth quoting at length certain sections from his study since their relevance is as strong today as when they were first published in 1979.

> There is no single or uniform West European approach to communication policymaking. Significant differences exist between countries and among various classes of communication services.
>
> Generalizations are accordingly hazardous, which is not surprising when one considers that policymaking is an attribute of political culture and that cultures are formed by the whole history of a people.
>
> But if there is no uniformity, there are common tendencies in Western European policymaking, which can be made to stand in relief when they are contrasted to the ways that communication policy is decided in North America.

> Americans would probably criticise European policymaking on several grounds: it does not foster service innovation or economic efficiency, it unnecessarily restricts consumers' freedom of choice, and it does not allow democratic involvement in the decision process. Europeans, on the other hand, would criticize the Americans for a wasteful insistence on both market competition and procedural regularity, claiming that each glorifies a process instead of the end result. What is wanted, they would say, is high quality and wise judgement – each of which can be better produced by an elite. (p. 14)

What we have in these quotes are some of the major differences in approaches to policy-making generally, but these differences spill over into more specific policy areas: in particular, areas of policy where the concern is with new, untried media such as cable. As Homet goes on to suggest, West European policy-makers are too concerned with eliminating risks in their management of technological change and thus they do not consider the possibility that flexibility is essential when faced with the unknown.

> There is ground for questioning many of the assumptions adopted by West European policy planners. Demand for new, presently unknown services may be inchoate but it is not impervious to stimulation. A global financing burden may be too large for governments but that need not rule out private entrepreneurs operating in, and subject to the disciplines of, the capital markets. Technical provision may be imperfect but standards can be designed flexibly to adapt to future evolutions. Above all, there is no reason to believe that today's uncertainties are any greater than will be those of tomorrow. (p. 51)

These statements are of interest for two main reasons. The first, and more immediate, is that Homet begins to identify differences in policy styles and policy-making between countries within Europe, and between Europe and the USA. These insights are extremely useful in the context of our specific example of cable television, and the ideas would clearly need to be followed up. The second reason why these quotes are of interest is that they tackle the policy-making question within the much broader context of technological change itself. In other words, there is an attempt to explore technological change, almost irrespective of the technology in question, within a societal context. In the last quote Homet contrasts market-driven solutions with state-directed ones and in this way raises a whole series of questions about how technologies evolve in different socioeconomic settings.

Providing such a broader theoretical overview of technological change is invaluable for a proper understanding of the evolution of technologies within societies. There is, therefore, some sort of theory which can be used to underpin the whole project in question, and to permit the work to develop in a coherent way and to be informed by theoretical insights. Without theoretical underpinning, research is not only incomplete but also unconnected to those sorts of issues about social change which are at the heart of communication research.

In the light of Homet's work, and with the schedule of work in mind, the following specific questions, or topic areas, may also need to be explored.

- When did serious interest in cable systems begin to manifest itself after 1970?
- What sorts of research or documentation may have influenced governmental 'thinking'? Briefly, and somewhat crudely, one can pinpoint three different strategies towards cable television, strategies which derive from three different documents: in Britain the *Cable systems* report of 1982 (ITAP, 1982), in France the Nora and Minc report of 1980 on the *Computerisation of society* (Nora and Minc, 1980), and in Germany the KtK report of 1976 (KtK, 1976). Each of these frames the issue in different ways: a free market liberal approach, a state-centred approach, a technologically driven telecommunication approach (Homet, 1979; Vedel and Dutton, 1990).
- What policies did governments pursue, and how were these received or viewed by interested parties such as the cable 'industry', advertisers, programme-makers, broadcasters, and so on?
- Were the policies implemented in their original form or were they amended? Why were they amended?
- Have the policies generally encouraged or discouraged the development of cable systems in the countries under investigation?

By setting out the sequence of events in this form, it becomes possible to interrogate the data with some theoretical notion in mind concerning the relationship between patterns of growth, policy regimes and the implementation of policies. We also need to take account of the fact that policies do change over time, in which case the original policy may have undergone some change, either of a mild or a more radical nature. The research would need to take care not to assume that a policy, once established, remains intact.

William Dutton and Thiery Vedel have recently published a piece of research which has attempted to confront the very issues that concern us here. By asking whether or not 'national cable policies (are) unique or converging?' (1992, p. 71), they have been able to focus not only on past policies and trends but also on more contemporary ones. By framing the question in the way they did, they created space for exploring the present state of the cable industries in relation to some (common) forces which, at the end of the day, may or may not lead to similarities in policy regimes. They were then better able to investigate whether such forces are more powerful than the policies – either original or amended – designed for those specific national systems of communication.

Finally, the research also permits in-depth analysis of the process, and meaning, of convergence.

Dutton and Vedel have argued that 'despite a multitude of cross-national differences in the specifics of cable policy, U.S., British, and French cable systems have developed along markedly similar paths.' (1992, p. 71) – see Figure 4.1. They go on to suggest that cable 'policy has travelled through four similar stages' since its invention. These stages can be set out in a chronological order and so can highlight the manner by which policies have changed, or adapted, to different circumstances.

(1) 'Initially, each nation witnessed a spontaneous, or market-led, introduction of cable systems . . .' (Ibid., p. 72).
(2) 'Eventually, the threatened interests ushered in public policies that restricted cable system development in each nation.' (Ibid., p. 73). The threatened interests included broadcasters, for example the BBC, and telephone companies, as in the US.
(3) 'At different points in time, public authorities in each nation then moved to promote cable system development to meet broader public interest objectives' (Ibid., p. 74).
(4) The last stage is the embrace of 'market-led expansion' for cable systems as enthusiasm for state-directed, publicly generated developments waned.

By looking at these stages, Dutton and Vedel argue that one can begin to detect a convergence both in an institutional sense but also with respect to the social values surrounding cable television, as, for example, in the changing image of cable in each of the countries in question from a medium of industrial significance to a primarily entertainment one (Ibid., p. 83).

But lest one suppose that such work is atheoretical, Dutton and Vedel stress that such work 'is central to the social study of technology, which has moved beyond a focus on the impacts of technological change to examine also the way social and political factors shape technology' (Ibid., p. 71). Furthermore, the convergence which has been identified also has to be explained in more than a simple descriptive fashion, and Dutton and Vedel's explanation draws on different bodies of interpretation, including:

- interpretations which explore the extent to which the nature of the technology in question helps to determine the pattern of its

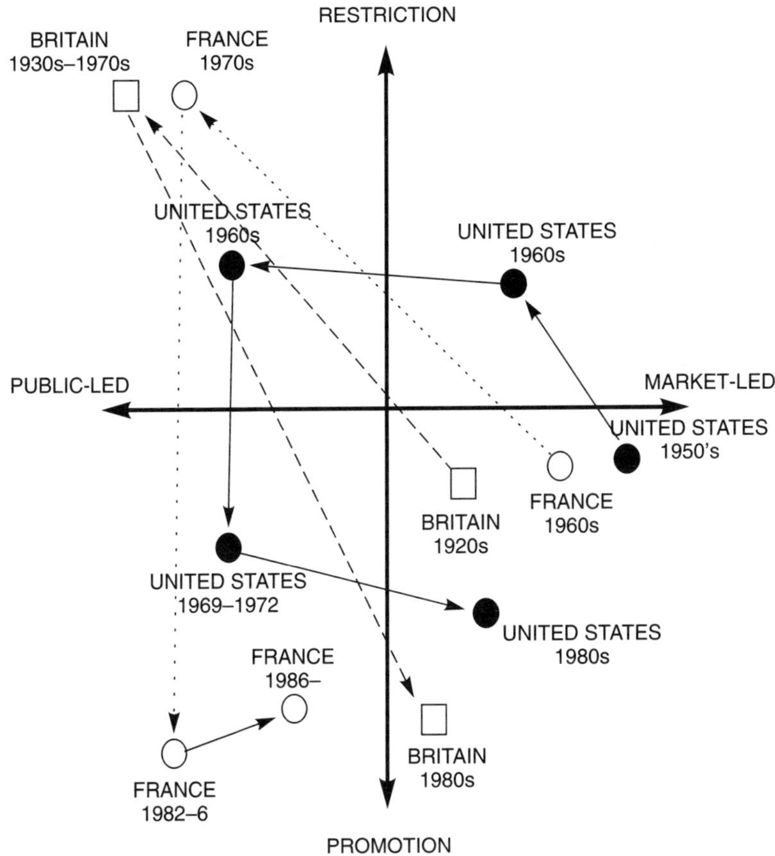

Figure 4.1 Paths of US, British and French cable policy

Note: The placement of nations on each continuum represents a consensus based on the judgmental ratings of the authors, who discussed the ratings with other experts on cable policy. It aims to reflect the relative positions of each nation, rather than any absolute position.
Source: Dutton and Vedel, 1992, p. 72.

development. This draws on work which looks at 'economic-cum-technological constraints' (Ibid., p. 83). For example, if its adoption and development is too expensive for any state to contemplate, that technology is more likely to develop within the private sphere;

- interpretations which emphasise the power given to certain cable industry groups to pursue their own specific interests (Ibid., p. 84);
- interpretations which emphasise the different preferences of different political groupings in power. So, convergence could perhaps be explained as 'a manifestation of partisan change with similar political interests in power pursuing similar policies' (Ibid., p. 84);
- interpretations which stress the international nature of the television industry; and
- interpretations which lean heavily on the notion that countries are imitating each other and thus adopting similar systems.

Dutton and Vedel's preferred explanation combines elements from the first and the last interpretation. There is, they argue,

> a case for some technological-cum-economic determinism in the sense that public authorities have been unable to mold cable technology and services in ways that fitted in with their early visions. In every country, market forces seemed to undermine public-led policies, particularly those aimed at promoting advanced technology and public services. Second, images of cable in other countries have shaped policies . . . but in less direct ways than suggested by notions of emulation. (Ibid., p. 86).

Their explanation is, in turn, open to further critical analysis. For example, what are 'market-led' forces if not a combination of other things? They could be nothing more than the ascendance of a certain political ideology (of deregulation) pursued by transnational groupings. Similarly, is it possible that the convergence which they have identified is merely a superficial one? Does their account have a predictive quality to it, and how does it fare in non-Western countries?

Although this process of continual questioning may appear to be an exercise for its own sake, it is a central part of the process by which better explanations come to be developed. Without this continuous process of inquiry, there is unlikely to be any advance in our knowledge of this, or any other, area.

From this example, we can begin to identify a series of stages in the completion of this particular piece of research. These are:

- selecting the topic of inquiry
- defining the problem to be investigated

- setting out a sequence of work or checklist of areas to be explored
- undertaking a literature search
- reviewing the literature
- refining the problem of the research
- providing a theoretical context for the work
- examining the problem in the light of the material collected
- carrying out a piece of original research, for example, interviews, questionnaires
- arriving at a conclusion which combines theory and analysis
- reviewing the conclusion and anticipating future research.

In practice, this schedule of work can be used in most settings, since it comprises the main stages which all research has to go through. Our second example, that of the future of public broadcasting in Europe, will illustrate the usefulness of the stages identified above.

4.4.2 Example 2: The Future of Public Broadcasting in Europe

The concern over the future of public broadcasting in Europe, a concern which is now commonly voiced by many, can be said to have its roots in a combination of technological and socio-political changes which have taken place since the early 1970s. These changes would include the advent of cable and satellite television which directly challenged the 'scarcity of broadcasting channels' argument which had hitherto underpinned terrestrial broadcasting in Europe, as well as the ascendancy of political preferences for more market-led and consumer-led solutions to public problems such as the future funding of public broadcasting.

Together, these technical and political changes challenged the unique position which public broadcasting organisations had previously occupied. They were no longer seen as the only possible providers of entertainment and information, and their cultural leadership and direction was undermined by those, mainly of the political right, who felt that the media audience as *consumers* of media products should become sovereign (see, for example, Peacock, 1986; Veljanowski, 1989).

One obvious and visible outcome of these changes has been the proliferation of commercially funded private satellite and cable television services across Europe (Table 4.1) although it should be added that the increase in the number of services does not of itself guarantee a widening of *the range of material* available to viewers.

Nevertheless, as the share of the television audience of the public broadcasters has declined, either because some viewers have turned to the new commercial services or because the national audience has become fragmented, the public broadcasters have had to develop strategies to meet the competition. Since, by and large, governments have refused to countenance an increase in the financial support offered to public broadcasters, these strategies could not include that of an across the board improvement in programme quality to match the competition. In practice, public broadcasters have had to compete by improving some of their programming (as far as the level of funding would allow); compete by broadcasting similar sorts or material, for example, soap vs. soap; by forming alliances, for example, BBC and Pearson, or by 'popularising' some of their content.

Table 4.1 Number of TV channels in Europe 1980/1990

	1980		*1990*		
	Public	*Commercial*	*Public*	*Commercial*	*Foreign cable*
Austria	2		2		12
Belgium	4		4	2	21
Denmark	1		2		25–30
Finland	2		2	1	
France	3		3	3	15–20
Germany	3		3/5	4	5–10
Greece	2		3	4	
Ireland	2		2	(1)	10–20
Italy	3		3	6	
Luxembourg		4		2(4)[a]	20–23
Netherlands	2		3	(1)	15–20
Norway	1		1	1	10–20
Portugal	2		2		
Spain	2		3[b]	3	
Sweden	2		2	3	15–20
Switzerland	3		3		12–20
UK	2	1	2	5+	

[a] Two area based in Luxembourg but beamed to other countries.
[b] One is regional

Source: K. Siune and W. Truetzchler (1992) (eds) *Dynamics of media politics* (London: Sage) p. 103.

This thumb-nail sketch of recent broadcasting history lays bare some of the main trends which a fuller, detailed study of the place of public broadcasting in Europe would have to flesh out. What parts would be fleshed out, and in what way, would depend very much on the specific research area which required investigation. In other words, one has to select and define the problem in question in greater detail. In this particular instance, the main problem area is 'the future of public broadcasting in Europe', and this gives a sense of the issues or questions which will have to be explored in the process of passing some sort of judgement on the transition from the past, to the present, and into the future of public broadcasting in Europe. A sketchy outline of these issues or questions would need to include:

- a broad European perspective on the emergence of broadcasting in Europe (although country-specific and comparative studies are also possible)
- a focus on public broadcasting – what is it in theory and in practice? Are there variations of a basic model?
- an analysis of technological change
- an analysis of socio-political change
- an analysis of changes in programme schedules and the contents of programmes before, say, the advent of the 'new' media and some years after
- an analysis of changing patterns of viewing
- a discussion of the likely pattern of future change.

One obvious difficulty with this structure is that it is, in fact, a very broad one; possibly too broad, since the European-wide emphasis would require an in-depth analysis of a large number of countries. This would suggest that it might be preferable to concentrate either on a single country or on two countries so as to provide room to compare how these changes are playing themselves out in different environments. This refinement of the problem would not only ease data collection but would also narrow it down so as to make it more amenable to a short piece of work.

The next step in the process would be to conduct a literature search. This would, most likely, reveal a large number of books, articles and magazines which dealt with the topic of broadcasting, public broadcasting, and contemporary socio-political and technological change. Some of that material is probably easier to access than others; audience data, and programme schedules may be more difficult to get hold of. In some countries this presents no problem, in others it does.

There are two major areas of inquiry which need detailed scrutiny. The first relates to the concept or idea of public broadcasting or public service broadcasting which is, for many, at risk. Although there are some common features which can be said to relate to the concept of public service broadcasting (Appendix 4.1), even a cursory glance at these will confirm that an element of evaluative judgement has gone into their construction. Public service broadcasting, certainly as it is interpreted within the British context, is suggestive of a certain positive cultural and ideologically committed enterprise. But this idea may not have its direct equivalent in other countries and it would be incumbent on the researcher to explore the different meanings of public broadcasting available across Europe (see Syvertsen, 1992, for example). If, for instance, public broadcasting is no more than a state-controlled, badly funded service which does not provide high quality broadcasting or a diversity of news content – this is a caricature of the old Greek ERT – its loss would be viewed differently from the loss of an organisation such as the BBC (see Kuhn, 1985, for comparative material).

The second difficulty which is likely to be encountered in carrying out this sort of research is the attempt to build in an element of analysis *over time*. If the argument is that public broadcasting has changed as a consequence of the advent of other commercial rivals, it would be necessary to demonstrate the changes. Have there been changes in where certain types of programmes are scheduled? Have there been changes in the proportion of certain types of programmes (information vs. entertainment, domestic vs. foreign productions, and so on) shown on various channels? What other changes, if any, can one point to? Some extensive and sophisticated content analysis will undoubtedly be called for!

Yet this part of the project is central to the research project as a whole, because it lies at the heart of the thesis about the transition which is alleged to be taking place in European broadcasting systems. Furthermore, it provides information and observations concerning the positive and negative aspects of the changes, if any, that have been, or are, taking place. Such differences will then have to be looked at in detail, since they provide a broad context within which we can try to understand the meaning of contemporary change. By defining the problem carefully, and by refining it in the light of the material which has been collected, and reviewed, a better structure is being put in place for the continued examination of the research problem.

The next few steps comprise the collection of data which would permit the argument to develop, and an explanation of the nature and causes of change. One such explanation could be grounded in a political economy approach which would stress the nature of ownership, the pursuit of profit and the more general capitalist nature of media industries; another could be more empirically grounded in its emphasis on the economic and social consequences of competition; yet another could stress the pursuit of ideological politics in favour of private enterprises and market solutions. The material collected must, however, make 'sense' in the context of the explanation or explanations preferred.

One good example of a recent piece of research on this particular topic which employs a variant of the sequence of work set out above is Jay Blumler's *Television and the public interest* (1992). In this work, we can see the stages outlined above fleshed out and supported by data. For this reason it is worth looking at it in a little more detail.

In the introduction, Blumler focuses on the 'current confrontations in West European television' and the problems which such 'confrontations' raise (pp. 1–5). At the heart of this short introduction is the preoccupation, as he puts it, 'with the likely fate in the new scheme of things of the reduced but still sizeable public service broadcasting organizations . . .' (p. 4). But to inquire into the future, to explore 'the likely fate', one has to determine the nature of the past and the present. What will be lost, if anything, and what is there to come?

These themes are explored in Blumler's next two chapters. The first is titled 'Public service broadcasting before the commercial deluge', and the second 'Valuable values at stake'. The sense of change, of things at risk, comes through very easily even from these chapter headings, though Blumler spends much time developing his position. In the first of the two chapters one can find a section on the 'legacy' of public service broadcasting, and an elucidation of 'points of vulnerability'. The second of these two chapters provides even more details ranging from data on the number of broadcast services available in Europe, to a fully worked out set of values – programme quality, diversity, cultural identity, and so on (see Appendix 4.1) – which are at risk, or likely to be at risk in the new commercial, market-led broadcasting environment.

The purpose of relating these themes is not to offer a critique of Blumler's work but, more simply, to illustrate how an argument about changes in broadcasting is constructed, and what sorts of data are necessary to support the argument. At the end of the day, he presents a position which, like that of Dutton and Vedel (1992), can be accepted either because the data is sufficiently strong for it to have some purchase or because it has a coherence to it which is not easily open to questioning. There is always, however, room for rejecting the argument because it is framed in a way which does not make sense or does not cohere in a logical way. There is a further possibility with respect to the Blumler study, namely that in certain circumstances, particularly where evaluative criteria are inherent in the argument, it may be possible to question the implicit (or explicit) position which is put forward. One could, for example, dispute whether the values of cultural identity or even quality broadcasting are themselves meaningful. In which case, the subsequent pursuit of the argument becomes meaningless. Put differently, if there is no fundamental agreement on what the problem is – are fundamental values really at stake? – the subsequent construction of the argument may be of little importance. (Interestingly, such a critique of the project can often be incorporated very meaningfully into the sorts of work described here.)

4.5 Conclusion and Summary

We have, in effect, once more completed the stages of research identified above, and with the problem having been defined and the research having been completed, the summary and discussion is then open to critical responses. This then generates further debate, and so on. And, as before, the intention is to arrive at a better understanding of the changes which are taking place in society.

There is one other point that is worth making about both the examples discussed here, namely that in both cases some of the research which has to be carried out is historical. In the first example, there is the need to look at the history of the cable industry and changing policies towards that industry; in the second example, there is a need to examine the evolution of public service broadcasting and to compare its contemporary manifestation with its dim and distant past. Historical research, then, need not be seen as something distinct in itself, although it can be treated as such. Very often it can contribute to our present understanding of the state of the communication industry, policies towards the media, and a whole range of other areas.

Nonetheless, in recent years some important works have been published which have raised important issues about communication within societies through an exploration of historical developments in communication systems. One example would be the 'social history' of broadcasting which has illuminated the role of the BBC in helping define British culture and British cultural practices (Scannell and Cardiff, 1989). Another would be works which have explored the impact of printing and the press on society in general, and on political representation in particular (Keane, 1991; Eisenstein, 1979).

These works, despite their primarily historical orientation, still demand that certain processes of research be observed. The focus of research still needs to be defined carefully, the review of the literature still has to be carried out meticulously, the arguments still need to be marshalled carefully, and so on. This is not to suggest that historical research is identical to research in the social sciences, but that some of the key principles of research may be very similar.

4.6 Summary

- Communication policy research addresses a wide range of contemporary concerns regarding the structure and organisation of communication systems in the past, in the present and in the future.
- Communication policy analysis seeks to examine the ways in which policies are generated and implemented, as well as the repercussions or implications of these policies for the field of communication as a whole.
- Communication policy analysis has recently focused on the 'convergence' of communication and telecommunications systems, for example, broadcasting and telecommunications, and the implications of this convergence for hitherto separate structures of communication.
- In communication policy analysis one needs to be aware of the many, and different, forces that play a part in the policy-making process.
- Before embarking on a particular piece of communication analysis, it is vital to undertake a comprehensive search of the relevant literature. This search would normally cover a range of related fields such as historical analysis, political and sociological writings, as well as governmental and other documents in the public domain.

- In communication policy analysis one needs to be aware of the different ways in which documents relating to communication policy appear in the public domain. Such documents could include government papers, announcements, committee reports, and so on. Statements by ministers, for instance, may also address policies towards communication systems.
- Conducting policy research requires the use of a combination of research methods, including archival research and interviewing of policy actors.
- Finally, communication policy analysis benefits greatly from the examination of the collected data within a strong theoretical framework which sets out to explore key relationships and processes.

Appendix 4.1: Some Different Ways of Looking at Public Service Broadcasting and its Values

(1) According to the Broadcasting Research Unit report (1985), there are eight principles of 'public service broadcasting'. These are:

- geographic universality – everyone should have access to the same services;
- catering for all interests and tastes;
- catering for minorities;
- catering for 'national identity and community';
- detachment from vested interests and government;
- one broadcasting system to be funded directly from the corpus of users;
- competition in good programming rather than for numbers; and
- guidelines to liberate programme makers and not to restrict them.

(2) Raymond Kuhn lists 'four elements':

- 'a commitment to balanced scheduling across the different programme genres, with no undue emphasis on any one . . . *One* institution has frequently had the task of satisfying *all* the audience's needs;

- the broadcast institution is a public body, with normally a high degree of financial independence from both government and commercial sources;
- the service is provided for all
- political output is obliged to be balanced and impartial.' (1985, pp. 4–5)

(3) Jay Blumler sets out seven 'vulnerable values' which could be at stake in the future (1992, pp. 22–42). These are:

- programme quality
- diversity
- cultural identity
- independence of programme sources from commercial influences
- the integrity of civic communication
- welfare of children and juveniles
- maintenance of standards.

References

Blumler, J. (1992) (ed.) *Television and the public interest* (London: Sage).

Broadcasting Research Unit (BRU) (1985) *The public service idea in British broadcasting* (London: BRU).

Dutton, W. and T. Vedel (1992) 'The dynamics of cable television in the US, Britain, and France', in J. Blumler, J. McLeod and K. E. Rosengren (eds) *Comparatively speaking: communication and culture across space and time* (pp. 70–93) (London: Sage).

Eisenstein, E. (1979) *The printing press as an agent of social change* (Cambridge University Press).

Homet, R. (1979) *Politics, cultures and communication* (New York: Praeger).

Information Technology Advisory Panel (ITAP) (1982) *Cable systems* (London: HMSO).

Keane, J. (1991) *The media and democracy* (Cambridge: Polity Press).

KtK Kommission fur den Ausbau des technischen Kommunikationssystems (1976) *Telekommunikationsbericht* (Bonn).

Kuhn, R. (1985) (ed.) *The politics of broadcasting* (Kent: Croom Helm).

Negrine, R. (1984) 'From radio relay to cable television: the British experience', in *Historical Journal of Film Radio and Television*, **4** (1), pp. 29–48.

Negrine, R. (1985) 'Cable television in Great Britain', in R. Negrine (ed.) *Cable television and the future of broadcasting* (Kent: Croom Helm).

Negrine, R. (1994) *Politics and the mass media in Britain* (London: Routledge).

Nora, S. and A. Minc (1980) *The computerization of society* (Cambridge, Mass.: MIT).

Peacock Committee (1986) *Report of the Committee on Financing the BBC.* Chaired by Professor A. Peacock (London: HMSO) Cmnd 9824.

Scannell, P. and D. Cardiff (1989) *A social history of broadcasting* (Oxford: Basil Blackwell).

Schneider, V., J. M. Charon, I. Miles, G. Thomas and T. Vedel (1991) 'The dynamics of videotext development in Britain, France and Germany', in *European Journal of Communication*, **6**(2).

Siune, K. and W. Truetzschler (1992) *Dynamics of media politics* (London: Sage).

Syvertsen, T. (1992) *Public television in transition. A comparative and historical analysis of the BBC and the NRK*, KULTs skriftserie no. 10 (Oslo).

Vedel, T. and W. Dutton (1990) 'New media politics: shaping cable television policy in France' in *Media Culture and Society*, **12**, pp. 491–524.

Veljanowski, C. (ed.) (1989) *Freedom in Broadcasting* (London: Institute of Economic Affairs).

5

Content Analysis

5.1 Introduction

Ask anybody what the media portray as the most pressing issues of the day, or how they portray illegal drug use, violence, politics, international conflict, and so on, or what images are represented of moral values, sex, foreigners, human relationships, etcetera, and in all likelihood most will readily offer relatively comprehensive accounts. We are all to varying degrees consumers of or casual observers of media contents. Chances are, however, that whatever answer is offered will be implicitly selective; that is, it will relate to a particular medium (for example television), or a particular type of media content (such as advertising, news, or serial drama), or a particular event or period in time.

If we wish to describe and analyse media content in a more comprehensive way, a way less prone to subjective selectiveness and idiosyncracies, then we must employ a systematic method. Content analysis is one such method for the systematic analysis of communications content. It is by no means the only method for studying media content (see Chapters 6–8 for introductions to other approaches). Indeed, during its long history of use it has repeatedly been criticised, *inter alia*, for its quantitative nature, for its fragmentation of textual wholes, for its positivist notion of objectivity, for its lack of a theory of meaning (see Kracauer, 1952, for an early critique; see also Burgelin, 1972, and Sumner, 1979). Rather than emphasising its alleged incompatibility with other more qualitative approaches (such as semiotics, structuralist analysis, discourse analysis) we wish to stress in this chapter that content analysis is and should be enriched by the theoretical framework offered by other more qualitative approaches, while bringing to these a methodological rigour, prescriptions for use, and systematicity rarely found in many of the more qualitative approaches.[1]

As a communications research method, content analysis is distinguished by its long pedigree. Krippendorf (1980) cites an eighteenth-century Swedish study of ninety hymns of unknown authorship as one of the earliest documented cases of quantitative analysis of printed texts. During the present century, some of the most spectacular early uses of content analysis were in propaganda analysis. Through the systematic analysis of German radio broadcasts, Allied intelligence was able to monitor, and in some cases predict, troop movements, the launch and location of new military campaigns, and the development and deployment of new weapons. While these studies were a case of using content analysis for finding out about the intentions of the originator of messages, the aim of content analysis in media research has more often been that of examining how news, drama, advertising, and entertainment output reflect social and cultural issues, values, and phenomena.

Indeed several of this century's most prominent sociologists have been attracted to the idea of using content analysis for monitoring the 'cultural temperature' of society, for establishing long-term cultural indicators comparable to the indicators used by economists and politicians in the monitoring of the economy. In the 1930s Harold Lasswell called for a 'continuing survey of "world attention" – as reflected in trends in media coverage of various social issues – to show the elements involved in the formation of public opinion' (Beniger, 1978, p. 438). In 1910 Max Weber had similarly proposed an ambitious long-term systematic study of press coverage of social and political issues to be carried out together with the monitoring of public opinion responses and changes (see Neuman, 1989). Weber's proposal did not, however, take off. One reason for this was undoubtedly the very considerable cost of sustained collection and analysis of media coverage. Another reason was that neither survey research or 'content analysis' had been developed into fully fledged methods at that time.

The development of content analysis as a formal method of social science inquiry took place in the years between the two World Wars, as well as in the major research programmes of Harold Lasswell and his associates around and during the Second World War. Developments in the method were spurred on by concerns about the contribution of the mass media to social upheaval and international conflict, a concern with the new electronic medium of radio, and the desire to make social inquiry 'scientific' in a manner comparable to the controlled, systematic, objective, and supposedly predictive, methods of the natural sciences.

From being used at the turn of the century mainly for keeping inventories of the contents of American newspapers and for journalistic studies (Holsti, 1969, p. 21), content analysis grew in the middle part of this century to become part of larger and theoretically much richer projects of social and political analysis. The method was increasingly integrated into larger research efforts involving not just the analysis of media content, but also other methods of inquiry (surveys, experiments, participant observation, qualitative and ethnographic audience research) and types of data.

In the latter half of this century, perhaps one of the most prominent examples of content analysis, integrated into a larger framework of analysis articulating media roles in the cultivation of public consciousness, is George Gerbner's cultural indicators programme. Originally outlined in 1969, this programme proposed the use of content analysis for the systematic monitoring of trends and developments in the symbolic environment of American television (Gerbner, 1995). The cultural indicators research by George Gerbner and his colleagues (Gerbner, Gross, Morgan and Signorielli, 1980 and 1994) combines detailed content analysis of television entertainment programming with surveys of public beliefs and attitudes to examine how far television 'cultivates' certain world-views in its audiences. In this respect, the cultural indicators/cultivation studies are typical of a considerable body of research which has used content analysis together with various types of studies of audiences to examine media influence on public beliefs, attitudes, opinion, and behaviour. Another prominent strand of research in this general area is agenda-setting studies (see Rogers and Dearing, 1988) which have attempted to establish how far the issues which dominate the media agenda (as established through content analysis of media coverage) come to dominate and influence what the public 'think about' or regard as the most important issues of the day (as established through surveys of public beliefs and opinion).

Content analysis also grew to become an important component in the armoury of studies of international media flows, carried out within wider debates and concerns about a New World Information and Communication Order and about cultural imperialism, development communication, globalization, and transnational information and image flows (Sreberny-Mohammadi, 1984).

As well as being used for mapping changing cultural and socio-political trends in the media – and the relationship between such trends and changes in public opinion and beliefs (Janowitz, 1976; Neuman, 1989) – content analysis became integrated into studies of media organisations, media professionals, sources of media information, and, generally, the production of news and other media content. Several of the classic studies of news production combine observational methods (in news organisations) and interviews (with media professionals and sources) with content analysis of the 'product': the news (for example, Gans, 1979; Fishman, 1980; and the Ericson, Baranek and Chan trilogy: 1987; 1989; 1991).

5.2 Content Analysis: Definitions and Problems

The development into a formal method of social science inquiry also brought up key questions/problems about the analysis of communications content generally and about this method in particular. These were problems revolving around the question of how far content analysis could be used for making informed inferences either from texts to conditions, intentions, and factors circumscribing the production of texts, or from texts to their social impact, influence, interpretation and reception. Essentially, these problems hinge on the fundamental question of 'meaning' and 'significance': how far is it possible to pin down the meaning of any text, whether it be the meaning as intended by the producers of texts or the meaning as it is 'read' and understood by consumers/recipients of texts?

In order to examine these questions in more detail, we need to look at definitions of content analysis. The classic and much quoted definition of content analysis comes from the first major review of the method, Bernard Berelson's *Content analysis in communication research*, published in 1952:

> Content analysis is a research technique for the objective, systematic, and quantitative description of the manifest content of communication (p. 18).

Much of the controversy over content analysis has focused on the notion that it must be 'objective'. Critics eager to debunk positivist science have focused on the objectivity requirement, arguing fundamentally, and rightly, that objectivity in content analysis as in any other kind of scientific research is an impossible ideal serving only to cover cosmetically and mystify the values, interests, and means of knowledge production which underpin such research. Content analysis, of course, could never be objective in a 'value-free' sense of the word: it does not analyse everything there is to analyse in a text (no method could, nor would there be any purpose in trying) – instead the content analyst starts by delineating certain dimensions or aspects of text for analysis, and in doing so, he or she is of course also making a choice – subjective, albeit generally informed by the theoretical framework and ideas which circumscribes his or her research – and indicating that the dimensions chosen for analysis are the important or significant aspects to look at. The criticism of positivist 'objectivity' criteria is by now both well-rehearsed and generally accepted, and it is indeed possible that a strictly positivist 'value free' notion of objectivity was never what was intended in the first place in definitions of the requirements of content analysis. Thus, it is perhaps symptomatic that later definitions of content analysis have omitted references to 'objectivity', requiring simply that content analysis be 'systematic' (Holsti, 1969) or 'replicable' (Krippendorf, 1980).[2]

Content analysis is by definition a quantitative method. The purpose of the method is to identify and count the occurrence of specified characteristics or dimensions of texts, and through this, to be able to say something about the messages, images, representations of such texts and their wider social significance. The problem, however, is how far quantification is taken in content analysis and to what degree the quantitative indicators that this technique offers are read or interpreted in relation to questions about the intensity of meaning in texts, the social impact of texts, or the relationship between media texts and the realities which they reflect.

As noted by Holsti (1969), early 'definitions of content analysis required that inferences from content data be derived strictly from the *frequency* with which symbols or themes appear in the text' (p. 6). Fifty years of communication research have, however, made it plainly clear that there is no such simple relationship between media content and its reception and social implications. Content analysis can help provide some indication of relative prominences and absences of key characteristics in media texts, but the inferences that can be drawn from such indications depend entirely on the context and framework of interpretation by which the texts analysed are circumscribed.

Thus, it would clearly be naïve to assume that a television serial showing ten incidents of cigarette smoking in every hour of programming is ten times more likely to influence viewers to smoke than a television serial showing only one incident of cigarette smoking in every hour. The relationship between the frequency with which some activity or phenomenon is portrayed and its wider social impact is far more complex than this, as long recognised in communication research, but this is not in itself an indictment against the practice of quantitative analysis; rather it points, in this example, to the need for placing what is counted in content analysis within a theoretical framework which articulates, in the form of a model of communication influence, the social significance and meaning of what is being counted.

On the question of quantification, we might similarly ask: is the over-representation of certain occupations, types of (a-)social behaviour, ethnic groups, and so on a case of media misrepresentation, distortion, and bias? Or, could the highly selective emphases of media images of reality be seen as an 'accurate' symbolic reflection (and perpetuation) of dominant social values? (see Gerbner, 1972).

The important point arising from these two questions is again that it is not the practice of counting and quantifying as such that needs to be questioned, but rather the 'meaning' or interpretation which is attached to the quantitative indicators provided by content analysis. There are two dimensions to this problem. The first concerns the practice of counting the frequency of occurrence of symbols; the second concerns what is seen as the fragmentation of meaning arising from the practice of singling out countable dimensions of texts for analysis. On the first aspect, critics of content analysis have thus argued:

> It is not the significance of repetition that is important but rather the repetition of significance. In which case the first question to answer concerns significance and perhaps then there can be some counting. But content analysis has no theory of significance. It merely assumes the significant existence (or existence-as-significance) of what it counts. It may be counting illusions or a fragmentary part of a real significance, but without a theory of significance it would not *know*: its concept of the significance of repetition gives it no knowledge of the significance of what is being repeated. (Sumner, 1979, p. 69)

There can be little disagreement that counting the insignificant has little purpose. Nor need we quarrel with the argument that the meaning or interpretation associated with certain symbols does not become any more 'right' or 'accurate' by counting the number of times the symbols appear. Thomas (1994) makes this point very lucidly:

> In recent years, the fuss over interpretational pluralism has pushed claims of indeterminate meaning to such extremes that we may have lost sight of the important difference between coding and interpretation.
>
> . . . [However] it is not at the level of coding at which the so-called reception problems reside. For instance, if there is a count of words or a coding of characters' hair color, or even noting violent acts (as explicitly defined), few would argue that these measurements alone are sites of contested meaning. The astute critic of content analysis would more likely say that the problem resides either in the unitizing (e.g., 'it's not that I can't identify a punch, it's that I question whether you should be counting punches') or in interpreting the data after they are collected (e.g., 'It's not that I can't identify a punch, it's that I don't agree that the distribution of punches signifies what you suggest it does'). (p. 693)

The second line of criticism concerns the argument that in counting individual units and their frequency of occurrence, content analysis fails to capture the way in which meaning arises from the complex interaction of symbols in texts. In the words of Burgelin:

> above all there is no reason to assume that the item which recurs most frequently is the most important or the most significant, for a text is, clearly, a *structured* whole, and the place occupied by the different elements is more important than the number of times they recur. (1972, p. 319)

True to his argument for a semiotic approach to the analysis of texts, Burgelin goes on to state:

> the meaning of what is frequent is only revealed by opposition to what is rare. In other words, the meaning of a frequently-recurring item is not essentially linked to the fact that it occurs ten times

> rather than twenty times, but it is essentially linked to the fact that it is placed in opposition to another item which occurs rarely (or which is sometimes even absent) . . . Structural analysis provides a way of approaching this problem, which traditional content analysis does not. (Ibid., p. 319)

Clearly, a content analysis which confines itself to counting the number of times a violent act is committed, or the number of dark-haired characters, or the number of times the word 'fundamentalism' appears will fail singularly to capture the meaning or significance of these symbols in the texts analysed. But then again very few content analyses confine themselves to such 'meaningless' counting. Content analyses count occurrences of specified dimensions *and* they analyse the *relationships* between these dimensions. Although content analysis initially fragments texts down into constituent parts which can be counted, it re-assembles these constituent parts at the analysis and interpretation stage to examine which ones co-occur in which contexts, for what purposes, and with what implications. Moreover, and in contrast to many 'qualitative'/'interpretative' approaches, content analysis, because it follows clearly articulated rules and procedures, lays open to scrutiny the means by which textual meaning is dissected and examined.

In summary then, it is argued here that much of the criticism which has been directed at content analysis touches on problems more to do with the potential and actual (mis)-uses and abuses of the method, than to do with any inherent weaknesses of this method as a method of data-collection.

5.3 Doing Content Analysis: the Key Steps

The process of content analysis can be broken down into a series of clearly articulated steps. While different scholars have divided these steps in different ways, from as few as four or five steps to ten[3], twelve or more steps, we propose here to describe the process of content analysis as consisting of six related steps:

(1) definition of the research problem
(2) selection of media and sample
(3) defining analytical categories
(4) constructing a coding schedule

(5) piloting the coding schedule and checking reliability
(6) data-preparation and analysis.

5.3.1 Definition of the Research Problem

The first step in content analysis, and one which logically precedes even the decision to use the method of content analysis, is to define what the research problem is: what is it that we would hope to be able to say something about by analysing a body of media texts? What aspect of communication, media roles, social phenomena, textual characteristics is it that the proposed research would aim to throw some light on?

Content analysis is a method for analysing texts. It is not a theory. As a method, it provides no pointers to *what* aspects of texts should be examined, or *how* those dimensions should be interpreted. Such pointers have to come from a theoretical framework, which would include a clear conceptualisation of the nature and social context of the documents which are to be examined. In relation to the analysis of media content this may concern questions about its production (for example, the influence of ownership, commercial interests, editorial policies, journalistic practices, news sources) and/or its consumption (for example, the role of news-coverage in relation to social, political, ideological, and economic processes, or in relation to individual audience or readership phenomena).

Content analysis is not and should not be carried out simply for the purpose of counting what can be counted in media content. Any number of dimensions of texts can be categorised and counted. It is only by making a clear statement of the research problem or objective that the researcher can ensure that the analysis focuses on those aspects of content which are relevant to the research. Indeed, it is not uncommon to see a great deal of time and effort being spent in content analyses on measuring the column inches of newspaper articles or the duration of news items in television news. These dimensions are easily, if laboriously, measured and counted. Yet, unless such space and time dimensions are particularly articulated as an important aspect of the research problem under investigation (that is, the research statement specifically hypothesises about the significance of the overall volume of coverage), they generally yield only relatively shallow pointers to the nature of the content being analysed.

A clear conceptualisation of the research problem – and the subsequent definition of what aspects and categories of content should be analysed – should always be anchored in a review of relevant literature and related studies. This is partly a question of not re-inventing the wheel unnecessarily and it is partly a question of taking advantage of comparisons, where possible, with previous analyses. Successive studies of the changing contents of British newspapers have, for example, benefited from keeping to procedures and categories which allow comparisons over time (see particularly Raymond Williams' analyses for the years 1961, 1965, and 1973 (Williams, 1976), and earlier comparisons by Silverman of the years 1927, 1937, and 1947, published as part of the 1949 Report of the Royal Commission on the Press). Other examples include studies of the portrayal of race and cross-racial relationships in prime-time television broadcasting (Weigel, Kim and Frost, 1995); studies of the portrayal of violence and the demographics of characters in popular television drama (Gerbner, and Gross, 1976; Gerbner, Gross, Morgan, and Signorielli, 1994); and numerous studies of the portrayal of alcohol and drinking on television (Breed and DeFoe, 1981, 1984; Hansen, 1986; Pendleton, Smith and Roberts, 1991; Wallack, Grube, Madden and Breed, 1990).

5.3.2 Selection of Media and Sample

It is rarely either possible or desirable to analyse absolutely all media coverage of a subject, area or issue. At the same time, it is precisely one of the major advantages of content analysis over, for example, semiotic analysis that it lends itself to the analysis of large bodies of text or media content. The media, however, produce gigantic volumes of text, sound and images. For conceptual and, more specifically, for practical reasons therefore content analysis must start with the selection and narrowing down of the type of coverage to be analysed. First, it is necessary to define clearly what body of media will be analysed, described and characterised. Next, it is often desirable and necessary to choose a representative sample from this body of media content. In practice the process of defining the media (the population) and sampling amounts, as Berelson indicated in 1952, to the following steps:

(1) the selection of media or titles;
(2) the sampling of issues or dates;
(3) the sampling of relevant content.

The Selection of Media or Titles

The term 'media coverage' is all-encompassing and could refer to anything from newspaper coverage, television, and radio, to magazines, cinema, bill-board advertising, or even electronic bulletin boards on the Internet. In practice, any content analysis of 'media coverage' would start by specifying more particularly which media (radio, television, press, and so on), and which channels or particular newspaper-titles within these media, were to be analysed. In general, of course, the choice of media and titles to be analysed would depend on the nature of the research problem or subject.

More specifically, the choice of media and titles involves a combination of considerations regarding: geographical reach (for example, national versus regional); audience size (for example, mass versus minority); audience type (for example, age, social class, profession, race, gender); format and content characteristics of media (for example, tabloid versus 'quality' press; political stance: for example, liberal versus conservative newspapers) – which, in turn, of course are related to the nature of the target audience; and, last but in practice often one of the most decisive factors, accessibility and availability of research material – these are decisive factors, particularly where retrospective analysis is needed.

Most content analysis studies tend to confine themselves to the analysis of only one or two types of medium: for example newspapers and magazines (Chapman, 1986), or newspapers and radio (Troyna, 1981), although there are studies which comprise all of the major media types; Ericson and his colleagues (1991), for example, sampled news coverage from newspapers, television, and radio.

The Sampling of Issues or Dates

Once the medium or media have been selected, the next step is to choose issues, dates, or periods which should be analysed. This depends essentially on whether the subject of analysis relates to a specific event (for example, specific nuclear accidents such as those at the Three Mile Island and Chernobyl power plants (Rubin, 1987; Friedman, Gorney and Egolf, 1987); a riot (Tumber, 1982; Hansen and Murdock, 1985); a war (Morrison, 1992; Morrison and Tumber, 1988)) or whether it concerns the mapping of some general dimension of coverage such as the portrayal of women, race, violence, science, environmental issues, health, alcohol consumption, risk, terrorism, foreign countries, drugs. In the former type, the period to be analysed is 'naturally' defined by the time and dates of the event concerned. Thus both the Falklands War in 1982 and the Gulf War in 1991 had relatively clearly defined start and end dates. Similarly with the British inner-city riots of 1981 and the Los Angeles riot of 1992.

It is important to bear in mind, however, that while event-specific coverage may be clearly defined by the dates of an event, the key to understanding the role and nature of media coverage would often necessitate analysis of coverage both before and after the dates or period of a specific event. In their classic study of an anti-Vietnam War demonstration in London in 1968, Halloran and his colleagues (Halloran, Elliott and Murdock, 1970), for example, noted that the media's emphasis on violence in their coverage of an essentially non-violent demonstration could be explained mainly as a self-fulfilling prophesy: media coverage in the period leading up to the actual demonstration had put great emphasis on the expectation that the demonstration would run out of control and lead to violent clashes. Consequently this became the main frame for the coverage of the demonstration itself. Similarly, the major frames governing the coverage of the Gulf War were put in place during the five to six month period between Iraq's invasion of Kuwait in August of 1990 and the counter-offensive by the coalition-forces in mid-January 1991 (Iyengar and Simon, 1994; Entman and Page, 1994).

The point of these examples is to emphasise that even where a content analysis focuses on the coverage of a specific event, clearly delimited by start and end dates, it may still be useful to sample coverage from both before and after the dates of the specific event. Likewise, and depending of course on the rationale and aims of the research, a helpful strategy for profiling and understanding the media coverage of a specific event may also include the sampling and analysis of coverage of a comparable event or comparable events. This strategy is, for example, a fundamental aspect of the 'Propaganda Framework'-approach advocated by Herman and Chomsky (Herman, 1985; Herman and Chomsky, 1988), who analyse US media coverage of political events which are similar in most respects but differ principally in terms of whether they appear in countries regarded by the US government as 'enemy' countries or 'friendly' countries.

In the analysis of more general types of coverage – not specifically tied to certain dates or periods – there are numerous, more or less systematic, ways of obtaining what we may call a 'reasonably representative' sample of material. 'Reasonably representative' here is taken to mean a sample which is not skewed or biased by the personal preferences or hunches of the researcher, by the desire to 'prove' a particular preconceived point, or by insufficient knowledge of the media and their social context. It is thus important, when deciding on a sampling plan, to be aware of the cycles and seasonal variations which characterise much media coverage.

In Britain, television programme schedules vary according to special holidays, seasons (Christmas), and diary events (for example, major sports diary events such as Wimbledon tennis). The summer period is often known in news terms as the 'silly season' where the 'man bites dog' variety of news has a higher likelihood of receiving coverage because of the lack of activity in the political, legislatory, and decision-making institutions of society. Television news-casts during weekends are normally much shorter than those of Mondays–Fridays. Many types of advertisements (alcohol, sun lotion, holiday package tours), across all media, are 'seasonal' to varying degrees.

While care should be taken to avoid relying on short sample periods which coincide with seasonal variations or other events affecting the nature of coverage, choosing a sample essentially amounts to combining a good knowledge of the media and their cycles with straightforward common sense. Thus, a study purporting to offer an analysis of the extent and nature of alcohol advertising on television should clearly not confine itself to, say, the second week of December, given that in countries which celebrate Christmas the level of alcohol advertising is particularly heavy in this period. Likewise, an analysis seeking to examine the extent and nature of British press coverage of Japan, would clearly end up with some very atypical conclusions if the analysis were confined to a week coinciding with the 50th Anniversary of VJ-day, or, less obviously, but equally skewed, coinciding with the occurrence of a major natural disaster (such as the earthquake in the Japanese city of Kobe at the beginning of 1995).

A sampling strategy often used for obtaining a representative sample of television coverage is that of one continuous week – Monday to Sunday – followed by a 'rolling' or composite week, that is Monday of one week, Tuesday of the following week, Wednesday of the following week, and so on. Another strategy used for both broadcast and newspaper sampling is to start by randomly selecting a starting date for the sample, and then to sample every nth day after that throughout the chosen period. In his analysis of the reporting of race in two regional newspapers, Troyna (1982), for example, started by randomly selecting a date in January and then selected every thirteenth issue of the two newspapers over a three-year period. It is clearly important that the sampling interval should not coincide with any natural cycle – that is, seven or any multiple thereof would yield a sample consisting entirely of media output from the same weekday and would thus not reflect the variation in media content across different days of the week.

The Sampling of Relevant Content

Once the medium or media and sample dates or period have been selected, there still remains the task of sampling relevant content. The definition of 'relevant content' should be derived principally from the articulation of the research problem and the theoretical framework of the study, but will also often involve more practical considerations, that is, how to limit the amount of material selected for analysis without compromising the requirement that it be 'representative'.

Some studies have thus looked at the portrayal of certain phenomena or issues across all types of television programmes – fiction and factual – broadcast during peak viewing hours (Cumberbatch and Negrine, 1992; Hansen, 1986); others have focused on specific genres such as television news (Ericson *et al.*, 1991; Heinderyckx, 1993; Cottle, 1993c), popular television drama (Signorielli, 1984), sports programming (Wonsek, 1992), or advertising (Nowak, 1992; Smith, 1994). In numerous content analyses of television news, the sampling has been confined further to include only the main evening news programmes rather than 'breakfast' news, lunch time news, early evening news, or indeed the brief hourly news featured by some television channels. Such sampling choices can generally be defended on the grounds of audience reach (which news programmes attract the largest audiences; – and during which parts of the television day do most people watch – the 'peak' viewing hours?) or by reference to the 'status' assigned to programmes either by the television organisations themselves or by audiences.

Similarly, the sampling in print media may be restricted to specific types or genres of content. Thus, general analyses of newspaper coverage of certain issues or phenomena tend to exclude advertising content, weather forecasts, stock-market and related financial listings, sports pages, cartoons, and perhaps more specialist newspaper sections, such as books, theatre, music, arts and cinema reviews, or education or holiday supplements. For studies which are principally interested in the operation of news values and factors governing the production of news such exclusions are reasonable on the grounds that these types of coverage are generally less directly driven by the news values and journalistic practices which apply in the main news sections of newspapers (although such boundaries are not always clear in relation to, for example, sports pages). As emphasised earlier, the selection of types of content must depend fundamentally on the rationale and objectives of the study.

Having chosen the medium or media to be analysed, sampled titles or channels from these, sampled dates and periods, and sampled types or genres of content, there still remains the task of identifying the articles, reports, programmes which are 'about' or refer to the subject or issue under scrutiny. Should a newspaper court case report, in which reference is made to DNA-analysis of hair-samples found on a murder-victim's clothing be included in a study of 'science' coverage? At what point can a television news item be said to be 'about' race, or to convey images of race? Should a television news report on the Irish political party Sinn Fein be included in a study of television coverage of terrorism, if it contains no direct reference to terrorism or links between Sinn Fein and the Irish Republican Army (IRA)? Perhaps the classic question to have exercised a very large body of communications research is, 'how do we define "violence" on television?' These questions illustrate the need to define clear selection criteria and rules for the inclusion or exclusion of media reports, articles, programmes.

Related to this is the definition of the 'unit of analysis', that which is counted. This can be the individual word, the sentence, the paragraph, the article, the news programme, the news item, an individual character, actor or source, the programme, the scene, the 'incident' (for example, a violent incident, the consumption of alcohol), and so on. As a quantitative technique, content analysis is about reporting how often different aspects of texts occur, what their prominence is relative to other aspects or dimensions (or compared with text-external indicators, for example, the relative prominence of the elderly in television drama compared with their proportional representation in the population). For such quantitative indicators to be at all meaningful it is therefore crucial to have clearly defined what is being counted.

5.3.3 Defining Analytical Categories

The 'task' of content analysis is to examine a selected (sampled) body of texts, and to classify the content according to a number of pre-determined dimensions. The conceptually most taxing aspect of any content analysis is to define the dimensions or characteristics which should be analysed. Though any number of text characteristics could be categorised, counted, and quantified, perhaps the main pitfall of content analysis is to get carried away with the measurement and counting of any number of text characteristics simply or mainly on the basis of what *can* be counted or on the basis of what lends itself easily to counting. The text characteristics which are singled out for analysis should relate directly to the overall research questions or hypotheses which prompted the choice of content analysis in the first place.

In an analysis of press coverage, for example, it is tempting to measure and code the area (that is, column inches) of each newspaper article analysed simply because this is easily done, if time-consuming. But unless the exact sizes of newspaper articles have (or are expected to have) a direct bearing on the research questions asked, time might be far better spent analysing and counting more substantive characteristics of text, and to use simply the number of articles (irrespective of size) as an adequate and sufficient indication of the extent of coverage in different newspapers or over time.

Likewise, it is not uncommon to see researchers who spend a great deal of time logging the number, size, and contents of photographs included in newspaper reports, only to ignore these data when it comes to the interpreting and writing-up of research results. Because the cataloguing or categorising of communications content is a time-consuming and laborious task, it is extremely important to include for analysis only those dimensions or characteristics of texts which can reasonably be expected to yield 'useful' information, and by 'useful' we mean information of relevance to the research questions.

What categories, then, should be included in a content analysis? In general terms, there is no single or straightforward answer to this question as the analytical categories will and always should depend entirely on the aims, objectives and foci of the research, on the theoretical framework and questions stated as part of the formulation of the research problem. More specifically, however, there are a number of categories which will tend to be standard in any content analysis, namely 'identifier' categories such as 'medium' (which newspaper, magazine, television channel does the text appear in or on), 'date' (day, month, year), 'position within the medium' (for example, 'page' in print media, or 'schedule time' in broadcast media), 'size/length/duration' of item (although, as indicated above, careful consideration needs to be given to the question of whether the analytical use to be made of this dimension warrants the time and effort invested in the coding). Another descriptive 'identifier' category often included in analyses of mass media content is a 'type/genre' classification; thus, newspaper content is often categorised along the lines of 'news report', 'editorial', 'letter to the editor', 'feature article', and so on; television programmes are categorised in terms of their genre: 'news', 'current affairs magazine', 'documentary', 'quiz show', 'talk show', 'drama serial', 'film', 'advertisement', and so on.

Although at one level, type/genre typologies can be regarded as basic identifier categories for general classification and comparison of media output, it is important to recognise that these also have much more far-reaching analytical potential. Thus, different media formats/types/genres set different limits for *what* can be articulated, by *whom*, through what format/context.

In addition to being informed by the general theoretical frameworks and research questions guiding one's research project, there is at least one further principle which should be borne in mind when constructing coding categories for a content analysis: a content analysis should never be merely a fishing expedition applying a preconceived category set to an 'unknown' body of text. Thinking up appropriate content analysis categories is as much a question of immersing oneself in the textual material to get a general 'feel' for its content and structure prior the construction of categories, as it is a case of deriving category ideas from the theoretical framework and questions which guide the research project. In other words, the researcher needs some familiarity with the content, structure and general nature of the material to be analysed in order to be able to set up categories that will be sufficiently sensitive to capture the nuances of the texts. There is thus not much point in using a subject coding system where 90 per cent of articles fall into just one category.

Going beyond these basic identifier categories there is inevitably a very considerable variation in the kinds of dimensions that different content analyses have analysed and counted, reflecting the many and varied research purposes for which the quantitative analysis of texts has been used. In the following, we examine some categories which are often deployed in sociologically-orientated analyses of media content.

Actors/Sources/Primary Definers – and Their Attributes

The analysis of characters/actors/sources is important both from a straightforward narrative or literary perspective, and from a more sociologically articulated theory of media representations and media roles. Whether informed by a hegemony framework, a constructivist perspective, social learning and modelling theory, or a social representations framework, the analysis of who is portrayed as saying and doing what to whom, and with what key attributes, is essential to an understanding of media roles in social representation and power relationships in society. Studies working broadly within a hegemony framework have successfully used content analysis techniques to show that public issues are defined in the mass media and for public consumption overwhelmingly by representatives for powerful institutions, agencies and interests in society, and that 'alternative' voices critical of the *status quo* are much less likely to gain a platform in the mainstream media. Deviance, social disturbances, terrorism, race, crime, and so on are defined in large measure by the law enforcement agencies, the judiciary, and the parties of formal politics.

In their comprehensive analysis of the representation of crime, law, and justice in broadcast and print news, Ericson and his colleagues (Ericson *et al.*, 1991) undertook a very detailed coding of the knowledge-providers and sources who, through the media, came to create the public definitions of these areas of coverage. They analysed:

(1) *the number of sources* used or represented in each news item;
(2) *the types of sources* (including 'journalists' themselves, but also 'government sources', 'private sector sources', 'individuals' not representing agencies or institutions, and 'unspecified sources' referenced through non-specific terms such as '"analysts", "reports", "observers", "intelligence sources", "authorities", "experts" . . .' (Ericson *et al.*, 1991, p. 199);
(3) *source contexts* (for example, interview, official meeting, press release, drama/actual event, and so on);
(4) *types of knowledge provided by sources*. Types of knowledge were categorised into primary (factual, asking 'What happened?'), secondary (explanatory, asking 'Why did it happen?'), tertiary (descriptive, asking 'What was it like to be involved in

what happened?'), evaluative (moral, asking 'Was what happened good or bad?'), and recommendations (asking 'What should be done about what happened?') (Ericson *et al.*, 1991, p. 204).

Ericson and his colleagues also looked at visuals and sound used in the representation of different sources. Among other things this enabled them to show that some types of sources were far more likely (relative to their overall prominence) to be pictured than others in the newspapers analysed, and that the use of photographs of sources varied considerably across the different newspapers in their sample.

While analysing and quantifying the types of actors or sources who are quoted or referred to in media coverage goes a long way toward showing how social power is expressed through and with the mass media, many content analysts have rightly pointed out that the analysis of actors and sources needs to go further to analyse the differential uses to which various 'voices' are being put in the media. In other words, how are the voices of those sources – often official, institutional sources – who initially define events and issues (the so-called 'primary definers') being used, elaborated, and framed by the media? Cottle (1993b, pp. 155–7) in his analysis of regional television news coverage, for example, points to the ways in which the different presentational formats of news create a hierarchy of opportunities or possibilities for primary definers to articulate their views. Thus, the 'restricted' format of the newsreader delivering a newsdesk presentation gives virtual monopoly to the newsreader's account, 'with the minimum of direct reference to outside voices, viewpoints and visuals' (Cottle, 1993b, p. 155). At the other end of the hierarchy of access for news sources is the 'expansive' format, which 'entails either live or full interview inclusion in which the interviewee is allowed to develop his or her point of view at some length, perhaps in engaged debate with an opposing voice' (Ibid., p. 156).

While quantitative analyses of the different 'voices' represented in the media form a useful starting point, the traditional notion of primary definition (Hall, Critcher, Jefferson, Clarke and Roberts, 1986) suffers from several problems. Most notably, this type of analysis does not normally distinguish between the potentially very different messages that come from the same group of primary definers, nor does it indicate the varying degrees of 'legitimacy' accorded different sources or voices by the media. In their analysis of television coverage of the Three Mile Island accident, Nimmo and Combs (1985), for example, discovered that whereas 'average citizens' were generally prominently represented, the narrative uses of 'average citizens' were very different from network to network:

> The CBS citizen interview normally involved persons expressing confidence in how things would turn out (for example, expressing appreciation for President Carter's visit to Middletown). ABC's average citizen interviews focused instead upon personal fears and anxieties. (Nimmo and Combs, 1985, p. 81)

Similarly, it has been suggested (Hansen, 1990) that in order to understand the relative 'weight' carried by different types of primary definers, it is necessary to take into consideration the 'newsmaking scenarios' or 'fora' through which such primary definers become news-worthy and articulate their claims. An example of the importance of this comes from research on media coverage of environmental issues, where content analysis of actors and sources have indicated that when environmental pressure groups appear as primary definers, they do so primarily through the forum of 'demonstration or public protest action' – a forum which carries considerably less legitimacy in Western democracies, than the forum of 'formal political activity/Parliament' or the forum of 'Science'.

Scientific, technical, medical and environmental controversies are defined largely by the mainstream establishment scientific and medical communities, by politicians, and by expert authorities, while the views of dissident scientists and experts are effectively sidelined – see for example content analyses of media coverage of genetics and biotechnology in both the United States (Pfund and Hofstadter, 1981) and Germany (Ruhrmann, 1992). It is, however, worth noting that in some areas of scientific controversy such as controversy about nuclear energy, content analysis has also been used to support the counter-argument that the media give a disproportionate amount of space and time to a small but highly vocal body of anti-nuclear scientists or experts who are not representative of the views of the scientific community as such (Rothman and Lichter, 1987).

Social constructivists are particularly interested in coding actors to see who successfully makes claims about social problems and thus help 'construct' and elevate new or low profile issues to centre public stage. Not only does this kind of analysis tell us about source–

communicator relationships, but also about source-power and power in public space. In a meticulous content analysis of media reporting on an oil-spill accident, Molotch and Lester (1975) thus were able to show that while an unexpected and unplanned news event such as an oil-spill provided temporary access for groups who would not normally be given media coverage, over time 'the fact of the spill . . . tended to be brought under control as the definition of its character increasingly fell into the hands of those news promoters with routine access to media' (p. 258).

Social stereotyping, mis-representation, and what Gerbner (1972) has termed the 'symbolic annihilation' (through under-representation or non-representation) of different groups and types of people in society have been central concerns of content analysts since the early part of the century. For example, in an early study of forty-three radio daytime serials (soaps) Arnheim (1944) found that working-class people were numerically underrepresented. In addition,

> the kinds of problems people had . . . were almost always interpersonal, while problems that might have been regarded as institutional were defined as individual and private. Change, if it occurred at all, was not brought about by planned collective efforts, but by chance, or a sudden, unexpected, and unexplained transformation of character, a moral conversion. In general, then, these daytime serials diverted attention away from the larger social institutions and failed to offer their fans any fresh insight or self-knowledge. (McCormack, 1982, p. 157).

Melvin DeFleur's study (1964) of the portrayal of occupational roles in television serials came to similar conclusions, showing that certain occupations were heavily over-represented while others were virtually absent. Numerous content analyses have been carried out to examine further the highly selective representation of occupations, the sexes, race and ethnicity in news and factual media content, drama and entertainment fare, and advertising.

Studies working within a cultivation approach or social modelling approach are concerned about the characteristics of those who are portrayed as the perpetrators of socially unacceptable behaviour, or of those who may serve as role-models for media audiences. Content analyses have been used for meticulously mapping not just the overall demography of television characters (in terms of sex, race, social class, age, and so on) but also the attributes and behaviours of characters along such lines as sexual conduct, moral values, drinking, smoking, drug-taking, and dietary habits.

Subjects/Themes/Issues

A key objective of many, perhaps even most, content analyses is to classify types or sub-categories of coverage within a general area of investigation. Thus, Ericson and his colleagues, while generally concerned with the representation of 'deviance and crime' (among other dimensions) in the news media, subcategorised deviant activities into five types: violence, economic, political, ideological/cultural, and diversionary (that is, '"morality crimes" or moral regulation regarding the distribution and use of alcohol and other drugs, pornography, gambling, and prostitution . . . [and] the regulation of leisure activities, such as video games and sporting events' (Ericson *et al.*, 1991, p. 249). Hartmann and his colleagues, in their analysis of British press coverage of 'race' in the period 1963–70, aimed to see 'whether any central defining themes could be identified that might be taken as indicating the meaning and significance given to race in the newspapers' (Hartmann, Husband and Clark, 1974). To this end, they arrived at a list of twenty-three categories of subject matter, including such subjects as 'housing', 'education', 'health', 'discrimination', 'crime', 'cultural differences', and so on.

The classification of what topics or themes or issues are covered within a general area of coverage chosen for analysis is of course a common starting point for studies of media content. Thus, studies of terrorism coverage would want to know what kinds or types of terrorism are covered; studies of war-coverage would want to examine what aspects receive most coverage (for example, 'technology/weaponry', 'political negotiations', 'dissent', 'troop morale', 'strategy and military progress', 'civilian suffering'); studies of health and medical coverage would often start by establishing what kinds of health, medicine or diseases receive coverage (see for example: Kristiansen and Harding, 1985; Entwistle and Hancock-Beaulieu, 1992); studies of science and technology coverage or of environmental issues coverage would similarly often start with a classification of the types of science, technology or environmental issues which receive prominence in media coverage (see Hansen and Dickinson, 1992; Clayton, Hancock-Beaulieu and Meadows, 1993; Cottle, 1993c). Studies of international news flows would start by mapping and classifying types of news coverage (see the classic study of news values by Galtung and Ruge (1981), and the multi-country UNESCO study of international news (Sreberny-Mohammadi, 1984).

Vocabulary or Lexical Choice

Since the very early days of content analysis, considerable interest has focused on the vocabulary or lexical choice in the texts studied. Indeed, some of the very first documented uses of content analysis were studies which focused on the occurrence of specific words/symbols in texts (see Krippendorf, 1980). In his pioneering work on quantitative semantics, Lasswell was essentially also interested in vocabulary and in the symbolic meaning of words. Much of his concern focused on the quantitative analysis of key symbols (such as 'liberty', 'freedom', 'authority') and he aimed to construct a dictionary of symbols and their uses in texts. The idea, that dictionaries of symbol or word use could be created for coding and content analysis purposes has also been central to developments in computer-assisted, electronic approaches to the analysis of texts since these were first formalised in the 1960s by Philip Stone and his colleagues through their General Inquirer program (Stone, Dunphy, Smith and Ogilvie, 1966; see also Hansen, 1995).

The analysis of vocabulary or lexical choice continues to be a central component of many content analyses, often drawing also on a wider linguistic and discourse analytic framework. Van Dijk, for example, commences his discourse analytic study of press reporting of race with a lexical content analysis of headlines:

> Words manifest the underlying semantic concepts used in the definition of the situation. Lexicalization of semantic content, however, is never neutral: the choice of one word rather than another to express more or less the same meaning, or to denote the same referent, may signal the opinions, emotions, or social position of a speaker. . . . To describe the civil disturbances in Britain in 1985, the headlines may use such words as *riots*, *disturbances* or *disorders* among many other words. . . . Not only do they [words in newspaper headlines] express the definition of the situation, but they also signal the social or political opinions of the newspaper about the events. That is, headlines not only globally define or summarize an event, they also evaluate it. Hence, the lexical style of headlines has ideological implications. (1991, p. 53)

In a similar vein, Picard and Adams (1991) used content analysis to analyse the characterisations of acts of political violence through such words as *hijacker*, *bombing*, *shooting*, *seizure*, *assassination*, and so on. Picard and Adams distinguished between 'nominal characterisations', 'words that label or describe the acts in a manner that merely indicates what happened' (p. 12), and 'descriptive characterisations', words that 'contain judgments about the acts or perpetrators within their denotative and connotative meanings' (p. 12). Stahl (1995) used a lexical content analysis of *Time* magazine over a ten-year period to examine the use of explicitly magical and religious language in coverage of computers and related technologies. David Fan (1988) and others (for example, Druschel, 1991; Lee, 1989; Einsiedel and Coughlan, 1993) have also used vocabulary-focused computer-assisted content analyses for examining media coverage of a diverse range of issues such as AIDS, drug-abuse, and the environment.

Value-Dimensions or Stance

Finally, a general category dimension which often forms part of content analyses is an attempt at classifying coverage in terms of value judgements, or assessment of the ideological stance, accuracy, or informativeness of coverage. In her analysis of Canadian press coverage of science and technology, Einsiedel (1992) thus analysed and coded the tone of stories in terms of whether they were predominantly 'positive', 'negative', 'neutral, or 'mixed':

> Coders were instructed to read the story as they normally would and to indicate the 'overall impression' they got from the story. This impression could result from information conveyed in a number of ways including: what was highlighted in the lead, the balance (or imbalance) of consequences described, and the type of information or description included. For example, if a new treatment was presented in terms of being a 'landmark discovery', or compared favourably with current methods but at lower cost, these elements would result in a positive evaluation. A story coded as 'mixed' in tone was one which had both types of consequences described but neither as dominant in the lead, in the range of consequences described or in the descriptors applied. (p. 93)

In a study of risk information provided by thirteen major newspapers in the United States, Friedman and her colleagues (1996) used content analysis to assess whether information about risk had been presented in depth, whether numerical risk information had been placed appropriately in context, and whether sufficient background information was given to enable readers to make sense of different expert interpretations of risk offered by the newspapers.

Holli Semetko (1989), in a study of television news coverage of the 1983 general election campaign in Britain, used a number of evaluative categories, including an evaluation of whether TV reporters' commentaries on politicians' campaign activities were predominantly 'reinforcing' (positive), 'deflating' (negative), 'straight' (descriptive), or 'mixed'. This coding sought to analyse and evaluate reporters' contextualising comments to determine whether:

> in describing the scene they appeared to reinforce or deflate the activities or statements of politicians; the reporter appeared to correct what a politician said; and whether there appeared to be any disdain in reporter comment. (p. 465)

In a study of bias in the *New York Times*' coverage of the US invasion of Panama, December 1989, Dickson (1994, p. 812) coded, inter alia, the valence of sources quoted:

> only those individuals, institutions, etc. who voiced an opinion on the invasion were coded. An opinion was defined as any statement that contains a value judgment about the invasion – its goodness or badness, rightness or wrongness, etc. These sources were then categorized according to whether they were positive, negative, or ambivalent toward the U.S. invasion of Panama.

Although evaluative categories in content analysis are often a variation on the relatively fundamental dichotomies of: 'favourable – unfavourable', 'positive – negative', 'accurate – inaccurate', 'critical – uncritical', there are clearly many more possibilities. Perhaps the main problem with evaluative categories is that they generally require a considerable degree of interpretation by the coder – they can rarely be deduced on the basis of single words or sentences, but require the coder to consider the 'overall tone' of a newspaper article or broadcast item. Unless very clear interpretation guidelines are laid down, content analysts often find it difficult to achieve a high degree of coder-agreement in the coding of evaluative categories.

5.3.4 Constructing a Coding Schedule

Defining the categories which are to be analysed, and constructing a formal coding schedule for the analysis and coding or classification of content are two dimensions of the same 'step' in content analysis. Once the categories have been chosen and defined, they need to be set out in a codable form on a coding schedule. A code-book which sets out clear guidelines and definitions for the coding practice also needs to be written before the content analyst can proceed.

A coding schedule is very similar to a survey questionnaire – it contains a listing of the variables which are to be coded for each programme or article (or whatever smaller unit of analysis may be used: for example, paragraph or sentence). For each variable, the coding schedule also sets out the values or coding possibilities associated with that variable: thus, the variable may be 'title of newspaper' and the values associated with this variable would be, for example, (1) *Guardian*, (2) *Daily Telegraph*, (3) *Independent*, (4) *Sun*, and so on.

Figure 5.1 shows an example of parts of a content analysis coding schedule used in a study of the coverage of the environmental pressure group Greenpeace in the British national daily newspapers (Hansen, 1993). Coding consists of applying a content coding schedule such as that shown in Figure 5.1 to the newspaper articles (or television programme, or other type of text) in the selected sample. In this case, one coding schedule had to be completed for each article in the sample. In practice, coding is a matter of (a) reading through each article, and (b) filling the coding boxes on the coding schedule with the appropriate codes (numbers) for each individual article. Let us briefly illustrate this.

Imagine that the article partially reproduced below is one of the articles selected for a study of press coverage of the environmental pressure group Greenpeace. This article, published on Thursday 14 September 1995 in the *Guardian* newspaper, is an editorial commenting on Greenpeace's strategic failure in its action against French nuclear testing at the Mururoa atoll in the Pacific.

Bearing witness on a broad front

Greenpeace's activists need to be a bit more disciplined. Labour is not the only organisation requiring a more centralised command structure. Greenpeace is in trouble too. A two-month campaign in

Content analysis coding schedule
PRESS COVERAGE OF GREENPEACE

NEWSPAPER [|]

1. Daily Telegraph
2. The Times
3. Independent
4. Guardian
5. Financial Times
6. Daily Mirror
7. Sun
8. Daily Mail
9. Daily Express
10. Today

DATE–MONTH–YEAR [| | | | |]

HEADLINE (copy verbatim):

. . . .
. . . .
. . . .

REPORTER/AUTHOR (copy name and designation (e.g. environment correspondent), if given, verbatim)

. . . .
. . . .

ARTICLE LENGTH (number of words) [| | |]

TYPE OF ARTICLE/ITEM [ ]

1. Main news story
2. Other news story
3. Feature article
4. Editorial
5. Letter
6. Advertisement
9. Other

GREENPEACE FOCUS [ ]

1. Greenpeace is the main focus
2. Greenpeace is a secondary focus
3. Greenpeace is mentioned only in passing
4. 'Greenpeace' is used as a metaphor or 'sign'/signifier
9. Other

If '4' or '9' proceed to next CASE; otherwise code the remaining categories.

GREENPEACE AS ACTOR [ ]

How is Greenpeace quoted or referred to? code only one;
where several options apply, code the 'highest' actor order,
i.e. 'quoted directly' > 'quoted indirectly' > 'referred to'.

1. Quoted directly
2. Quoted indirectly
3. Referred to but not quoted either directly or indirectly
9. Other

WHAT IS THE ARTICLE/STORY ABOUT?

Code the main subject and up to two subsidiary subjects of the article. Keep a running list of subject codes, adding new codes as required, as the coding progresses

Main subject [| |]

Subsidiary subject 1 [| |]

Subsidiary subject 2 [| |]

Figure 5.1 A content coding schedule

> the Pacific was scuppered on the first day by over enthusiastic activists, who disobeyed orders by taking the pressure group's main boats into the 12-mile exclusion zone around Mururoa Atoll, allowing the French to capture both boats, the group's helicopter and a flotilla of inflatables.
> As our environmental correspondent reports from Tahiti today, months of planning and millions of pounds of investment in supplies were lost in a single day when the MV Greenpeace was seized [. . .].

Applied to this article, the first part of the coding schedule shown in figure 5.1 would look when completed as shown in Figure 5.2.

5.3.5 Piloting the Coding Schedule and Checking Reliability

Before embarking on a full-scale content analysis it is crucial to 'try out' the coding schedule on a small sub-sample. 'Piloting' and 'fine-tuning' the coding schedule is important in content analysis, just as it is important to pilot one's research instruments, strategy, or data collection tools in any other type of sociological analysis. Test coding of a small sub-sample of the material which is to be analysed often helps to reveal inadequacies and/or inconsistencies in the category systems of the coding schedule. The four types of problem which follow are fairly typical.

(1) *Categories need to adhere to a single level of classification.* Examples of categories which mix different levels of categorisation within a single frame often include: confusing macro-categories and sub-categories within a single coding category, for example, types of product advertising on television (cars, cosmetics, food, drinks, beer – 'beer' is of course a subcategory under 'drinks'); confusing 'race' and religion (Caucasian, African-Caribbean, Asian, Christian – any person belonging to one of these 'races' can of course also be a 'Christian') or 'age' and 'sex' (male, female, children).

(2) *A category system which aims to code and classify the main subject focus may turn out to be insufficiently and inadequately differentiated.* In a study of media coverage of science, Jones *et al.* (Jones, Connell and Meadows, 1978), for example, found that approximately three-quarters of the coverage fell into just a single category, 'Medicine and Human Biology'. Where three-quarters

Content analysis coding schedule

PRESS COVERAGE OF GREENPEACE

NEWSPAPER [0|4]

1. Daily Telegraph
2. The Times
3. Independent
4. Guardian
5. Financial Times
6. Daily Mirror
7. Sun
8. Daily Mail
9. Daily Express
10. Today

DATE–MONTH–YEAR [1|4|0|9|9|5]

HEADLINE (copy verbatim):

Bearing witness on a broad front. . . . .

. . . .

. . . .

REPORTER/AUTHOR (copy name and designation (e.g. environment correspondent), if given, verbatim)

. . . .

. . . .

ARTICLE LENGTH (number of words) [|4|7|5]

TYPE OF ARTICLE/ITEM [4]

1. Main news story
2. Other news story
3. Feature article
4. Editorial
5. Letter
6. Advertisement
9. Other

GREENPEACE FOCUS [1]

1. Greenpeace is the main focus
2. Greenpeace is a secondary focus
3. Greenpeace is mentioned only in passing
4. 'Greenpeace' is used as a metaphor or 'sign'/signifier
9. Other

If '4' or '9' proceed to next CASE; otherwise code the remaining categories.

GREENPEACE AS ACTOR [3]

How is Greenpeace quoted or referred to? code only one; where several options apply, code the 'highest' actor order, i.e. 'quoted directly' > 'quoted indirectly' > 'referred to'.

1. Quoted directly
2. Quoted indirectly
3. Referred to but not quoted either directly or indirectly
9. Other

Figure 5.2 A partially completed content coding schedule

or more of the coded items end up in a single category, relatively little is learnt from the content analysis about the nature of the coverage coded; in other words, this suggests that the categorisation is not sufficiently sensitive or detailed to adequately capture the nuances of the material.

(3) *A coding schedule may set out a large and highly differentiated list of actors, primary definers or sources to be coded.* In practice it might turn out that only a very small proportion of these ever appear in the articles or texts analysed. Rather than spending unnecessary time and effort on putting zeros in coding boxes, the coding schedule should be changed to include only those actors who are likely to appear in the coverage. Of course, it is impossible to know in advance of doing the actual analysis precisely who will appear and who will not, but a general familiarity (see also the argument above, that such familiarity is a prerequisite for the construction of sensible and text-sensitive coding categories in the first place) with the body of texts to be analysed should enable the researcher to narrow down the types of actors, subjects, contexts, issues, and so on that are likely to occur in the texts.

(4) *Ability to relate different categories and dimensions to each other.* A mistake which is commonly made when researchers first set out to construct a coding schedule, particularly for the analysis of advertisements, is to confuse the advertisement as a unit of analysis with the character(s) appearing in the advertisement as the unit of analysis. If coding categories are constructed along the lines of: subject of advertisement, scheduling time of advertisement, number of male or female characters, age of characters, race or ethnic origin of characters, dress-code of characters, and so on – the problem here is that although the analysis would provide data on the distribution of male or female characters, young or old characters and so on it would not be possible to say whether the young ones were predominantly smartly dressed black male characters, the older ones predominantly white, conservatively dressed, female characters an so on; in other words, this coding strategy would not facilitate cross-referencing of the actor characteristics.

Piloting should also include some checks on how reliable the coding process is. Reliability in content analysis is essentially about consistency: consistency between different coders (*inter-coder reliability*), and consistency of the individual coder's coding practice over time (*intra-coder reliability*). If checks on reliability reveal considerable divergence in how the same material is being categorised by different coders, or by the same coder over time, then it is necessary to tighten up the coding guidelines, to make the coding instructions and definitions clearer. There are several different ways of checking or measuring reliability in content analysis, from a simple check on the percentage of coding decisions on which coders agree, to more complex formulae which take into account the degree to which a certain level of agreement would occur simply by chance in a set number of coding decisions (Scott's Pi is one such statistic which is relatively easy to apply (Scott, 1955) – see also Holsti (1969), Ch. 6, for a more detailed discussion of reliability testing).

5.3.6 Data-Preparation and Analysis

Where a content analysis is extremely simple and rudimentary, it may be possible to analyse the results 'by hand'. That is, the frequency with which different specified dimensions occur can be determined by looking through the completed coding schedules and counting up the number of times each dimension has been coded. However, for most intents and purposes the data collected through content analysis should be entered into a computer data file and analysed with the help of any one of the several computer programs available for statistical analysis of data.

While the task of entering content coded data into a computer may at first seem a laborious process, the effort is soon handsomely 'repaid' in terms of the gain in efficiency (speed and reliability of analysis) with which the data can be analysed. But perhaps a far more persuasive argument for analysing content data by computer concerns the much greater flexibility than that afforded by 'manual' analysis. Thus, it is not always clear, when first embarking on a content analysis, which dimensions of coverage should be compared, or which media, genre, or time comparisons might yield interesting patterns. With the content analysis data on computer, it is possible to work 'inductively' with the material, to discover unexpected trends, and to return repeatedly to the data to explore new ideas, co-occurrences, and patterns which may not at first have been obvious candidates for analysis.

Entering the content analysis data into a computer file is a simple, if rather tedious, matter of typing the codes from the coding boxes on the completed content coding schedules into a file (a document) on a computer (see Chapter 11 for more detail on this). Once the data have been entered into a computer file, and checked for typing errors and consistency, the analysis can begin. The analysis of data can be done with any one of the by now quite large variety of statistical analysis packages and spread-sheet packages available on the market. A powerful package which has traditionally been popular, and continues to be so, with social scientists for content analysis purposes is SPSS (Statistical Package for the Social Sciences), but other widely available programs include SAS (Statistical Analysis System), Minitab, and spreadsheets (for example, Microsoft Excel) which increasingly have facilities for complex statistical analysis.

How should the data be analysed? There is no single answer to this question, just as there was no single or simple answer to the question 'which categories or dimensions of content should be coded?'. Fundamentally, the data analysis needs to address the questions or hypotheses set out in the definition of the research problem, which may, for example, give some indication of the main axes of comparison which need to be examined. Such 'axes' may include comparisons of different television channels, radio channels, or types of newspapers ('broadsheet' versus 'tabloid', 'left-wing' versus 'right-wing', 'independent' versus 'government-controlled'); they may be comparisons of coverage during different time periods; or they could be comparisons of the cultural images in television soap operas originating from different countries.

Though the definition of the research problem should indeed give a good indication of what kind of analyses need to be done, it is also important to be flexible and open-minded in the process of analysing the data. In other words, it is quite possible that while examining basic trends in the coded categories, it becomes apparent that some dimensions seem to co-occur, or that some dimensions only appear in certain parts of the coverage. Such discoveries, in turn, call for further analyses, perhaps with a different grouping of dimensions, or with different axes of comparison.

A good starting point for any content analysis is to begin by establishing simply the distribution or frequencies for each of the main categories analysed (for example, types of newspapers, actors, topics, types of reporters) before moving on to conduct more complex analyses comparing two or more dimensions with each other (for example, the distribution of topics by each type of soap opera; the types of actors by each time-period analysed).

5.4 Conclusion

Content analysis is a flexible research technique for analysing large bodies of text. It follows a clearly defined set of steps, one of its attractive features, but is also vulnerable to abuse. Fundamentally, those choosing to use content analysis for the study of media content should recognise that content analysis is little more than a set of guidelines about how to analyse and quantify media content in a systematic and reliable fashion. What it does not, and cannot, tell us is what dimensions (categories) of content to analyse, or how to interpret the wider social significance or meaning of the quantitative indicators generated by content analysis. Both of these aspects need to be drawn and developed from the theoretical framework circumscribing one's study, a framework which amongst other things must articulate the relationship of the texts analysed to their wider context of production and/or consumption.

5.5 Summary

- Content analysis is a method for the systematic and quantitative analysis of communications content.
- Content analysis is well suited for analysing and mapping key characteristics of large bodies of text, and it lends itself well to the systematic charting of long-term changes and trends in media coverage.
- While early uses of content analysis aimed principally at finding out about the intentions of the originators of media messages, the aim of content analysis in media research has more often been that of examining how news, drama, advertising, and entertainment output reflect social and cultural issues, values, and phenomena. Content analysis is well suited to integration into larger research efforts involving, not just the analysis of media content, but also other methods of inquiry (surveys, experiments, participant observation, qualitative and ethnographic audience research).
- Although content analysis initially fragments texts down into constituent parts which can be counted, it re-assembles these constituent parts at the analysis and interpretation stage to examine which ones co-occur in which contexts, for what purposes, and with what implications. Moreover, and in contrast to many 'qualitative' or 'interpretative' approaches, content analysis, because it follows

clearly articulated rules and procedures, lays open to scrutiny the means by which textual meaning is dissected and examined.

- The process of content analysis can be broken down into six related tasks or steps: (1) define the research problem; (2) select media and sample; (3) define analytical categories; (4) construct a coding schedule; (5) pilot the coding schedule and check reliability; (6) data-preparation and analysis.
- The conceptually most taxing aspect of any content analysis is to define the dimensions or characteristics which should be analysed. While any number of text characteristics could be categorised, counted, and quantified, perhaps the main pitfall of content analysis is to get carried away with the measurement and counting of any number of text characteristics simply or mainly on the basis of what *can* be counted or on the basis of what lends itself easily to counting. The text characteristics which are singled out for analysis should relate directly to the overall research questions or hypotheses guiding the research.
- While the categories singled out for analysis will depend on the purpose and objectives of one's research, content analyses in mass communication research have often included, in addition to basic 'identifier categories', one or more of the following substantive dimensions: (a) actors/sources/primary definers – and their attributes; (b) subjects/themes/issues; (c) vocabulary/lexical choice; and (d) value-dimensions and/or ideological/political stance.
- The method of content analysis offers a set of guidelines about how to analyse and quantify media content in a systematic and reliable fashion. What it does not, and cannot, tell us is what dimensions (categories) of content to analyse, or how to interpret the wider social significance or meaning of the quantitative indicators generated by content analysis. Both of these aspects need to be drawn and developed from the theoretical framework circumscribing one's study, a framework which amongst other things must articulate the relationship of the texts analysed to their wider context of production and/or consumption.

References

Arnheim, R. (1944) 'The world of daytime serial', in P.F. Lazarsfeld and F.N. Stanton (eds) *Radio research 1942–43*, pp. 38–45 (New York: Duell, Sloan & Pearce).

Beniger, J. R. (1978) 'Media content as social indicators: The Greenfield Index of agenda setting', *Communication Research*, **5**(4), 437–53.
Berelson, B. (1952) *Content analysis in communication research* (Glencoe, Ill.: Free Press).
Breed, W. and J. R. DeFoe (1981) 'The portrayal of the drinking process on prime time television', *Journal of Communication*, **31**(1), 58–67.
Breed, W. and J. R. DeFoe (1984) 'Drinking and smoking on television 1950–1982', *Journal of Public Health Policy*, **5**(2), 257–70.
Burgelin, O. (1972) 'Structural analysis and mass communication', in D. McQuail (ed.), *Sociology of mass communications*, pp. 313–28 (Harmondsworth: Penguin).
Chapman, S. (1986) *Great expectorations: advertising and the tobacco industry* (London: Comedia).
Clayton, A., M. Hancock-Beaulieu and J. Meadows (1993) 'Change and continuity in the reporting of science and technology: a study of *The Times* and *The Guardian*', *Public Understanding of Science*, **2**(3), 225–34.
Cottle (1993a) 'Mediating the environment: modalities of TV news' in A. Hansen (ed.), *The Mass Media and Environmental Issues*, pp. 107–33 (Leicester: Leicester University Press).
Cottle (1993b) *TV news, urban conflict and the inner city* (Leicester: Leicester University Press).
Cumberbatch, G. and R. Negrine (1992) *Images of disability on television* (London: Routledge).
DeFleur, M. L. (1964) 'Occupational roles as portrayed on television', *Public Opinion Quarterly*, **28**, 57–74.
Dickson, S. H. (1994) 'Understanding Media Bias – the Press and the United-States Invasion Of Panama', *Journalism Quarterly*, **71**(4), 809–19.
Druschel, B. E. (1991) 'Sensationalism or sensitivity: use of words in stories on acquired immune deficiency syndrome by Associated Press videotex', in M. A. Wolf and A. R. Kielwasser (eds) *Gay people, sex and the media*, pp. 47–62 (Binghamton, NY: Haworth Press).
Einsiedel, E., and E. Coughlan (1993) 'The Canadian press and the environment: reconstructing a social reality', in A. Hansen (ed.), *The mass media and environmental issues*, pp. 134–49 (Leicester University Press).
Einsiedel, E. F. (1992) 'Framing science and technology in the Canadian press', *Public Understanding of Science*, **1**(1), 89–101.
Entman, R. M., and B. I. Page (1994) 'The News before the Storm: The Iraq War Debate and the Limits to Media Independence', in W. L. Bennett and D. Paletz (eds), *Taken by storm: the media, public opinion, and U.S. foreign policy in the Gulf War*, pp. 82–101 (University of Chicago Press).
Entwistle, V., and M. Hancock-Beaulieu (1992) 'Health and medical coverage in the UK national press', *Public Understanding of Science*, **1**(4), 367–82.
Ericson, R. V., Baranek, P. M. and Chan, J. B. L. (1987) *Visualizing deviance: A study of news organization* (Milton Keynes: Open University Press).
Ericson, R. V., Baranek, P. M. and Chan, J. B. L. (1989) *Negotiating control: A study of news sources* (Milton Keynes: Open University Press).

Ericson, R. V., P. M. Baranek and J. B. L. Chan (1991) *Representing order: Crime, law, and justice in the news media* (Milton Keynes: Open University Press).

Fan, D. P. (1988) *Predictions of public opinion from the mass media: computer content analysis and mathematical modelling.* (New York: Greenwood Press).

Fishman, M. (1980) *Manufacturing the news* (Austin and London: University of Texas Press).

Friedman, S. M., C. M. Gorney and B. P. Egolf (1987) 'Reporting on radiation: A content analysis of Chernobyl coverage', *Journal of Communication*, **37**(3), 58–79.

Friedman, S. M., C. M. Gorney and B. P. Egolf (1992) 'Chernobyl coverage: how the US media treated the nuclear industry', *Public Understanding of Science*, **1**(3), 305–23.

Friedman, S. M., K. Villamil, R. A. Suriano and B. P. Egolf (1996) 'Alar and apples: newspapers, risk and media responsibility', *Public Understanding of Science*, **5**(1), 1–20.

Galtung, J. and M. Ruge (1981) 'Structuring and selecting news', in S. Cohen and J. Young (eds), *The manufacture of news*, rev. edn, pp. 52–63 (London: Constable).

Gamson, W. A., and A. Modigliani (1989) 'Media discourse and public opinion on nuclear power: a constructionist approach' *American Journal of Sociology*, **95**(1), 1–37.

Gans, H. J. (1979) *Deciding what's news* (New York: Vintage).

Gerbner, G. (1972) 'Violence in television drama: trends and symbolic functions', in G. A. Comstock and E. A. Rubinstein (eds), *Media content and control: television and social behavior*, (vol. 1, pp. 28–187 (Washington, DC: US Government Printing Office).

Gerbner, G. (1995) 'Toward "cultural indicators": the analysis of mass mediated public message systems', in O. Boyd-Barrett and C. Newbold (eds), *Approaches to media: a reader*, pp. 144–52 (London: Arnold).

Gerbner, G., and L. Gross (1976) 'Living with television: the violence profile', *Journal of Communication*, **26**(2), 173–99.

Gerbner, G., L. Gross, M., Morgan amd N. Signorielli (1980) 'The "mainstreaming" of America: violence profile no 11', *Journal of Communication*, **30**(3), 10–29.

Gerbner, G., L. Gross, M. Morgan and N. Signorielli (1994) 'Growing up with television: the cultivation perspective', in J. Bryant and D. Zimmerman (eds), *Media effects: advances in theory and research*, pp. 17–42 (Hillsdale, N.J.: Lawrence Erlbaum).

Glasgow University Media Group (1976) *Bad news* (London: Routledge & Kegan Paul).

Hall, S., Critcher, C., Jefferson, T., Clarke, J. and Roberts, B. (1978). *Policing the crisis* (London: Macmillan).

Halloran, J. D., Elliott, P. and Murdock, G. (1970) *Demonstrations and communication* (Harmondsworth: Penguin).

Hansen, A. (1986) 'The portrayal of alcohol on television', *Health Education Journal*, **45**(3), 127–31.

Hansen, A. (1990) 'Socio-political values underlying media coverage of the environment', *Media Development*, **37**(2), 3–6.
Hansen, A. (1993) 'Greenpeace and press coverage of environmental issues', in A. Hansen (ed.) *The Mass Media and Environmental Issues*, pp. 150–178 (Leicester University Press).
Hansen, A. (1995) 'Using information technology to analyze newspaper content', in R. M. Lee (ed.) *Information technology for the social scientist*, pp. 147–68 (London: UCL Press).
Hansen, A., and R. Dickinson (1992) 'Science coverage in the British mass media: Media output and source input', *Communications*, **17**(3), 365–77.
Hansen, A. and Murdock, G. (1985) 'Constructing the crowd: populist discourse and press presentation', in V. Mosco and J. Wasko (eds) *Popular culture and media events*, (Vol. III, pp. 227–57) (Norwood, NJ: Ablex).
Hartmann, P., C. Husband, and J. Clark (1974) 'Race as news', in J. D. Halloran (ed.) *Race as news*, pp. 90–173 (Paris: Unesco Press).
Heinderyckx, F. (1993) 'Television news programmes in Western Europe: a comparative study', *European Journal of Communication*, **8**(4), 425–50.
Herman, E. S. (1985) 'Diversity of news: "marginalising" the opposition', *Journal of Communication*, **35**(3), 135–46.
Herman, E. S. and N. Chomsky (1988) *Manufacturing consent: the political economy of the mass media* (New York: Pantheon).
Holsti, O. R. (1969) *Content analysis for the social sciences and humanities* (Reading, Mass.: Addison-Wesley).
Iyengar, S. and A. Simon (1994) 'News Coverage of the Gulf Crisis and Public Opinion: A Study of Agenda-Setting, Priming, and Framing', in W. L. Bennett and D. Paletz (eds) *Taken by storm: the media, public opinion, and U.S. foreign policy in the Gulf War*, pp. 167–85 (University of Chicago Press).
Janowitz, M. (1976) 'Content analysis and the study of sociopolitical change' *Journal of Communication*, **26**(4), 10–21.
Jones, G., I. Connell and J. Meadows (1978) *The presentation of science by the media* (Primary Communications Research Centre, University of Leicester).
Kracauer, S. (1952) 'The challenge of qualitative content analysis', *Public Opinion Quarterly*, **16**(Winter), 631–42.
Krippendorf, K. (1980) *Content analysis: an introduction to its methodology* (London: Sage).
Kristiansen, C. M. and C. M. Harding (1985) 'Mobilisation of health behaviour by the press in Britain', *Journalism Quarterly*, **61**(2), 364–70, 398.
Lee, J. A. (1989) 'Waging the seal war in the media: Toward a content analysis of moral communication' *Canadian Journal of Communication*, **14**(1), 37–56.
McCormack, T. (1982) 'Content analysis: the social history of a method', in T. McCormack (ed.) *Culture, code and content analysis*, Vol. 2, pp. 143–78 (JAI Press Inc).
Molotch, H. and M. Lester (1975) 'Accidental news: the great oil spill', *American Journal of Sociology*, **81**(2), 235–60.

Morrison, D. (1992) *Television and the Gulf War* (London: John Libbey).

Morrison, D. and H. Tumber (1988) *Journalists at war: the dynamics of news reporting during the Falklands Conflict* (London: Sage).

Neuman, W. R. (1989) 'Parallel content analysis: old paradigms and new proposals', in G. Comstock (ed.), *Public communication and behavior*, Vol. 2, pp. 205–89. (San Diego, Calif.: Academic Press).

Nimmo, D. and J. E. Combs (1985) *Nightly horrors: crisis coverage in television network news* (Knoxville, Tenn.: University of Tennessee Press).

Nowak, K. (1992). Magazine advertising content in Sweden and the United States: stable patterns of change, variable levels of stability. In J. G. Blumler, J. M. McLeod, & K. E. Rosengren (eds), *Comparatively speaking: communication and culture across space and time* (Newbury Park, Calif.: Sage).

Pendleton, L. L., C. Smith and J. L. Roberts (1991) 'Drinking on television – a content-analysis of recent alcohol portrayal', *British Journal Of Addiction*, **86**(6), 769–74.

Pfund, N. and L. Hofstadter (1981) 'Biomedical innovation and the press', *Journal of Communication*, **31**(2), 138–54.

Picard, R. G. and P. D. Adams (1991) 'Characterizations of acts and perpetrators of political violence in three elite U.S. daily newspapers', in A. O. Alali and K. K. Eke (eds) *Media coverage of terrorism: Methods of diffusion*, pp. 12–22 (London: Sage).

Rogers, E. M. and J. W. Dearing (1988) 'Agenda-setting research: where has it been, where is it going?', in J. A. Anderson (ed.), *Communication Yearbook*, Vol. 11, pp. 555–94 (London: Sage).

Rothman, S. and S. R. Lichter (1987) 'Elite ideology and risk perception in nuclear energy policy', *American Political Science Review*, **81**(2), 383–404.

Royal Commission on the Press (1949) *Report of the Royal Commission on the Press, 1947–1949* (London: HMSO).

Rubin, D. M. (1987) 'How the news media reported on Three Mile Island and Chernobyl', *Journal of Communication*, **37**(2), 42–57.

Ruhrmann, G. (1992) 'Genetic engineering in the press: a review of research and results of a content analysis', in J. Durant (ed.) *Biotechnology in public: a review of recent research*, pp. 169–201 (London: The Science Museum).

Scott, W. A. (1955) 'Reliability of content analysis: the case of nominal scale coding', *Public Opinion Quarterly*, **Fall**, 321–5.

Seiter, E. (1986) 'Stereotypes and the media: a re-evaluation', *Journal of Communication*, **36**(2), 14–26.

Semetko, H. A. (1989) 'Television news and the 'Third Force' in British politics: a case study of election communication', *European Journal of Communication*, **4**(4), 453–79.

Signorielli, N. (1984) 'The Demography of the Television World', in G. Melischek, K. E. Rosengren, and J. Stappers (eds) *Cultural Indicators: An International Symposium*, pp. 137–57) (Vienna: Österreichischen Akademie der Wissenschaften).

Singletary, M. W. (1993) *Mass Communication Research: Contemporary Methods and Applications* (New York: Longman).

Smith, L. J. (1994) 'A Content-Analysis Of Gender Differences In Childrens Advertising', *Journal Of Broadcasting & Electronic Media*, **38**(3), 323–37.
Sreberny-Mohammadi, A. (1984) *Foreign news in the media: International reporting in twenty-nine countries*, Vol. 93 (Paris: UNESCO).
Stahl, W. A. (1995) 'Venerating the Black-Box – Magic In Media Discourse On Technology', *Science, Technology & Human Values*, **20**(2), 234–58.
Stone, P. J., D. C. Dunphy, M. S. Smith and D. M. Ogilvie (1966) *The General Inquirer: A computer approach to content analysis* (Cambridge, Mass.: MIT Press).
Sumner, C. (1979) *Reading ideologies: an investigation into the Marxist theory of ideology and law* (London: Academic Press).
Thomas, S. (1994) 'Artifactural Study In the Analysis Of Culture – a Defense Of Content-Analysis In a Postmodern Age. *Communication Research*, **21**(6), 683–97.
Troyna, B. (1981) *Public awareness and the media: a study of reporting on race* (London: Commission for Racial Equality).
Tumber, H. (1982) *Television and the riots* (London: British Film Institute).
Van Dijk, T. A. (1991) *Racism and the press* (London: Routledge).
Wallack, L., J. W. Grube, P. A. Madden and W. Breed (1990) Portrayals of alcohol on prime-time television', *Journal Of Studies On Alcohol*, **51**(5), 428–37.
Weigel, R. H., E. L. Kim and J. L. Frost (1995) 'Race-Relations On Prime-Time Television Reconsidered – Patterns Of Continuity and Change', *Journal Of Applied Social Psychology*, **25**(3), 223–36.
Williams, R. (1976) *Communications*, 3rd edn (Harmondsworth: Penguin).
Wonsek, P. L. (1992) 'College basketball on television: a study of racism in the media', *Media, Culture & Society*, **14**(3), 449–61.

Notes

1. For examples of studies which have combined qualitative approaches, such as semiotics and discourse analysis, with content analysis, see the Glasgow University Media Group (1976), Chapman (1986), Gamson & Modigliani (1989), Hansen & Murdock (1985), Van Dijk (1991).
2. 'Content analysis is any technique for making inferences by systematically identifying specified characteristics of messages' (Holsti, 1969, p. 14)
3. 'Content analysis is a research technique for making replicable and valid inferences from data to their context' (Krippendorf, 1980, p. 21)
4. Singletary (1993) for example lists 10 steps as follows: 1. select topic, 2. decide sample or census, 3. define concepts or units to be counted, 4. construct categories, 5. create coding form, 6. train coders, 7. collect data, 8. measure intercoder reliability, 9. analyze data, 10. report results.

6

Analysing the Moving Image: Narrative

6.1 Introduction to Moving Image Analysis

A useful place to start any analysis of the moving image is with a consideration of the all-pervasive nature of both narrative and genre in moving image products. One could go as far as to say that every moving image product has a relationship to narrative, and that all products can be classified and understood in terms of genre. Thus the analysis of these two areas is central to the study of the mass media generally, and to moving image content particularly. This chapter aims to provide the moving image researcher with key tools for narrative analysis, and Chapter 7 offers an introduction to genre analysis.

'Moving image' as a relatively self-explanatory term can best be understood in relation to the media that it covers: film, television, video, animation. A problem with the term is that it does not indicate the importance of sound, both to production and analysis. There may be several technical arguments about the quality of reproduction between video and film, or about the ability to manipulate light; at the end of the day though, most of the production techniques are the same for the different media. Indeed, in a world of multi-media production the barriers between media are already crumbling; most moving image products are now 'finished' on computer anyway. Thus this chapter and the next address analytic and methodological procedures applicable to all types of moving image product.

Narrative and genre analysis have long held a prominent place in the study of literature and film, although 'like all terms derived from literary criticism their description and usage are much argued and debated over' (Newbold, 1995, p. 442). Thus, it is only over the last few years that attempts have been made to apply the strategies of narrative and genre analysis not only to the study of film, but to the study of all moving image products. It is symptomatic of the origins of these methods of research, that they have tended to be applied particularly to fictional products such as gangster movies (Warshow 1964) and westerns (Wright 1975) in film, with soap opera (Ang 1985) and drama (Berger 1991) prominent in the study of television. What these two chapters seek to establish is that the concepts of narrative and genre are tools for opening up texts, and are key devices for examining meanings in *all* moving image products, from news and current affairs to advertising and situation comedies.

Moving image products utilise a language into which both producers and audiences are socialised; they must understand and master it in order to be able to use the medium effectively. That is, for communication to take place they must share the same or similar codes. It is the task of the moving image researcher to reveal and understand this shared language, and the structures, codes and conventions from which it is built.

Central to the analysis of both narrative and genre is an application of the researcher's own reading, that is, a structured approach, not only based on formula and application of models, but largely dependent on the development of skills of description and classification. Thus, such methods appear under the qualitative approaches banner, enshrining as they do certain principles of researcher interpretation, what Kracauer (1953; see also Larsen, 1991) called for in terms of qualitative, hermeneutic or humanistic procedures. Research of this nature involves *an act of interpretation* on the part of the moving image researcher. For Kracauer, quantitative analysis fails, because – in trying to break down meaning into quantifiable units of words, expressions or statements – it destroys or obstructs the object of study, rendering the examination of the text as a meaningful whole impossible (see the discussion of this critique in Chapter 5). Using the procedures provided by narrative and genre study, the moving image researcher is able to break down signifying components and structures without breaking up the object of study as a meaningful whole. The usefulness of narrative and genre analysis is not only in the revealing of deep structures in texts, but also in the identification of ideological positions and ideological messages within texts.

6.2 Understanding Moving Image Language

The first step to be taken in any moving image analysis, is that of standing apart from the text or texts that you are approaching, and *stopping them dead*. In order to analyse the moving image, it is first of all necessary to halt its progress, to separate yourself from the apparent seamless and constant flow of images and story, and then to start to dismantle the individual component parts that make up the whole.

To be in a position to examine visual style, to extract the narrative and generic content, or to conduct other content research such as representation research, it is first of all essential to gain a thorough knowledge of the codes and conventions that make up the language of the moving image. Moving image codes are best understood as the rules which govern the construction of the moving image and thus the way moving image language communicates; for example, the use of the reverse-angle shot in the construction of a conversation between two people, or the use of slow-motion to heighten and extend dramatic sequences. Conventions, on the other hand, are those established practices which have become associated with particular types of moving image product, be they film or television. A convention of the Western genre would be the shoot out, or the 'look' of a Western town. A convention of television might be on-screen news readers sitting down facing the camera.

The process of identification of the codes and conventions that constitute a moving image product is the first step in the decoding or analysis of a text. It cannot be stressed enough how important for moving image analysis is a thorough knowledge of the various methods and techniques of visual and audio construction, for it is through these that particular meanings are generated and a language is derived and understood.

The elements or significant (signifying) parts of this language are divided into the technical and symbolic:

- **technical** – camera angles, camera movement, shot duration, lighting, depth of field, editing, sound, sound effects, music, special effects, framing, and so on.
- **symbolic** – colour or black and white, costume, objects, stars, performance, setting, location and so on (those features of moving image language which are contained within that which the audience sees rather than those which are part of its 'seamless' technical construction).

These elements are combined into signifying systems or codes, in the same way that a wardrobe provides a person with a combination of clothes to wear, depending upon the occasion, or the statement the person wishes to make. So moving image language provides the producer with a number of alternative ways to construct a scene, and create meaning for the audience. The technical elements work to create moving image language through the following devices in order to construct the largely subconscious pattern of a narrative or genre that an audience is concerned with.

6.2.1 Technical Elements

Camera Shots

The essential building blocks in the technical armoury are the camera shots. A brief discussion of these will be useful in becoming technically and visually aware.

- **The close-up** provides a shot of a part of a person (head, arms, legs and so on) or object, which because of its size on the screen bestows a high dramatic sense to it, or great symbolic value within the scene to it. The close up is also used to direct the audience's attention and to establish identification or empathy with characters. It provides emphasis in moving image construction.
- **The extreme close-up** has similar qualities, although its more clinical detail of faces and objects serves to heighten tension and drama greatly.
- **The medium shot** or **mid shot** is the typical shot in studio television, and emphasises some detail on a person usually taken from waist up. The person or object remains to some extent isolated from his/her/its environment, unlike the long-shot.
- **The long-shot** is often used to relate a person to his or her particular environment. Two types of related long-shot particularly strive to do this:
  — *the cover shot*, which is used to relate one character to others,
  — *the establishing shot* which is particularly designed to provide a sense of the locale, essential in the western genre, where the opening sequence establishes the hero in 'his' or 'her' landscape.
- **The point-of-view shot** – see below, p. 135.

Camera Angle

Camera angle, or the viewing position of the camera, is its placement in relation to the object or person on view. Angle can be used for both aesthetic and psychological values; most importantly it can add to the spatial relations and thus diminish the two-dimensionality of an image on the screen.

- The main use of the camera is in the **straight on** position.
- **Low-angle** is where the camera is placed below eye-level and looks up at the subject often ascribing to it power and stature.
- **High-angle** is where the camera looks down on its subjects, making them look small, insignificant and vulnerable.
- The two other angles are the **oblique angle** and the **Dutch angle**, both concern camera tilt, the first to the left or right, the second, horizontally and vertically.

Lenses

The variety of lenses used are important in that they can alter the type of image seen on the screen.

- **The wide-angle lens** is most commonly used on the long shot, since it provides a large focus range. However, if used in close-up shots, the wide-angle lens can create a sense of distortion.
- **Fish-eye lenses** achieve this to an even greater extent, imbuing the scene with the sense of tension and drama, perhaps indicating a disrupted or disturbed world, excellent for horror genre products. The fish-eye lens is so effective because it works against the conventions of standard lenses.
- **Telephoto lenses**, although rare in film-making, are favoured by documentarists, in that they enable subjects to be recorded from some distance without disturbing their surroundings.
- **The zoom lens** is now the standard lens in television use, and allows the camera person to change the range of the shot from telephoto to close-up without stopping the camera. The effect of this could be to direct audience attention to any number of objects and/or people within a shot.

Depth of Field

Depth of field is important in guiding the viewer's eye to particular areas or characters on the screen.

- **Close-up focus** or **distant focus** is largely determined by the kind of lens being used and the aperture.
- **A deep focus shot**, however, in allowing for a great depth of field where everything within the frame is in focus, theoretically leaves the audience to focus where they wish on the screen. Great claims are made for Orson Welles' use of deep focus in *Citizen Kane* (1941).

Camera Movement

This is also of central importance, for it is the ability to follow moving action, or scan around a scene, which in part separates the moving image camera from the still camera.

- **Panning** is the movement of the camera on the horizontal plane which allows the actions of a character to be followed or, in an establishing shot, the locale to be scanned.
- **The tilt shot** – movement of the camera in the vertical plane – is often built into a panning shot. An early example of this is in Edwin S. Porter's *The Great Train Robbery* (1903), where we follow the train robbers as they leave the train and run along the track (this is done by panning), and then the camera tilts as we follow them down a ravine. If pans and tilts are used objectively, they can allow the audience to follow some action in a voyeuristic sense, as if they themselves were observing it at a distance. Both panning and tilting allow the director to sustain a shot, keeping its momentum and thus its dramatic effect without having to cut.
- Pans and tilts can also be used in a subjective way, when part of a **point-of-view** (POV) shot, where we see the world from the central character's side, seeing what they see, scanning a room, or looking at the floor.
- A **tracking** or **dolly** shot provides the same continuation of shot that a director may require from a pan or tilt, following the action on a dolly pushed on tracks or mounted on a moving vehicle or on a crane. This allows fast-moving action to be followed either close in, or at a distance; unlike the zoom which appears to move through space, the dolly stays with the events as they happen. Dolly shots may also be used to intensify or distance the emotions of a character by physically moving in for a close-up, or drawing away

to a long shot, thereby showing him or her isolated or surrounded by other characters.

Length of Take or Duration of Shot

This can alter the audience's sense of time and space.

- **Long takes** tend to incorporate tracking and panning or tilting shots. They are particularly favoured by some documentarists as they relate real time rather than screen time.
- **Length of shot**, particularly of a close up, can heighten the drama and intimacy or even disturb the audience.

Editing

The development of **cutting** or **editing**, and **montage editing** in particular, is the understanding of the relationship between shots. The simplest form of editing is the **straight cut**, where one shot is instantly replaced by a second, which might then be replaced by a third, or it might be **crosscut** to another line of the developing story. Perhaps above all other technical codes, it is the recognition of editing techniques that enables us to halt the apparently seamless quality of the moving image. It is the editor who, through these creative techniques, is ultimately responsible for the construction of the scenes into the plot and narrative. The editor's role can also affect the *tempo*, and thus the dramatic effect of the product. Editing plays a key role in the *construction of space and time*, and thus in the making believable or the verisimilitude of the piece. The construction of time and space, as we will see later, is subordinated to the logic of the narrative and in particular its cause–effect chain.

In Eisenstein's version of montage, it is the relationship between the shots that not only drives the narrative and creates meaning, but is also the source of film art, in that they are arranged creatively by the editor/director in order to generate emotional and intellectual impact by their juxtaposition. In *Battleship Potemkin* (1925) Eisenstein juxtaposes shots of a crucifix, a sword and the Russian imperial crest, thus creating the association of the church, the military, and the Tsar, with the oppression of the sailors on the battleship.

Shots linked together become **scenes**; that is, a series of shots in one setting. Scenes become sequences, or self-contained blocks of dramatic action. These linked together become the plot and the narrative.

Special Effects

Special effects exploit the qualities of the moving image medium in ways during the production and post-production phases so as to persuade the audience of the reality, verisimilitude, or sheer spectacle of the product.

- Production techniques might involve pyrotechnics, optical effects, or trick photography.
- Post-production might include animation, superimposition, or computer graphics.
- Other special effects might involve the use of chromakey or a matte (or masking) shot, in order to insert or combine images.

Framing

In the development of the moving image the importance of framing is in the positioning of people and objects which contribute to the narrative. The principal elements of framing relate to camera distance, lens choice, camera movement and camera angle. The recognition that what passes before the viewer is not on the whole there by accident but is deliberately placed, is essential to any decoding or analysis. This is also true of the positioning of the camera, whereby each scene is shot according to the intention of the director.

Lighting

Lighting can be used not only to create the sense of time and place, but also mood and character. Furthermore, a great deal is made of the use of natural light in 'realist' films and documentaries. High-key lighting and low-key lighting, generally refer to the quality of lighting; thus:-

- **High-key** lighting describes a generally equal amount of lighting across a scene, while
- **Low-key** indicates that there is less light on the entire scene, creating greater contrasts and areas of light and shade.

The convention of lighting is that high-key will usually be used in musical or comedy products and television studio programmes, whereas low-key occurs in mysteries and thrillers such as film noirs.

6.2.2 Symbolic Elements

Colour and/or Black and White

The use of colour and/or black and white film can convey both realistic and expressive messages. They can convey atmosphere and underscore the theme of a moving image product. Warm colours are red, yellow and gold, while cold colours are blue and green. For example, in Jean-Jacques Beineix's *Betty Blue* (1986), changes in colour as the film progresses indicate changes in the relationship between the two central characters, as well as changes of mood within the film itself. The use of sepia in moving image products is often a code for the past or old film.

Costume and Objects

- **Costume** has been the mainstay of both genre and narrative production since the beginning of moving image history. It is used not only to connote time and place, but also to provide spectacle to products.
- **Objects** are also a key symbolic source of information in moving image products. They can have both connotive and mythic (see Chapter 8) resonance. For example, the sheriff's badge in the western genre ties him to the community he serves as well as marking him out as the 'good' guy. Hence, at the end of Fred Zinnemann's *High Noon* (1952) sheriff Will Kane's action in throwing down the sheriff's badge, has particular meaning and significance within the film and the genre.

Stars and Performances

Stars are particular icons who carry symbolic power, and are identified with particular genres and personality traits. Arnold Schwarzenegger is associated with action/adventure films and portrays hero/anti-hero type figures.

An actor's **performance** is best understood and analysed by considering its physicality. That is, that the attention of the audience is drawn in by the movement, physique, facial features and personality displays of the actor. Because the large screen exaggerates movement, restraint is a central part of an actor's performance. Subtle emotional and character shadings reveal the quality of a performance as well as the verisimilitude of the character.

Sound

Sound codes can be split into two kinds:

- Ddiegetic sound, that is sound that emanates from the scene such as sound effects and dialogue.
- **Non-diegetic sound** is sound that does not emanate from the scene we are watching, and is essentially music or a voice over.

Sound effects are often used to create realism, but these similarly can be divided into two kinds: (i) atmospheric sounds, background noises such as the wind, or birds singing, and so on; and (ii) sound effects that are justified, that is, they are sounds relating directly to what we are seeing, explosions or gunshots and so on.

Both sound effects and music can be examined in their *generic context*. Sounds like gunfire, a bugle or Indian yelps may relate directly to westerns, as may certain types of music and ballads.

- Music can be diegetic in that it may be part of the drama of a film based on an orchestra, for example. Most often music is **functional**: it is there to help direct the mood of the audience, to reinforce the pace of the screen action, or to provide a musical motif behind the moving image.
- The **dialogue** in any film is going to be of crucial importance to any style of moving image research. Dialogue can exist in two forms, as voice over, or if we see the faces that are talking, synchronic lip movement. Dialogue is most often scripted speech. However, many film-makers in the 'realist' tradition look for their actors, be they professional or non-professional, to improvise speech so as to heighten the realism of the product they are trying to create.

Mise-en-scène

This literally means 'putting into a scene' and can be seen as everything that is within the frame; the content of the frame, the image, set-design, costume, objects and their placement, the spatial relations (those who are dominant within the frame, the relationship between characters seen in terms of the distance between them) is crucial here. It is through *mise-en-scène* that all the above technical devices combine and work, and are thus best understood by the audience and the researcher. We shall return to more specific analysis of the *mise-en-scène* later. However, it is worth while noting here that analysis of *mise-en-scène* will involve the description of a particular scene in all its detail utilising the above elements in order to analyse the construction and thus the meaning. The research may then successfully rest on the full description of the scene in total, or feeling that the *mise-en-scène* conveys.

Setting and Location

We can round off this section with a discussion of two main areas of consideration in *mise-en-scène*, the setting and the location.

- **The setting** crucially establishes the time and the place of the story. Many of the symbolic elements mentioned above are essential to help establish the setting and thus the wider *mise-en-scène*. Specific genres in particular are tied to specific settings. Westerns, for instance, with their wilderness landscapes, or gangster films with their predominantly urban settings.
- **Location work** is then important, since it is the shooting of a scene outside of the totally constructed studio situation. Realist film and programme-makers in particular endeavour to use location shooting much more than studio work in order to establish a feeling of authenticity; the work of Italian neo-realists, and British Social Realist film-makers are good examples here.

The technical and symbolic elements in bold above are reproduced at the end of this chapter in checklist form.

It must be noted that these technical and symbolic devices do not work in isolation and in any one scene many of these codes will have been working together in order to create the encoded meaning. The moving image researcher adapts his or her understanding of all these codes to the particular object of study. A thorough analysis is built on the relationship between moving image elements, technical as well as symbolic, and the codes and conventions of production.

The technical and symbolic elements and the codes and conventions considered in this section are major contributory factors in the opacity of much moving image production, that is, its need to conceal its own construction. It is the role of the moving image researcher to make overt these hidden constructions, to describe and then analyse their workings. In order to analyse them the researcher has to separate himself or herself from the stream of images and sounds. Any analysis of the moving image must be aware of and address construction, codes and conventions in order to be able to *understand*, *describe* and *categorise* that which is being studied.

6.2.3 Considerations Before Starting Research

Before starting on narrative and genre analysis, several practical points are worth considering.

- Be aware of the copyright laws affecting the recording and use of film and television material.
- Films are available from a few commercial companies, and other organisations, such as the British Film Institute. However, these can be very expensive to hire and need the correct facilities to be viewed.
- Video equipment is essential. It is relatively cheap, and very flexible. Video recorders will allow you to pause, rewind, fast forward etc., all necessary to thorough analysis.
- Be wary of stills reproduced in books or commercially available; these are often publicity shots, and not actual stills from the film or television programmes. They may be useful though, as they often capture the essence of the product.
- Watch a film or programme at least three times. The first time any of us watch a moving image product, no matter how hard-boiled researchers we may be, we always watch the story. It is only on the second and third viewing that we start to thoroughly see the construction with, of course, the help of the pause button.
- How many films or programmes need to be discussed? This will ultimately depend on factors such as the questions pursued, the size of the study, finances available, and time available. But for a small-scale study, about four ninety-minute films will be more than enough. A maximum for any study could be about twenty films analysed in depth. These, though, ultimately depend on the nature of the study.

6.3 Examining Narrative

In a general sense, narratives are all around us, the world comes to us in the form of narratives, they are central to the way we organise and understand the world. The study of narrative, or narratology, refers us here to the examination of those specific structures in moving image products that are familiar to both producer and audience (although they are often taken for granted by both). This is important, since it is in this way that narratives form a central part of the organisation of the communication between producer and audience.

Narrative so dominates moving image construction that, as we shall see, all the technical and symbolic elements described in section 6.2 above are subordinate to its construction. It is undoubtedly the case that consideration of the structure of narratives dominates narratology and narrative analysis. This kind of analysis will inevitably be concerned with the delineation of patterns: patterns of dramatis personae, of plot and of oppositions. Ultimately the moving image researcher will be interested in considering those patterns both within single texts and between texts. The usefulness of narrative research is in the analysis of not only the structure of texts, but also the construction of meaning and especially ideologies within texts. The methodological strategies set out here are designed to help the moving image researcher analyse not only the meaning contained within narratives, but also how, through the very structure of narratives themselves, ideological effects can be imputed.

The basic approaches to examining narrative derive essentially from two sources.

- **The syntagmatic approach**, is based in the formalist work of Vladimir Propp and examines the sequential development of narrative plot.
- **The paradigmatic approach**, emerges from the structuralist work of Lévi-Strauss and considers the patterns of oppositions that exist within the narrative and how they contribute to the development of the story.

Both Propp and Lévi-Strauss believed that you could not only unravel and reveal the governing threads and ties of narrative, but in doing so you could also systematise narratives. This systematising as well as the delineation of patterns and meanings are then inevitably the central tasks of narrative analysis.

Any review of strategies for narrative analysis will discuss a number of systems or procedures which can be used to examine a moving image product. Not all of these have to be used by the researcher; rather, each methodology should be adapted to the particular needs of the study in hand. As we have stated, the major methodologies emerge from the formalist and structuralist approaches, but inevitably these will need to be developed alongside additional interpretative analysis in order to provide as complete a methodological engagement as is possible. Much of the work, then, will involve the construction of lists of elements identified, or relationships established, accompanied by a detailed description and analysis of the relationships between the various technical elements, symbolic elements and codes and conventions, as discussed in section 6.2.

6.3.1 Story, Plot and Narrative

All the events, both inferred and presented in the narrative, are referred to as the story. The plot is part of the narrative, the substance of the story told in visual and audio presentation, as well as the added material such as music, graphics and credits. Thus while films such as Orson Welles' *Citizen Kane* (1941) may have a simple story – a boy inherits a fortune, runs a newspaper, becomes a recluse and dies – the plot itself is very complex in its construction, with its convoluted shifts in time and space. The previous section has illustrated some of the main technical and symbolic devices by which the plot is constructed, our concern now is with how these elements are combined within the structure of the narrative and thus can best be researched.

If we begin by understanding the narrative as a relationship of cause and effect, forming a chain of events which occur in the moving image's construction of time and space, then we can start to identify and examine the dynamics of narrative and the structure of the narration, that is, the events that combine to create the direction that the story-telling takes. As we shall see, this form of analysis is useful, since it identifies the structures that narratives have in common, and may be used to identify underlying assumptions and structures in all stories.

In this section we shall concentrate on what is perhaps the dominant form of moving image narrative structure, which is variously referred to as:

— the institutional mode of representation,
— the classic realist text, or
— the standard Hollywood narrative.

The key features of this are outlined below, and are discussed in terms of methodology as this section progresses.

- A single diegesis: there is one main storyline.
- A central pattern of enigma and resolution is followed.
- All questions posed at the start of the narrative, or as it progresses, are answered.
- The chain of events follows a logical sequence, and has an inner logic.
- Verisimilitude: all events are believable.
- The audience should empathise with the central characters.
- The focus of the narrative is on individuals rather than society or groups.
- Technical and symbolic elements are subordinate to the construction of the narrative and the need to drive it along.

This type of narrative relies on the narrative structure of the nineteenth-century novel and classical theatre, which is organised into a standard three acts. Hence, one of the central points for analysis here is the structure of the narrative, comprised of an identifiable beginning, a middle, and an end. These can also be called opening, conflict and resolution. The narrative is constrained by this format, with information on the development of the story being tightly structured and released to the audience in intelligible leaks at set points throughout the narrative. The job of the moving image researcher is then to identify and isolate these moments in the narrative structure.

The first step in this might well be to identify the narrative structure using a simple model to overview the whole story (see Figure 6.1). These models draw our attention to the elements to be addressed in the research, and can be used to identify and discuss narrative structures across a number of moving image products. What is done here is a simple form of segmentation: that is, the separating out of the narrative into its component plot elements. In Figure 6.1, we have considered the vary basic model of beginning, middle and end, in order to demonstrate a number of points about narrative structure.

Segmentation of plot is also a useful device in uncovering what are the central moments of the plot and considering their place in the narrative. For example Annette Kuhn (1993) provides a breakdown of Michael Curtiz's film *Mildred Pierce* (1945) into seven segments, reflecting how the temporal development of juxtaposed flashbacks can be separated off in order to examine the narrative structure (Figure 6.2 illustrates this).

What is discussed as the institutional mode of representation has produced a structure that dominates moving image production and consumption throughout the world. Central to its approach, as we saw above, is the chain of events in a cause and effect relationship, which revolves around the resolving of a central enigma.

Beginning	HERO VILLAIN PROBLEM EMERGES
Middle	PROBLEM INTENSIFIES QUEST AND/OR BATTLE
End	VICTORY PEACE CHANGED SITUATION

If we now apply this to an example of a typical film noir story we get:

Beginning	Detective Murderer Client meets detective
Middle	Client and/or detective menaced Detective hunts for murderer Detective fights murderer
End	Detective is victorious Problem solved Detective and/or client have developed in some way

Figure 6.1 Model of narrative structure

1	2	3	4	5	6	7
narrative present	flashback 1: indefinite narrative past (Mildred)	narrative present	flashback 2: indefinite narrative past (Mildred)	narrative present	flashback 3: narrative past (Detective)	narrative present

1. The Murder. Mildred is found on the beach and taken to the police station.
2. Mildred tells detective events in her past.
3. Detective interrupts.
4. Mildred proceeds with her story.
5. Mildred's daughter is brought into the police station.
6. The 'truth' is revealed by the detective and the murder is solved.
7. Mildred leaves the police station with her former husband.

Source: Kuhn 1993, p. 30.

Figure 6.2 Annette Kuhn's breakdown of *Mildred Pierce*

A key tool for identifying and analysing this structure, and for a consideration of how the reader moves through it, is based on the process Todorov (1977) identifies in his 'equilibrium formula'. This formula emphasises the linear nature of most narratives. That is, the way that narratives start with some form of state of equilibrium, followed by disruption, and end with the equilibrium being regained. The following pattern can be identified by the equilibrium formula:

Equilibrium/plenitude →
Disruption/disequilibrium →
Quest [opposition force versus unifying equalising force] →
Disequilibrium →
New equilibrium.

For example, if we apply this with variations to Fred Zinnemann's *High Noon* (1952), then we come up with a model that looks like this:

Equilibrium and state of Plenitude (quiet western town, a unifying marriage taking place)
Disruption and disequilibrium (outlaws arrive in town to wait for leader, who is coming on the noon train to gain revenge)
Opposition force (outlaw leader Miller just released from prison) versus **unifying/equalising force** (Sheriff Will Kane)

Quest (Sheriff looks for help, decides to/has to stand alone)
Disequilibrium (gunfight with outlaws, Kane saved by wife's intervention)
New Equilibrium (outlaws killed, town safe, but characters different because of experience).

We might also synthesise out and identify some of the key elements in this formula, such as the equalising effect of the disrupting force (outlaw Miller, plus three accomplices) with the unifying/equalising force (Sheriff Will Kane). We might also emphasise the positive narrative closure. The importance of such characters for analysis will be worked with later when we discuss Propp's notion of **role**, and Lévi-Strauss' **binary oppositions**.

A simpler form of Todorov's formula might be applied to Bernardo Bertolucci's *Last Tango in Paris* (1972), where Maria Schneider is in a state of equilibrium and plenitude looking for a new flat, Marlon Brando arrives, causes disruption and disequilibrium in her life. After Brando has gone, a new state of equilibrium is established for Schneider. The central enigma or disruption has been resolved through the narrative, the closure device being the death of the Brando character.

The same pattern applies to moving image advertising, where a state of equilibrium, or an inferred state of equilibrium, is disrupted by some oppositional force, perhaps dirt, body odour, hunger, or a poor self-image, which is then dealt with by an equalising force, or product, leading to a new (and much improved) state of equilibrium.

With some variation, this model can be applied to all moving image products within the Hollywood narrative framework. This, as we have seen, includes everything from two-hour feature films to thirty-second adverts. This type of method or approach is interested (1) in the underlying rules and structures within single narratives and groups of narratives, and (2) in how movement within texts is achieved. Ultimately this type of method leads us on to further theoretical as well as other methodological questions related to such topics as ideology and myth, as discussed by Lévi-Strauss (1966) and Roland Barthes (1972).

It is important at this point to note that if the object of research is to ascertain and understand ideological content, then the equilibrium formula points our attention to how conflicts are resolved and closed narratively. The point of consideration here is whether closure is achieved through the re-establishing of the *status quo*, through socially acceptable means, such as marriage, or institutionally through imprisonment, or through acts of socially sanctioned violence? The equilibrium formula can inevitably be used as a critique of the 'symbolic world' created by the media, as compared to the real 'lived world' of the audience.

Questions of whether narratives can be seen as universal continually reoccur in theoretical and methodological work, since common features and functions of narrative can be seen across national and cultural boundaries. However, each of these is to some extent adapted to their particular cultures. The work on myth by both Roland Barthes and Lévi-Strauss mentioned above, describes how narratives have a common function for the societies in which they operate, in that contradictions within them that cannot be altered in reality, become resolved in a symbolic sense through their myths and stories. It is this notion of symbolic resolution which causes us to examine narratives not solely in terms of their internal structures and devices, but also in terms of the ideological underpinning of texts.

6.3.2 Roles and Functions

A useful tool for examining both universal narrative, and myths and ideology in moving image products, can be found in Vladimir Propp's *Morphology of the Folk-tale*. Although first published in 1928, it still affords the researcher not only useful insights, but also methodological categories and formulas. Propp's analysis of fairy tales can also be seen as a central component of both work on narrative, and work on genre. As Berger (1992) indicates in his analysis of genre, 'many of the elements found in the most important genres are found in fairy tales and different genres focus upon different aspects of fairy tales' (p. 38).

Propp identifies a series of rules for narrative. He provides us with two common components of fairy tales and narratives that we can utilise in moving image research:

(i) *Roles* which are filled by characters;
(ii) *Functions*, which constitute the plot.

Seven roles or dramatis personae can be identified, some of which can be filled by the same character, and may also be filled by more than one character:

(1) the villain
(2) the donor or provider

(3) the helper
(4) the princess and her father
(5) the dispatcher
(6) the hero
(7) the false hero.

If we apply this to an obviously fairy-tale-based narrative, such as the legend of King Arthur, in John Boorman's film *Excalibur* (1981), then the villain can be seen as Morgana, the donor as Merlin, the helper as the knights of the round table, the princess as Guinevere, the dispatcher as Merlin, Arthur as the hero, and Lancelot as false hero. The same schema can be applied to numerous other moving image products, from cartoons to adverts, documentaries (especially wildlife ones with their anthropomorphic structure), and even news, where heroes and villains populate the discourse.

The functions of characters constitute the fundamental components of the tale and tend to follow the same sequence in the development of the narrative. *A function is the significant act of a character within the course of the action in the narrative.* The ordering of these functions is of some importance to our understanding of the meaning within the text. The number of character functions is limited – Propp identified thirty-one functions, or parts of the narrative organised by the plot, although he also suggests many subcategories for the functions. It is the presence or absence of these which may form the basis of a classification of plots. Graeme Turner (1993) provides us with the most usefully abridged version of these narrative functions, which are reproduced in Figure 6.3.

For Propp, not all narratives have *all* of these functions, but they will have some, and those they do have will be composed of functions from this list, following the order he outlines. From this list, then, it is useful to synthesise our own functions which will be identified within the subject of the research. Inevitably many functions will not be applicable, but equally those that are will form the core of any analysis of narrative structure. This can fruitfully be combined with the roles to produce the following type of analytic framework:

Hero leaves home and sets out on quest
Villain acts against hero and/or community
Hero and villain join in direct combat
Villain is defeated
Hero is married and/or crowned.

1.	A member of the family leaves home.	PREPARATION
2.	A prohibition or rule is imposed on the hero.	
3.	This prohibition is broken.	
4.	The villain makes an attempt at reconnaissance.	
5.	The villain learns something about his victim.	
6.	The villain tries to deceive the victim to get possession of him and his belongings.	
7.	The victim unknowingly helps the villain by being deceived or influenced by the villain.	
8.	The villain harms a member of the family.	COMPLICATION
8a.	MA member of the family lacks or desires something.	
9.	This lack or misfortune is made known; the hero is given a request or command and he goes or is sent on a mission/ request.	
10.	The seeker (or the hero) plans action against the villain.	
11.	The hero leaves home.	TRANSFERENCE
12.	The hero is tested, interrogated, and as a result receives either a magical agent or a helper.	
13.	The hero reacts to the actions of the future donor.	
14.	The hero uses the magical agent.	
15.	The hero is transferred to the general location of the object of his mission/quest.	
16.	The hero and villain join in direct combat.	STRUGGLE
17.	The hero is branded.	
18.	The villain is defeated.	
19.	The initial misfortune or lack is set right.	
20	The hero returns.	RETURN
21.	The hero is pursued.	
22.	The hero is rescued from pursuit.	
23.	The hero arrives home or elsewhere and is not recognised.	
24.	A false hero makes false claims.	
25.	A difficult task is set for the hero.	
26.	The task is accomplished.	
27.	The hero is recognised.	RECOGNITION
28.	The false hero/villain is exposed.	
29.	The false hero is transformed.	
30.	The villain is punished.	
31.	The hero is married and crowned.	

Source: from Turner, 1993, pp. 69–70.

Figure 6.3 Narrative functions

If we then apply this to an example such as John Ford's film *The Quiet Man* (1952), we get the following:

Prize fighter (John Wayne) sets out to return to his native Ireland to find a quiet life.
He meets landowner (Victor McLaglen), and falls out over a property deal.
Various conflicts ensue, especially over the villain's sister (Maureen O'Hara).
Conflict culminates in fist fight and defeat of McLaglen.
McLaglen gives consent to Wayne's marriage to O'Hara.

Moving image texts will rarely contain all the elements here defined by Propp; however, they can all be identified as variants on these central themes. These variants work simply because of our knowledge and expectations of narrative structures. If we take an extreme example, of the cult film *The Wicker Man* (1973) by Robin Hardy, the hero (a police sergeant) leaves home on a quest (to find a missing girl). The hero meets villain (Lord Summer Isle), villain acts against hero (by laying a false trail), defeats hero and proceeds to offer him up as a sacrifice to the pagan gods. Although the hero sows a seed of doubt against the villain before his demise, the denouement of the story appears to run counter to Propp's fairy tale functions. Or a less stark example might be *The Terminator* (1984) by James Cameron, in which the hero is a heroine, and the film does not end with marriage and/or crowning of the heroine, although there is a conclusion of sorts in the destruction of the terminator. *Terminator 2: Judgement Day* (1991) Cameron's sequel, however, ends with the future secured through the self destruction of the *Helper*. Two useful, although more traditional, applications of Propp's work can be found in Berger (1991), and Silverstone (1981).

In any analysis of this sort, it is essential to relate not only what exists in terms of the structure, but crucially that which does not register or exist. This in itself is equally as enlightening. The Film *Bob Roberts* (1992) by Tim Robbins is the story of a scheming corrupt politician, and does not have a central character who can be described as a *hero*; indeed, many of the acts of the central character are perceivable to some extent as acts of villainy, but as the story unfolds we relate to the narrative in terms of our knowledge of the 'roles' being played out in a perverse sense before our eyes, and thus engage the meaning of the film.

This type of analysis or classification will be useful for research down several avenues of interest, not least of which is an examination of whether this style of narrative structure is in fact universal. It might also be of use in comparing and examining the structure of different cultural moving image products, as well as assessing the change in the structure of moving image products over a period of time.

Propp provides a yard-stick against which we can hold up our own objects of analysis and through a sophisticated development of Propp, identify the component parts, their absence or estrangement, and thus the meaning of the text. It is this element of meaning that is of the utmost importance for the moving image researcher. Once the roles and functions which effect our perception have been identified, and their sequence established, the meaning contained within the text (as communicated) is then identified and understood in some considerable detail and depth.

6.3.3 Binary Oppositions

Propp's original concerns lay within the texts themselves. Lévi-Strauss, on the other hand, is concerned with the relationship between myths and the societies they serve and reflect. Myths for him are the coded messages that societies produce for their members, which exist in the deep structure of narratives. It is the job of the researcher to unpack or reveal these messages hidden in the deep structure. Lévi-Strauss is not interested in sequence or chronology, but in the relationships between basic categories of character, setting and actions. Part of the methodological process, then, is the focus on categorising oppositions, which draws our attention to the latent or hidden content of moving image products. Binary oppositions are useful in helping us to tease out or define the essence of a text, be it for the analysis of myths and ideologies or simply to identify the core points around which a text evolves.

Some general oppositions found in a range of moving image products might well be:

Black v. White
Male v. Female
Good v. Evil
Life v. Death
Dirt v. Cleanliness
Strong v. Weak

RAF v. Luftwaffe
Left v. Right
East v. West
William Hague v. Tony Blair
Blue v. Red
Blue v. Grey

Man v. Nature	Cowboy v. Indian
Sea v. Land	Virgin v. Whore
Civilisation v. Wilderness	Christian v. Pagan

Constructing lists to elicit meaning is important here. However, explaining the relationships and portrayal using the tools and descriptions established in the second section of this chapter, is crucial to a thorough analysis. A useful application of this method is made by Turner (1993) in his examination of Susan Seidelman's *Desperately Seeking Susan* (1985).

A simple analysis of a film noir such as Fritz Lang's *The Big Heat* (1953) might start with the listing of the central oppositions which serve to structure the narrative:

Determination v. Compromise	Little Man v. Large Organisation
Cops v. Gangsters	Good Cops v. Bent Cops
Suicide v. Murder	Life v. Death
Male v. Female	Love v. Hate
Wives v. Molls	Home life v. Night Life
Light v. Shade	Honesty v. Corruption
Rich Criminals v. Poor Cops	

This might then proceed with a specific examination of some crucial moment of the film, or of the opening sequences and the closing or resolution of the narrative, where the opposition are established and then worked through. For instance, *The Big Heat* begins with the wife and the moll being compared; but for all their obvious differences, they 'would have got on fine'. This then sets up one of the central oppositions that develops throughout the film, both within the narrative and through the technical construction.

Binary oppositions also provide a useful tool for auteurship studies, identifying recurrent themes and oppositions in the work of directors such as John Ford (Caughie, 1981; Place, 1974).

6.3.4 Actants

The work of A. J. Greimas is worthy of consideration at this point, since it provides a methodology that lies between the two poles of Propp's formalism and Lévi-Strauss's structuralism. Described as structural semantics, Greimas is concerned with the construction of meaning, the language of narrative. So he is interested in identifying the various elements of the narrative, examining their interrelationships and analysing how they change and develop as the narrative progresses.

In his approach, it is the act and the action which register in the methodology, the act being the *verb* in the construction of the narrative sentence. His 'actorial' model contains only six of what Propp called 'roles'. These are:

Sender	Receiver
Object	Subject
Helper	Opposer

Each of these categories might contain more than one character. Also, each character may well cross into one or more categories as the narrative progresses. For instance, consider them in terms of Proppian roles: sender as a category might include father/dispatcher; receiver would be the hero; object could be described as the sought-for person; the subject may also contain the hero; the helper remains the helper/provider; and the opponent becomes variously the villain and the false hero.

These fundamental agencies, which in Greimas are ultimately abstractions, being neither roles nor characters, are then organised into pairs of oppositions, or actants as he calls them, that is; sender/receiver, subject/object, and helper/opponent. It is the logic of syntax which decides this construction in Greimas work, a criticism of Propp that sees his dramatis personae as too closely connected to the narrative. This may well aid empirical research as described above, but does not help in the examination of the relationship between them. Greimas' categorisation, or classes of actants, tries to combine logical structuring with functional recognition and empirical analysis. That is, the content as well as the spheres of action and the relationship between them are all taken into account.

With his interest in grammar, the semantics and the syntactics of narrative, Greimas is closer to Ferdinand de Saussure, the founding father of linguistics, than to Propp or Lévi-Strauss. The defining characteristic of narratives for Greimas is not the Proppian sequence of functions, but the relationship between actants. It is this relationship that we can most usefully utilise in methodology. The work of Greimas may be seen as reductionism, though, since it takes the rich complexity of both Propp and Lévi-Strauss and discards much in the combination of the two approaches. The moving image researcher may thus wish to use Greimas as a starting point and then work backwards, as it were, filling out detail by utilising Propp and Lévi-Strauss. As has been emphasised throughout this book, the use of combined methodologies is often more revealing than dogmatically sticking to one approach, thus combining, or at least working in the light of, Propp and Lévi-Strauss may well be advantageous when using Greimas.

The clearest examination of Greimas' work can be found in Schleifer (1987), while Silverstone (1981) discusses at length the theoretical contortions of Greimas' work, as well as conducting a useful application not only of Greimas, but also of Propp, to a British television series of the 1970s entitled *Intimate Strangers*.

6.3.5 Logical Sequence and Narrative Space

The thrust of the methodologies discussed here has been towards the identification of the patterns and purposive nature of narrative examined as a chain of events following a logical sequence. Texts are seen as constructed; that is, the unfolding of narrative is far from being accidental or natural, rather, it is the result of information being manipulated, edited and released for specific narrative purposes. As we have mentioned, temporal and spatial relations are directed towards the logical narrative sequence of cause and effect, rupture and remedy, enigma and resolution. Inevitably, all patterns that are established and all questions that emerge and are developed during the narrative are answered.

The 'space' of the film or moving image product is taken up by that which is narratively important. The 'space' is the site of action. Everything within the frame is used by the drive of narrative; all objects, settings and events are extensions of, and related to, the characters. They are foregrounded to emphasise their key narrative role, and concentrated on by the camera, leaving other less important elements out of focus. Even where deep focus is used, the placing of the characters within the frame is often sufficient to guide the viewers' eye to what is narratively important.

The chain of events is narratively driven by the actions of central characters (functions and roles). The audience is drawn into the plot through empathy with central characters: this is achieved through close-up shots, and point-of-view shots. The star system also encourages this identification. The focus is thus individual rather than collective/societal endeavour (with the one exception of Eisenstein, who attempted to portray the 'mass' as hero in his films, such as *The Battleship Potemkin* (1925)). This individual focus can be ideologically understood in terms of the emphasis on individualism in Western societies. One of the metaphysical themes of the western genre film, for example, is the nineteenth-century doctrine of 'manifest destiny' which explicitly expresses individual responsibility. The analysis of stars or characters in moving image production will often be in terms of their meaning and the values they embody. Much gender research will examine the role of male and female characters and stars, considering what their particular prominence in the narrative is saying to male or female audience members about their role in society (Dyer (1987) is of particular interest here). Much research in this area focuses on ideology, not only *vis-à-vis* individualism and gender roles, but also the portrayals of race, age, religion, sexuality, and so on.

6.3.6 Television Narratives

As discussed, in most fictional moving image products the idea of closure and resolution of tension forms a central dynamic of the narrative structure. However, television soaps, situation comedies and serials place heavy emphasis on the future. The demands of the television industry to keep the audience are very strong, hence the use of the cliff-hanger, multiple narrative threads, introduction of new characters, and temporary resolutions. Indeed, it can be said that many of the devices discussed above, although useful to specific programme analysis, may well find many of their central assumptions challenged if not reversed by the televisual medium. Indeed Feuer (1986) argues that the apparatus of television may even act against the logic of causality and closure.

Ellis (1982) points to the influence of non-fictional moving image forms, which have now almost without exception transferred to television, on the types of television fiction forms mentioned above. For Ellis, there is now only one TV mode of narration. As he says:

> The non-fiction and fiction modes of exposition of meanings seem to have converged within TV, under the impulsion of the characteristic broadcast TV forms of the segment and the series, and the pervasive sense of the TV image as live. This has produced a distinctive regime of fictional narration on TV which owes much to its non-fiction modes. After all, the first true use of open-ended

> series format would seem to be the news bulletin, endlessly updating events and never synthesising them (Ellis, 1982, p. 145).

For Ellis, this leads to television narrative being extensive rather than sequential, and offering the audience a continual refiguration of events. McMahon and Quin (1986), building on Ellis, characterise television narrative by expansion and circularity. That is, there is greater emphasis on character than in the film medium, and the narrative structure of television is that in each episode the programme ends where it had begun. This latter point is especially the case with police or detective series such as *Columbo* or *Inspector Morse*, or even *The X-Files*, where the end of each episode finds the characters and setting restored after their disruption, and ready to face next week's episode.

For the moving image researcher interested in this area, an examination of series structure will provide a most useful route. Todorov and the equilibrium formula is particularly applicable to the type of serial analysis mentioned above, while the consideration of characters, roles and actants will also prove useful. John Fiske (1993) provides a very useful analysis of television dramas, using Propp. Television news and advertisements will often succumb to an analysis of binary oppositions, revealing much about their nature and role in ideological and mythic construction. As we said at the beginning of this chapter, *all* moving image products are constructed of narratives, be they 'extensive' or 'sequential', and thus can be examined as such.

6.3.7 Considering Alternative Narratives

It is finally worth turning our attention to what are called counter or alternative narratives. A useful binary technique for the analysis of narrative is to consider the differences between standard Hollywood narrative and alternative narrative structures. Here the production values are opposed to those of traditional narrative orthodoxy, both ideologically and structurally. Thus, by contrasting them, you make the Hollywood approach overt, in a sense helping you to reveal it, to demystify it, to *stop it dead*. The key is to analyse how these alternative narratives challenge the expectations of the audience, gained through their experience of narratives, and the codes and conventions of production that seek to soothe, pacify, and reinforce ideologies. By assembling a list of criteria that tells you what one thing is, you then develop a thorough understanding of its opposite.

Here it is useful to adapt Peter Wollen's (1985) work on Jean-Luc Godard and counter or alternative cinema, considering and applying the patterns or oppositions he identifies.

(1) **Narrative Transitivity versus Narrative Intransitivity**
One thing following another in the course of narrative construction *versus* Gaps, interruption, episodic construction, digression, and narrative break up
(2) **Identification versus Estrangement**
Empathy and emotional involvement *versus* Direct address, multiple central characters, mass as hero, overt commentary on people and events
(3) **Transparency versus Foregrounding**
Neutral window on the world, seamlessness *versus* Making overt and explicit the technical and constructed nature
(4) **Single Diegesis versus Multiple Diegesis**
Homogenous world *versus* Heterogeneous world
(5) **Closure versus Aperture**
Self-contained, beginning/middle/end *versus* Open-ended narratives, over-spill and intertextuality
(6) **Pleasure versus Unpleasure**
Entertaining, satisfying *versus* Dissatisfaction, provocation
(7) **Fiction versus Reality**
Actors wearing costume and make-up telling a story *versus* Real life, non-professional actors, breaking-up representation

These can be applied generally to narrative, specifically to Hollywood products, or more specifically as Wollen (1985) does, to counter cinema. They will go some way towards helping to reveal the building blocks of ideological production in moving image products by making overt that which is usually taken for granted.

6.4 Conclusion

The structures and strategies discussed in this chapter describe tools which systematise analysis, and provide the basis for a variety of textual research interests. Foremost among these, as we have indicated, are discussions of the structure of narratives, the mechanisms of construction of narratives, how meaning is produced in the texts, and how ideologies are constructed and reinforced by the very nature of narrative.

The various methods outlined in this chapter should be considered not simply standing alone, but as possible combinations or triangulations for research. This chapter has focused particularly on one crucial aspects of moving image analysis. It has, however, tried to indicate that the approaches outlined are only part of what could be a much wider research endeavour in these areas, encompassing first and foremost genre study, as well as semiotics, audience research, and industry studies. This chapter highlights textual work, but moving image research methodologies are not exclusive, and the best research will triangulate methods or use a multi-method approach, combining perhaps with other mass communication research strategies discussed in this book. When analysing moving image products, the analysis of narrative structures is important, and description and classification are central to the endeavour. However, to discover how the audience moves through the narrative, an experimental situation or interviews or questionnaires might be carried out at the end, or at various points during the study. Ultimately the results could be combined with the informed analysis of the narrative or genre along the lines discussed in this chapter and in Chapter 7.

6.5 Summary

- The aim of narrative research methodologies is to extract and understand the meaning, myths and ideologies inherent in moving image content.
- Being informed by theoretical considerations rooted in literary and film theory, the methodological discussions are based in qualitative approaches to moving image content.
- Narrative analysis can be broken down into concerns with categorisation, classification, the construction of typologies, and description.
- Successful analysis of the moving image is reliant upon the researcher having a thorough knowledge of the construction of the moving image product that he or she is analysing. An understanding of the technical and symbolic elements in moving image construction is the best way to achieve this.

- There are two basic methodologies in narrative research: (i) the *syntagmatic* approach, which examines the sequential development of the narrative; (ii) the *paradigmatic* approach which is concerned with the patterns of oppositions that arise within narratives.
- Narrative and genre methods are well suited to being combined, as well as used in conjunction with other still and moving image methods of inquiry such as semiology and content analysis.

6.6 Checklist of Technical and Symbolic Elements

In production terms, this list is by no means exhaustive. It does, however, cover the main production elements that moving image researchers are likely to come across on a day-to-day basis. The importance of the emphasis on these particular technical elements lies in their signifying power in moving image production.

- **Camera shots**
  Extreme Close-up
  Close-up
  Medium or Mid-shot
  Long-shot
  — Cover shot
  — Establishing shot
  Point-of-view shot
- **Camera Angles**
  Straight on
  High angle
  Low angle
  Oblique angle
  Dutch angle
- **Camera Lenses**
  Wide-angle lens
  Fish-eye lens
  Telephoto lens
  Zoom lens
- **Depth of Field**
  Close-up focus
  Distant focus
  Deep focus

- **Camera Movement**
  Panning
  Tilt
  Tracking or Dolly shot
- **Length of take/Duration of shot**
- **Cutting or Editing**
  Montage editing
  Straight cut
  Crosscut
- **Special effects**
- **Framing**
- **Lighting**
  High-key lighting
  Low-key lighting
- **Sound**
  Diegetic sound
  Non-diegetic sound
  Functional music
  Dialogue
- **Colour/Black and White**
- **Costume**
- **Objects**
- **Stars**
- **Performance**
- **Setting**
- **Location**
- Mise-en-scène

References

Ang, I. (1985) *Watching 'Dallas'* (London: Methuen).
Barthes, R. (1972) *Mythologies* (London: Jonathan Cape).
Berger, A. A. (1991) *Media Analysis Techniques* Revised edition (London: Sage).
Berger, A. A. (1992) *Popular Culture Genres: Theories and Texts* (London: Sage).
Caughie, J. (ed.) (1981) *Theories of Authorship* (London: Routledge & Kegan Paul/ BFI).
Corner, J. (1991) 'Meaning, Genre and Context: the Problematics of "Public Knowledge" in the New Audience Studies', in J. Curran and M. Gurevitch (eds) *Mass Media and Society*, pp. 267–84 (London: Edward Arnold).

Dyer, R. (1987) *Heavenly Bodies: Film Stars and Society* (London: BFI).
Ellis, J. (1982) *Visible Fictions* (London: Routledge & Kegan Paul).
Feuer, J. (1986) 'Narrative Form in American Network Television', in C. MacCabe (ed.) *High Theory/Low Culture: Analysing Popular Television and Film*, pp. 102–14 (Manchester University Press).
Feuer, J. (1992) 'Genre study and television', in R. C. Allen (ed.) *Channels of Discourse Reassembled: Television and Contemporary Criticism* 2nd edn pp. 138–60 (London: Routledge).
Fiske, J. (1993) *Television Culture* (London: Routledge).
Kracauer, S. (1953) 'The Challenge of Qualitative Content Analysis', *Public Opinion Quarterly*, vol. 16, no. 2, pp. 631–42.
Kuhn, A. (1993) *Women's Pictures: Feminism and Cinema* (London: Verso).
Larsen, P. (1991) 'Media Contents: Textual analysis of fictional media content', in K.B. Jensen and N.W. Jankowski (eds) *A Handbook of Qualitative Methodologies for Mass Communication Research*, pp. 121–34 (London: Routledge).
Lévi-Strauss, C. (1966) *The Savage Mind* (London: Weidenfeld & Nicolson).
McMahon, B. and R. Quin (1986) *Real Images: Film and Television* (Melbourne: Macmillan Australia).
Newbold, C. (1995) 'Analysing the Moving Image', in O. Boyd-Barrett and C. Newbold (eds) *Approaches to Media*, pp. 442–5 (London: Arnold).
Place, J. A. (1974) *The Western Films of John Ford* (Secaucus, N. J.: The Citadel Press).
Propp, V. (1975) *The Morphology of the Folktale* (Austin: University of Texas Press).
Schleifer, R. (1987) *A. J. Greimas and the Nature of Meaning: Linguistics, Semiotics and Discourse theory* (London: Croom Helm).
Silverstone, R. (1981) *The Message of Television: Myth and Narrative in Contemporary Culture* (London: Heinemann Educational).
Todorov, T. (1977) *The Poetics of Prose* trans. by Richard Howard (Ithaca, NY: Cornell University Press).
Tudor, A. (1974) *Theories of Film* (London: Secker & Warburg).
Turner, G. (1993) *Film as Social Practice*, 2nd edn, (London: Routledge).
Warshow, R. (1964) *The Immediate Experience* (Garden City, NY: Anchor).
Wollen, P. (1985) 'Godard and Counter Cinema: Vent d'Est, in B. Nichols (ed.) *Movies and Methods*, Vol. 2, pp. 500–8 (Berkeley, Calif.: University of California Press).
Wright, W. (1975) *Six-guns and Society: A Structural Study of the Western* (Berkeley, Calif.: University of California Press).

7
Analysing the Moving Image: Genre

7.1 Introduction to Genre Analysis

The notion of genre, as indicated in the introduction to Chapter 6, is a powerful concept in moving image production. It determines how media organisations are constructed with departments of news, current affairs, light entertainment, sport, and so on; It delineates products such as westerns, science-fiction, comedy; it organises and marshals audience expectations. Genre theory in media research has become so powerful that it dictates not only the interests and research agendas of many institutions, but also what is taught and how it is taught. News is an interesting example here, with much interest being shown in the construction of the genre (Gans, 1979; Bell, 1991; Helland, 1995), the international nature of the genre (Boyd-Barrett, 1980; Sreberny-Mohammadi *et al.*, 1984; Gurevitch, 1991), and the effects of the genre on the audience and the information/political agenda (Glasgow Media Group, 1976, 1980, 1982; Katz, 1992; Butler, 1995). Thus it is of some considerable relevance to the media researcher to be able to examine, understand, and use the methodological tools available for genre analysis.

Genre theory in moving image analysis owes a considerable debt to film criticism, which itself partly emerged from literary criticism. Genre theory in film developed out of a growing dissatisfaction with the auteur theory in the 1950s and 1960s. This theory saw the creation of meaning for the audience being situated in one aspect of the production process, the work of the director. Genre critics maintained that audiences watch films and understand them in relation to other films that they have seen. Cook (1985) puts the relatively recent emergence of genre theory down to a rejection of industrial associations and the original connection of genre with 'conventions', which were seen in a pejorative sense. She makes the point that 'Film criticism in its attempt to divest itself of its literary or sociological heritage, sought to demonstrate the presence of individual artists (*auteurs*) *despite* rather than in relation to industrial conditions' (p. 58). As we shall see later in this chapter, there has been a revival of interest in the contribution of auteur theory to genre analysis.

Genre study has developed over the last thirty years as a central tool of moving image analysis. This is especially the case in seeking to examine texts and their relationship to the audience, to other texts, and to wider moving image production in the culture industries. The examination of genre texts has two possible directions.

- The first is concerned with value, and considers the *aesthetic quality* of genre products and their contribution to moving image art. This is often concerned with identifying and isolating a genre's formal characteristics and associating particular products with a particular genre. It might also be concerned with the establishment of the notion of genre itself.
- The second use of genre study is in discerning the genre's *social role* as a transmitter or reflector of social norms, values and meanings.

The questions raised from both these directions of genre research, and the associated methods and techniques of analysis, are becoming more and more important for both textual and culturally-based approaches in both mass communication and media research.

7.1.1 Areas of Possible Genre Research

There are a number of very broad concerns in genre study; although not exclusive or exhaustive, the list below indicates some of the areas that a moving image researcher may wish to consider. The choice of study will often be dependent not only on the genre(s) to be analysed and the number of texts to be studied, but also upon the hypothesis, resources and particular competencies of the researcher.

- Tracing the history and development of a genre
- Studying genre text's formulaic components
- Examining intertextuality, that is, how a text relates to other texts in the same or different forms (in fiction or non-fiction); or across different media (film, television, radio, newspapers, magazines, novels, even in advertising)

- Analysing the symbolic and technical codes used in genre production
- Establishment of sub-genres, post genres or neo-genres
- Consideration of intercultural generic texts; western genre films from Hollywood, Italy, Spain or Japan for instance
- The study of other culture's genre products, such as Masala film in India, or Jidai-geki film in Japan
- Debate between auteur and genre analysis
- Comparison of 'classical' texts and 'B' movie texts
- Genre and allegory. Examining the deep structures of generic texts; the reflection of social and cultural values; that is generic texts as signifying processes
- Audience studies of viewer choice and expectations (These are research questions of response, identification, pleasure, and so on, that are worth pursuing by a variety of methodologies.)
- Industry studies or analysis of production context: marketing strategies often revolve around genre; commercial cinema has throughout its history organised itself around the production of generic formulas. (Perhaps when considering approaches to genre methodologies, useful insights might be gained by interviewing media professionals about the generic structure of their industry. Also, producers, programmers and industry people might be interviewed about their own decisions concerning generic products, and the desirability and persistence of certain formulas.)

To do all these would call upon a large number of approaches, from structuralist to formalist, from culturalist to psychoanalytic and sociological. This list does, however, serve to illustrate the variety of uses to which genre analysis can be put. It also points up the fact that there are not only many different possible applications of genre, but that there are also, by implication, different interpretations of the term itself.

It is important to note at this stage that genres cut across media and can fruitfully be examined with reference to literature, painting, magazines, advertising, radio, and so on. Much of the visual style and plot conventions of moving image westerns for instance, were established in nineteenth-century dime novels, from which the genre largely emerged, as well as the wild west shows of people such as Buffalo Bill and the western paintings of artists such as Bierstadt in the 1860s and Remington in the 1890s. These then burgeoned into early film products (Edwin S. Porter's *The Great Train Robbery* in 1903 being the first narrative western), radio series (*The Lone Ranger* began as a radio show in 1930), cartoons, and advertising. The importance of considering other media in research is stressed here, in that any analysis of moving image genres must take into account the fact that both audiences and producers come to the moving image with knowledge of genres gathered from many other sources.

7.1.2 Concerns Affecting Genre Research

Genre analysis, much more than narrative analysis, has a number of problems or difficulties of which the moving image researcher should be aware from the very start.

The first is the *problem of definition* or *circularity*. To establish a genre, you have first to isolate its content, and you can only do this if you already have a pre-existing set of criteria. Put another way, to establish the horror genre we need to examine certain kinds of films, but how do we know which films to isolate unless we already know what a horror film is? Studies can get around this by gathering a number of commonly held assumptions as to what constitutes a particular genre and then developing a more detailed analysis from there. As we shall see later, it is necessary to rely on assumptions, common sense or shared agreement, in order to provide a starting point, otherwise the apparent futility of the whole exercise may well overwhelm the researcher.

There are always concerns as to where one genre ends, and another begins. The problem of *linearity of genre divisions*, is where sets of criteria and descriptions may well be too static to accommodate a changing developing genre. Thus there is the possibility of failing to reveal relationships with other genres, and the diversions from the established charted route that may have occurred.

Related to this, is the problem that the *labelling of genre systems may be too large* to incorporate subdivisions, hence the development of sub-genres, cycles, or post-genres, such as the post-western. The crime genre tends to be sub-divided into police drama, private eye, thriller, film noir and so on. There is some disagreement as to whether some of these are not genres in their own right, while others may be simply styles of film, not genres at all. However, there is then the problem of so increasing the number of these categories as to make them almost unusable.

The final problem, *repetition within genre products* is a familiar old cry, and concerns the nature of genre being merely the repetition of the same worn-out formulas, to an audience lacking a variety of non-generic products to choose from in modern-day moving image presentation.

7.1.3 Approaches to Genre Analysis

The problems outlined above will be discussed further as the chapter proceeds. Bearing them in mind, the moving image researcher should begin cautiously to approach the notion of genre itself, through theory, in order to discern his or her own particular approach and definition of the term 'genre'. This will depend of course upon his or her hypothesis and preferred methodology. In order to organise appropriate tools and concepts, we have divided the methodologies into two main areas of genre research with subdivisions in order to provide any specific focus that may be required. Methodologically these two can be separated by their concerns:

- the first with *categorisation and codification* of principal elements, and
- the second with what we shall call *exchanges*, that is, the relationships between society, industry, genre and audience.

Categorisation and Codification

Let us take genre in the broadest sense to mean a type or kind of moving image based on similarity of product which relies on a limited array of recognisable visual styles, formal characteristics, and conventional patterns in order to operate. In research we shall first of all be considering the key areas of moving image construction, such as visual elements, iconography, codes and conventions, as well as fixed plot or narrative and *mise-en-scène*. Genre analysis in moving image research first and foremost will be about establishing and identifying *a set of principal elements* by which we can associate or connect one type of moving image product with others of its like or kind. This approach, which is at the heart of much genre analysis, is also described as the categorisation or coding system.

This style of analysis can be broadly based around *aesthetic* concerns. The aesthetic approach might include an analysis of the look or style of a genre, and the creativity and artistic values inherent in them. Solomon (1976) examines what he sees as the 'best' examples of genre, in order to understand how artists shape their creative materials within the constraints of genre.

Exchange Approaches

Once a genre has been established, analysis in moving image research may secondly be considered in the light of what we have called 'exchange' approaches. These approaches are inclined towards the need for a more eclectic approach to genre methodologies, calling not only for textually-based analysis, but also for the use of other social survey techniques.

- Research based on the *ritual* approach would look at how society speaks to itself through the exchange between genre, industry and audience.
- The *ideological* approach would examine the meaning of genre products in relation to the structure, myths, and values of society. The work of Will Wright (1975) on the western genre, with his application of Lévi-Strauss' work on myth, is particularly important here, as we shall see later.

This chapter is recommending that the moving image researcher considers the above methodological approaches not as the result of a dialectical process leaving a trail of discarded and discredited methods behind it, but as an opportunity to combine appropriate concrete methodological procedures depending upon the type of analysis he or she wishes to undertake. This should be done with the theoretical debates in mind, as well as the problems of method outlined above. We shall also be recommending drawing upon both narrative and semiotics-based methods to enhance existing genre methodologies.

7.2 Researching Principal Elements

Central to any analysis of genre is the recognition that genre is not an imitation of life or reality, but of other moving image products, indeed, of other mass media products. Although some of the filmic genres such as the western or gangster film may be based on historical reality, it is the self-reflexivity and intertextual relationship between the products of a genre that is crucial to our establishing, understanding and analysing of them. The first and most obvious place to start research is with the establishing of a genre. There are two approaches here:

- the 'essentialist' approach.
- the 'categorisation' approach.

The Essentialist Approach

The 'essentialist' approach of Robert Warshow was the first to attempt this kind of methodology. An ideal for each genre was constructed; for the western, it was the attributes of the western hero which formed the essence of the genre. This approach was, however, criticised for being overly prescriptive and assuming a normative function (Alloway, 1971). But this need not be the case if your 'essential' model is constructed from a large enough sample, and is recognised as a starting point or a yard-stick. A discussion of generic cores, for instance, has the same essentialist assumption – that is, that you can identify a central element around which a genre revolves. The generic core of the western is seen as being the landscape. All western narratives revolve around the landscape: the bounty from it, and the battle with it; the people it has moulded; and the need to explore and conquer it. The generic cores of other genres revolve around occupations, the private eye or the cop, for instance. The essentialist approach, then, is to identify the core or centre of a genre and through description build a case for the uniting of several like films or moving image products under the one banner.

The Categorisation Approach

The 'categorisation' approach is best formulated by the apparently and deceptively simple task of constructing a list of key elements that are found in any moving image genre product. Start by analysing products that are held by consensus to be associated with the particular genre that you are interested in. John Ford's *Stagecoach* (1939) is universally seen by critics as a western, *Dracula* (1958) by Terence Fisher as a horror, *Star Trek* as a sci-fi, *East Enders* as a soap opera, and *The Price is Right* as a quiz show. You can then proceed to apply this list to moving image products which are seen as belonging to the same genre, or which you would like to be able to associate with a particular genre. Inevitably your list of key elements will grow and evolve as you proceed. Be flexible. Remember that the aim is to be descriptive, not prescriptive. The list will be based on your own particular set of skills and criteria. It will never be exhaustive or the final word on that particular genre; it is designed to open up a genre for analysis and debate, not to finish the argument.

A useful starting point in the construction of a list of key elements in a genre is the technical and symbolic elements discussed in Chapter 6. The most important elements for genre analysis are often seen as the symbolic ones, since they correspond to what Braudy (1992) calls pre-existing motifs; what Sobchack (1986) relates to iconography; and most interestingly what Buscombe (1970) describes as an 'outer form' as opposed to the 'inner form' of content. However, consideration of the technical elements serves to draw our attention to the signifying systems or techniques that are used to convey generic information. The combination of these key elements constitute the main signposts for recognition and division between genres.

Buscombe (1970), in his search for the defining criteria of westerns lists four particular 'outer forms': the setting, clothes, tools of the trade, and miscellaneous physical objects (pp. 36–7). Our own list of symbolic elements emphasises colour/black and white, costume, objects, stars, performance, setting, location and finally *mise-en-scène* (which will be discussed later as a way of combining these elements into a more holistic analysis).

Using this schema will allow you to build up a composite picture of the genre. You can either do this in table form as in Table 7.1, or in simple list form. It is important to supply illustrations as well as examples to back up the points that you are making about each individual element. Table 7.1 considers the principal elements of the western genre. You do not have to use all the technical and symbolic elements discussed in Chapter 6, only those you find are significantly represented in the genre; for instance, camera angles are very significant for film noir, but less so for the western. The table considers the genre as a whole, but, as we have said, it can first of all be used to set up some key elements from one film, and then developed.

There are of course many variations and developments of these elements to be found within the western genre. However, films such as John Ford's *The Man Who Shot Liberty Valance* (1962) with its mid-shot dominated, largely dark, urban location, still operates as a western because its differences are recognisable from the existing patterns and formations of western genre products. Other films such as *High Noon* (1952), or Sam Peckinpah's *The Wild Bunch* (1969) set out deliberately to challenge many of the key elements in order to jar the audience into some kind of recognition of the values portrayed by the western genre.

Table 7.1 Elements of the western genre

Elements	*Genre*
Camera shots	The long shot and the establishing shot dominate the western, as it is principally a genre of landscape; the long shots of monument valley in John Ford's *Stagecoach* (1939) epitomise this.
Camera lenses	The wide angle lens is important in the western as it effectively shows the central character in the foreground set against his or her environment.
Camera movement	The western is a genre of movement, east to west in the narrative. The wagon trains, the cattle, the Indians and cavalry are always on the move. The camera apes this movement, tracking the action, as well as observing it from a distance and panning the various scenes.
Framing	The framing of people and objects is important. For example, showing an Indian chief astride his horse against the skyline gives him symbolic power. The final shot of John Wayne framed by the door in *The Searchers* (1956) by John Ford is one of the most famous shots in cinema, and shows Ethan Edwards as still the outsider, living apart from the community.
Lighting	Westerns are always brightly lit: even on location they are characterised by high-key lighting, emphasising the clear-cut nature of the genre; there are no hidden depths or shadows, what you see is what you get.
Sound	All elements of sound are heavily used in the western genre, whether it is diegetic gunshots, or dramatic non-diegetic music. The sound of the Coyote at the beginning of Henry King's *The Gunfighter* (1950) implies a relationship between the lifestyle of the single animal and the central character.
Costume	Stetson hats, feather head-dresses, leather waist coats, leather chaps, gingham dresses, boots, boot-lace ties are all central symbolic elements of the western genre. In analysis the meaning of each needs to be examined. For instance, as the character played by Gregory Peck in *How the West Was Won* (1963) (Henry Hathaway, George Marshall and John Ford) changes to a river boat gambler, so his costume changes from the open-neck shirt to the attire of a gambler, signified by expensive, city clothes and a boot-lace tie, dress associated with the east more than the west.

Table 7.1 cont.

Objects	Horses, six-guns, Winchester rifles, sheriff's badges, lassoes, bows and arrows, stagecoaches, whiskey bottles and shot glasses, are also central to the meaning of the western genre. For example, the bow and arrow used by the Indians in *Stagecoach* implies a savage and uncivilised culture as opposed to the sophisticated Colts and Winchesters used by the cavalry.
Stars	John Wayne, James Stewart, Gary Cooper, Glen Ford, all become instantly recognised and associated with particular characterisations in the western genre. John Wayne is the obvious example, as a symbol of an unswerving good guy in films like *True Grit* (1969) by Henry Hathaway and Andrew V. McLaglen's *Chisum* (1970).
Setting	Saloon, jail, main street, Indian encampment, railway coach or engine. The main street of a western town is the setting most often used for the climactic scene of the plot, the shoot out. This is taken to the extreme in Sergio Leone's *A Fistful of Dollars* (1964), with many shoot outs taking place before the final climactic one.
Location	The desert is the abiding landscape of the western genre, it is both friend and enemy to the western hero, hiding in it, or enduring it as in John Ford's *Wagonmaster* (1950).

The construction of a list such as this will prove useful in engaging debates such as whether film noir is a genre or not. A list of the key elements of film noir can be constructed, and films compared. Alternatively, lists from genres such as the crime, thriller, or detective can be compared with films labelled as film noir in order to ascertain some clues to their category.

The classification or principal elements approach is based on the similarities assumption, that the similarities in moving image products define them as genres. The temptation to create normative and overly prescriptive categories is an ever-constant threat to the genre researcher. Some fluidity of categories should be retained in order to maintain their descriptive quality and allow for the coverage of genre developments. This is especially true about working at the turn of the millennium when the fragmentation of traditional genres has led to many categorising conundrums. Any scheme of research developed has to be flexible enough in its categories to take into account variations and developments on traditional patterns.

7.2.1 Iconography

It is worth while taking a moment here to discuss briefly a crucial tool in genre analysis – iconography. Indeed, Buscombe (1970) sees iconography as the defining criterion for genre recognition. Iconography is employed in genre films to aid rapid audience understanding; as a short cut, avoiding the need for complex explanation. As with all aspects of genre, iconography only really works effectively if the audience is already well versed in the particular genre. Too often in genre work the icon is simply referred to in terms of the literal or denotive level of meaning. Thus lists of 'icons' are constructed, guns, horses, cars, hats and so on, without comment or reference to their actual meaning within the text or the genre. Iconography is central to genre recognition and meaning, since as a sign it refers the researcher to the meaning beyond its mere physical form, to the deep or the connotive level. Hence a six-gun is more than a weapon, it attains a quasi religious meaning in the hands of an avenging sheriff cleansing the west of evil. When we analyse the icon of a horse in a western it has to be seen as more than simply a mode of transport; it represents a man's freedom, his control, his power and indeed his masculinity. Someone on a horse, however, could signify many films or film types, from historical epics such as William Wyler's *Ben Hur* (1959) to adventures such as *National Velvet* (1944) by Clarence Brown. However, give the person on the horse a Stetson hat, a six-gun and a sheriff's star, then the establishment of the western genre will be made, and audience expectations will arise from that. A discussion of iconography in genre analysis can begin to point the researcher away from classification towards the analysis of myth and meaning. This idea will be developed further when we consider genre as ritual and ideology.

The examination of iconography is a central component of moving image genre research, since it is the description and analysis of this visual aspect that separates film and television analysis from the more literary approaches to genre and narrative. Iconography differs from genre to genre, and is thus a key element in separating off one genre from another, and must form a central core of our analysis. Iconographical meaning in the moving image is often dependent on and derived from the films themselves. Readings of iconography are therefore often dependent upon a thorough and detailed knowledge of the iconography and visual language of a genre as a whole.

7.2.2 Mise-en-scène

Although deriving originally from auteur theory, a discussion of *mise-en-scène* provides the moving image genre researcher with the opportunity to combine the above elements and iconographic descriptions either into a general analysis of multiple texts in a genre, or of single scenes from a genre product. *Mise-en-scène*, that is, everything within the frame – set, objects, costume, spatial relations (between characters and their importance and position), movement and so on – as well as the sound, is important for genre research as it provides clues towards the identity of the genre we are involved in and thus triggers audience expectations. Analysis of *mise-en-scène* will build on the description and interpretation of key elements and iconography, discussing how they combine to create their meaning. In discussing and describing the *mise-en-scène* of any genre it is worth remembering that everything within a frame is placed there, and carries a meaning, nothing is there by accident, they are the result of the moving image construction process. So take account of them, they will add depth to your analysis.

7.3 Genre and Narrative Work

So far we have concentrated our analysis on the 'outer form' of genre, that is, what we actually see (and hear). The inner form, that is the subject and audience, will be discussed as the chapter progresses. However, there is a major component of genre analysis to be added to this schema; the understanding of patterns of narrative structure. Although narrative analysis was dealt with in Chapter 6, we need to consider here particular elements of narrative analysis which are applicable to genre study.

It is undoubtedly the case that despite their generic differences, genres as diverse as westerns, musicals and science fiction may well share the common structures of 'classic realist' Hollywood cinema. Any examination of narrative and genre may well start out from this common base, using the methods discussed in the previous chapter; but this general approach may soon prove unsatisfactory, providing only cursory information, since unlike non-generic texts the components of a genre film arrive already heavily laden with thematic significance derived from their generic associations. It is the various structures and nuances of particular genres, their characteristics and narrative conventions, that supply the significance for genre narrative analysis.

The popularity of genre products, and indeed much pleasure in genre consumption, is based on the combination of the contradictory poles of familiarity and novelty – that is, audience recognition or surprise at an old route taken, or a new route discovered. This reaction is guided to some extent by the generic map contained in the audiences' generic memory, and sign-posted with the established conventions of the genre.

7.3.1 Narrative Conventions of Genre

The points below illustrate how the symbolic elements described in Chapter 6 relate to the narrative conventions of genre. An analysis of narrative conventions may prove more useful to the identification of contemporary genres, since the technical and symbolic codes may not in many cases be too dissimilar. The look of a soap opera, for instance, may be fairly similar to a situation comedy. There are a limited number of narrative conventions, and not all will be represented in any one story. However, the combination of any number of them will create the formula or pattern of the identifiable genre story. The relationship between narrative conventions and audience expectation is what allows for the construction of genre classification.

- Conventional period – the western genre takes place in the nineteenth century.
- Conventional heroes, villains and heroines – cowboy, sheriff, Indian, outlaw, cavalry officer, ranchers daughter, etc.
- Conventional representations or stereotypes – cantankerous old man, saloon girl/whore, innocent child, savage Indian, etc.
- Conventional locations – the plains, the western town, the Indian encampment, etc.
- Conventional settings – inside the saloon, the covered wagon, the jail, the tepee, etc.
- Conventional objects – six-guns, saddles, bow and arrow, sheriff's badge etc.
- Conventional modes of transport – horse, stagecoach, train, buggy
- Conventional costume – gingham dresses, Stetson hats, leather chaps, feather head-dresses, etc.
- Conventional dialogue – 'head 'em up and move 'em out', 'Ye Ha', 'this town ain't big enough for the two of us', etc.
- Conventional sounds – cavalry bugle, gun shots, saloon piano, stampeding cattle, yelping Indians, etc.
- Conventional music – western ballad (such as those sung by Frankie Laine), western fiddle and guitar music, etc.

- Conventional set-pieces – the gunfight on the street, the saloon poker game, the bank/train robbery, etc.
- Conventional themes – revenge for the murder of a friend or relative
- Conventional plots – gunfighter comes to town; gunfighter causes trouble; sheriff challenges gunfighter; sheriff wins gunfight; peace restored to town

The examination of conventions goes beyond Buscombe's (1970) 'outer forms', since his emphasis is understandably on what we see on the screen, as we are dealing with a visual medium. Any moving image product also contains sound, and this can equally be analysed as signs, icons and conventions. By starting from and examining the narrative conventions, we can begin to see how they relate to each other and form the narrative structure. To illustrate this we can reproduce the model drawn up as Figure 6.1, p. 145, and now shown in Figure 7.1.

Beginning	HERO VILLAIN PROBLEM EMERGES
Middle	PROBLEM INTENSIFIES QUEST AND/OR BATTLE
End	VICTORY PEACE CHANGED SITUATION

If we now apply this with the addition of the narrative conventions to an example of a typical western genre gunfighter story, we get:

Beginning	Sheriff deals with local drunks as only problem Gunfighter arrives at behest of local rancher Gunfighter causes trouble/kills someone
Middle	Sheriff confronts gunfighter, but lacks evidence Gunfighter will not leave town, threatens sheriff Gunfight on main street
End	Sheriff is victorious Peace is restored, rancher flees Sheriff/ town developed in some way

Figure 7.1 Model of narrative structure applied to the Western

Genres can be seen as being constructed from a combination of technical and symbolic elements (icons, *mise-en-scène* and narrative conventions and structures), which the audiences recognise almost instantly and understand through the operation of their generic memory, which type of moving image product they are engaging. Generic narrative conventions organise viewer's expectations; that is, their experience of similar products that they have come across elsewhere (in any medium). Genre essentially demonstrates how audiences watch moving image products in relation to others that they have seen, and are then able to categorise them. These are categories that, as we shall see in the next section, circulate between author, industry and audience, and can thus be identified and analysed by the moving image researcher at any stage, not only by analysing and describing the content of products, but also if desired, by use of questionnaires or interviews with producers and audiences.

7.4 Genre Development

With the developments of genre in mind, it is worthwhile considering a longer view approach to genre. Using the work of Focillon (1942), Metz (1974), and Schatz (1981) we can develop a schema for establishing a generic pattern of development. We can even go so far as to assert that to be recognised as a genre a form must be identified as passing through four phases of existence, the *experimental* evolving to the *classical*, from there to self-conscious *parody* and finally to *deconstruction* and critique of the genre itself.

- The **experimental** stage contains the earliest contributions to the genre – these can be identified by their establishment and use of principal elements, conventions, iconography, and so on.
- The **classical** stage may well be the point of maximum output – it will certainly involve the clearest identification of the above key elements.
- **Parody** concerns the stage at which films begin to become self-reflexive, and self-conscious; the parody may be comic or just highly stylised.
- Finally, **deconstruction** is where the generic elements and conventions calls attention to themselves by being placed out of their original context.

To these four, we might add a fifth category of

- **postmodernism**, which would have a pastiche base, drawing on all the above four categories and creating a kind of product which is based on nostalgia, fragmentation of content, relativism of values, erosion of time/place and symbols, hyper-signification or the over use of intertextual and symbolic messages, and recycled themes.

Obviously each of these phases can be analysed for their own intrinsic value, but if we here consider them as a whole, then we can demonstrate how the schema works. In Table 7.2 two examples have been chosen for each classification. This model can be applied to all moving image genres, from sitcoms to news and documentaries. Indeed, some of the most interesting work may well be done with non-fiction products rather than the fictional genres. Again, as with much of the work in this section, the discussion and analysis of the content of these phases is the essence of the methodology. There will inevitably be some disagreements about the content of each phase; this serves to open the debate rather than restrict it, and that is all to the good.

The advantage of this approach is that by identifying particular examples of the phases of a genre we are able to develop an overview which points us not only to where a genre is going, but also its genesis. Some of the problems highlighted earlier derive from perhaps being too close to individual films and too concerned with the minutiae of genre identification and establishment. This schema provides us with some very broad historical brush-strokes from which to develop a genre analysis which is concerned with genre development rather than individual texts.

7.5 Aesthetic Approaches

Before leaving the concerns of principal elements, with its classification methodologies, it is worth considering the central concern with aesthetics of the approaches discussed above. Concerns with aesthetics or the artistic nature of genre unite the principal elements

Table 7.2 Phases of genre development

	The Western	*Film Noir*
Experimental	*The Great Train Robbery* *The Iron Horse*	*The Cabinet of Dr. Caligary* *Metropolis*
Classical	*Stagecoach* *Shane*	*The Big Sleep* *Double Indemnity*
Parody	*Young Guns* *Butch Cassidy and the Sundance Kid*	*Body Heat* *Klute*
Deconstruction	*Outland* *Blazing Saddles*	*Bladerunner* *Near Dark*
Postmodern	*Unforgiven* *Posse*	*The Colour of Night* *Basic Instinct*

research, with its pursuit of textually-based analysis. One of the key debates to which the aesthetic approach draws our attention strikes at the very heart of the criticism of genre as repetition. Indeed, much early debate in film criticism saw genre as an inadmissible concept, since aesthetic quality was seen to be associated, as in art, with originality. Originality was perceived to be unattainable in a mass production system such as Hollywood. Hence the emphasis of the aesthetic approach has been as Feuer states, 'to define genre in terms of a system of conventions that permits artistic expression, especially involving individual authorship' (Feuer, 1992, p. 145). Solomon (1976) while accepting some charges of the repetition argument, states that, 'to achieve genre art, film-makers must be committed to exploring new facets of the familiar setting, elaborating on their insights into the mythic structures of the genre' (p. 7). Solomon's aesthetic methodology is based around identifying the best products of a genre; those which incorporate generic elements to the fullest degree, never going beyond the limits of genre formula. 'The artistic and intellectual insights necessary for such products are stored' according to Solomon 'in the minds of film-makers such as Alfred Hitchcock and John Ford' (Ibid., p. 2).

This to some extent leads us to a reconciliation between genre and auteur theory and methods. The methodology suggested by a study of *mise-en-scène* is perhaps the most useful tool here, in that it can be examined as an authorial signature. This is especially the case in Hollywood genre productions where the studio had control over the scripts, so it was up to individual directors to make their mark through the inventiveness with which they constructed a scene.

7.6 Exchange Approaches

The categorisation approach as outlined above is not as simple as it might first have appeared. It is also not the only method of genre analysis, and demonstrates some limitations when it comes to ascertaining deep structure in moving image products. Andrew Tudor feels that 'genre terms seem best immediately employed in the analysis of the relation between groups of films, the cultures in which they are made, and the cultures in which they are exhibited' (Tudor, 1974, pp. 148–9). Cook (1985) saw that with the revival of Marxist aesthetics in the 1960s and 1970s genre analysis 'enables film criticism to take account of conditions of production and consumption of films, and their relationship to ideology' (p. 59).

This section considers what we have called exchange methodologies – methodologies that seek to understand the role of genre as an exchange between society, industry, audience and content. Genre film is successful because it is perceived to give the audience what it wants. Genres are constructed with the audience reaction in mind; that is, a horror is designed to be horrific and to scare, a comedy to amuse, and a thriller to thrill. The audience registers its interest in particular types of products by viewing figures or film attendance. The industry then provides more of that type of product, since it will to some extent guarantee a return on investment, and will certainly attract advertising. New genres, or twists and turns in existing genres, will develop and diversify as the older versions are no longer seen to be acceptable or interesting to the audience.

A further development of this exchange relationship is where genre can be examined as a form of representation and meaning production. Genre products provide the audience, within a familiar setting, with the recognisable values and norms of its culture. This analysis figures most strongly in the work of structuralists, as the ritual and ideological approaches provide methodologies for this kind of analysis.

Four conceptual models are worth bearing in mind, since they provide an overview of the relationships at work in this section. The first two concern the relationship between the originator, the art product, and the audience. Both models are linear in form and to some extent predate genre criticism:

Artist/author → Art product → Audience
Social reality → Art product → Audience

These two models can be broadly identified as:

- the authorship model and
- the social reality model

Both can be seen to be reflected to some extent in methodologies discussed in this chapter, be it in the emphasis on the role of the author, or in the consideration of genre as reproducing ideologies in society.

The third model, derived from Ryall (1987), is perhaps more directly associated with genre criticism, since it posits a more fluid relationship between the genre product, the audience and the artist.

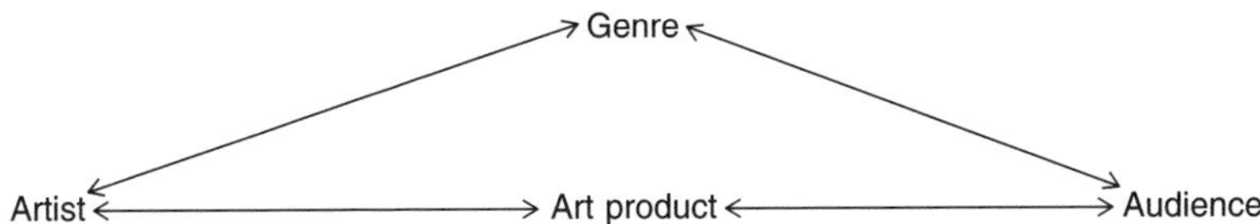

The model can also be re-drawn, emphasising the industry rather than the artist, and removing the separate focus on the art product:

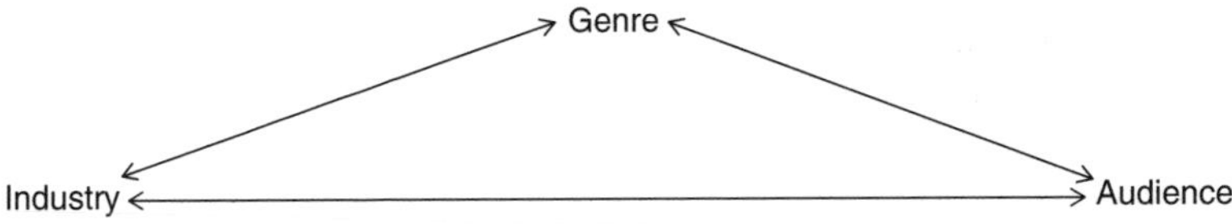

All these models can be applied to genre products, since they emphasise the relationship between the producer, the product and the audience. However, only the last two can really be seen as pure genre models, since they emphasise the idea of an exchange between the key components of genre, producer and audience.

7.6.1 Ritual Approach

In this approach, film-going and television-viewing become kinds of rituals, where people, in similar vein to church attendance, go to hear their values and beliefs confirmed in a familiar setting. Particular genre products are recognised in particular cultures, not only because of their set of characteristics, but also because they are seen to reflect the values of that society; they are understood in the context of a certain set of cultural values and assumptions. The ritual approach considers genre to work in the same way as language does in society, where the values and beliefs of a society are communicated between industry and audience. Genres are seen as signifying systems, as communications to be considered in the same way that a linguist would examine the nature and construction of language. Individual films can then be examined in the same way that sentence construction is broken down by a linguist.

The language analogy provides a useful methodology for investigating these relationships, and calls upon us to identify the meaning behind the grammar of genre products. Here, the moving image researcher can refer to the key elements of genre as described in the above section. Most importantly, a genre film can be examined in a ritual sense by considering the social meaning of these key elements, its iconography and its plot conventions and narrative structures. As Schatz states,

> a genre then, represents a range of expressions for film-makers and a range of experience for viewers. Both film-makers and viewers are sensitive to a genre's range of expression because of previous experiences that have coalesced into a system of value-laden narrative conventions. (Schatz, 1981, p. 22)

So the moving image researcher might analyse the meaning behind the iconography of the horse or six-gun in a western as we did above, drawing out and relating the social meaning of masculinity in the western genre. The conventions of technology in sci-fi movies might be discussed in terms of their utopian statements about the role of science and scientists in society. The narrative structure of any genre may be considered in terms of Todorov's (1977) equilibrium formula, where the importance of the resolution is tied to the *status quo* being re-established through culturally accepted means; be it officially sanctioned violence, marriage, or subjugation of a minority group.

The ritual approach, more perhaps than any other outlined in this chapter, demands that the genre researcher turns his or her attention to complementary methodologies in order to get a thorough sense of the relationships between genre, audience and production. One approach here might be an analysis of the particular use of genre in professional practice; this might be how products are constructed into genres with the audience reaction in mind. Helland (1995), through interviews and observation, looks at the genre of news, considering how producers' perceptions of the genre affect the way that a television station constructs its news product. Genre research in the ritual approach may also be of use in considering audience choice, especially asking questions about decisions on what to view, or which thematic channels to buy into from satellite or cable. Another area of interest for a survey might be how genres are constructed in gender terms. Why are soaps and quiz shows seen as female genres, and westerns as male genres?

7.6.2 Ideological Approach

According to Feuer 'the ideological approach views genre as an instrument of control' (Feuer, 1992, p. 144); that is, genres are seen to reproduce the ideologies of capitalism, nationalism, individualism, sexism, racism and class structure. Genres limit and constrain the possibilities of meaning within what is acceptable within ideology. Tom Ryall emphasises the difference between the ritual and ideological approaches most succinctly when he says, 'instead of a symmetry between the genre film and the audience's beliefs and expectations, there is a symmetry between the genre film and the interests of the ruling order' (Ryall, 1987, p. 15).

It may be through familiarity with genre themes and conventions that genre moving image products work ideologically. The very familiarity of content, conventions and form makes genre viewing a reinforcing and comforting experience. It is ideological in the way that it closes down alternative meanings and ways of acting in favour of a consensual *status quo*. It is also through the revealing of these themes, conventions, and indeed iconography (including stereotypical representations), that the moving image researcher is able to examine genre and its ideological dimension. Thomas Schatz (1981) considers the resolution of genre products to be their most significant feature, and provides us with the following plot structure of genre products:

- *Establishment* (via various narrative and iconographical cues) of generic community with its inherent dramatic conflicts;
- *Animation* of those conflicts through the actions and attitudes of the genre's constellation of characters;
- *Intensification* of the conflict by means of conventional situations and dramatic confrontations until the conflict reaches crisis proportions;
- *Resolution* of the crisis in a fashion which eliminates the physical and/or ideological threat and thereby celebrates the (temporarily) well-ordered community. (from Schatz, 1981, p. 30)

Symbolically-opposing value systems are eliminated and the existing system affirmed. Schatz states that:

> genre films function to stop time, to portray our culture in a stable and invariable ideological position. This attitude is embodied in the generic hero – and the Hollywood star system itself – and is ritualised in the resolution precipitated by the hero's actions. Whether it is a historical western or a futuristic fantasy, the genre film celebrates certain inviolate cultural attributes. (1981, p. 31).

For Schatz it is these basic cultural oppositions or inherent dramatic conflicts that are genre products most basic determining features. Will Wright's *Six Guns and Society* (1975) also directs our attention to ideology and conflict in texts, using Lévi-Strauss's notion of binary oppositions in order to identify four basic oppositions that re-occur in the Western genre:

Good v. Bad
Strong v. Weak
Civilisation v. Wilderness
Inside Society v. Outside Society

These oppositions can be discerned in the texts themselves, and should be illustrated as part of the analysis. Wright's work can serve to reveal the structure of modern myths, and how society symbolically comes to terms with its tensions, and maintains itself in the face of contradictions. Wright's method, as with Schatz's, illustrates how the structure of moving image products is part of this process. The structuralist approach points us towards the key meanings in a text, allowing us to reveal the underlying structure or logic to a moving image product, providing us with the tools to *stop it dead*; permitting us to analyse and classify that which would remain hidden if we were to approach it purely on its own denotive level.

The overall theme of the 'ideological' approach is that all genre products are saying basically the same things to and about society. They can thus be researched with this in mind. Schatz provides us with a useful model to apply when considering ideological narrative strategies in genre productions. He considers that the characteristics of genres can be described in two 'rites'; rites of order and rites of integration (Table 7.3). The usefulness of this model is that it allows different genre films to be analysed together under the same classifications, pulling out similar ideological frames under which they work, as well as similar narrative structures which also lead to a consideration of the ideological nature of genre.

Table 7.3 Schatz's model of ideological strategies in genre production

	Order	*Integration*
	(Western, gangster, detective)	(musical, screwball comedy, family melodrama)
Hero	individual (male dominant)	couple/collective (female dominant)
Setting	contested space (ideologically unstable)	civilised space (ideologically stable)
Conflict	externalised – violent	internalised – emotional
Resolution	elimination (death)	embrace (love)
Thematics	meditation – redemption macho code isolated self-reliance utopia-as-promise	integration – domestication maternal – familial code community co-operation utopia-as-reality

Source: Schatz, 1981, p. 35.

7.7 Conclusion

Central to genre methodology is a concern with the content of moving image products. As we have seen, this is largely based on definition, description and classification: that is, definition of its various ingredients, description of key conventions as well as description of both single and multiple moving image products, and finally, classification of components such as technical and symbolic elements, iconography, narrative and so on. It is all these contributory categories that the moving image researcher seeks to isolate and reveal for analysis. Genre research examines the networks and relationships of codes and conventions, rules and norms that guide and control genre production and reception.

This chapter has considered genre methodologies ranging from concern with the smallest units of analysis within the key elements, to the largest categories as suggested by Schatz. Only in Schatz's work have we begun to examine what unites genres; the major focus has been concerned with what divides them. This chapter then, calls for genre methodology work to concern itself with two not unrelated spheres of interest.

The first is to examine genres as a whole, considering what unites them on a formal moving image level (narratives structures, key elements, ideologies and so on) as well as their outreach to other mediums and sources. That is, genre methodology should encompass the investigation of generic roots (in whatever medium), as well as considering the wider aspects of genre influence, such as the star and personality systems, advertising and marketing, moving image industry policy, audience choice and perception, use of genre-related products in society itself, and the dynamics of genre growth and transmission.

Secondly, the drawing together of genre approaches into a fluid and eclectic pattern of research methodologies and analysis, rather than the static and divided approaches of the past, is essential for thorough research. This would crucially involve a reconciliation between the genre approaches outlined in the first half of the chapter – *principal elements* – and those in the second half – *exchange approaches* – as well as considerations of genre art and the auteur theory, alongside ideology in genre and audience reception. A more eclectic approach to methodology would include not only breaking down walls between media, but especially calling for a truly moving image-based approach, rather than one solely concerned with just one of film, television, video or animation.

Finally, it is worth reiterating that complex textual critical analysis, as we have seen in both this and Chapter 6, can be constructed by combining and triangulating methods. Although in the separation of narrative and genre analysis into two chapters we ourselves are guilty of compounding an artificial separation, it is hoped that we have been able to curtail too harsh a criticism by pointing to many of the methodological benefits to a combined multi-method approach to texts.

7.8 Summary

- The aim of genre research methods is to extract and understand the meaning, myths and ideologies inherent in moving image content.
- Being informed by theoretical considerations rooted in literary and film theory, the methodological discussions are based in qualitative approaches to moving image content.
- Genre analysis can be broken down into concerns with categorisation, classification, the construction of typologies, and description.
- Successful analysis of the moving image is reliant upon the researcher having a thorough knowledge of the construction of the moving image product that he or she is analysing. An understanding of the technical and symbolic elements in moving image construction is the best way to achieve this (see Chapter 6).
- Genre research methods can be divided into two main approaches, *principal elements*, and *exchanges approaches*. The first is concerned with categorisation and codification of genres, the second with the relationship between society, industry, genre. and audience.
- Narrative and genre methods are well suited to being combined, as well as used in conjunction with other still and moving image methods of inquiry such as semiology and content analysis.

References

Alloway, L. (1971) *Violent American Movies* (New York: Museum of Modern Art).

Bell, A. (1991) *The Language of News Media* (Oxford: Blackwell).

Boyd-Barrett, O. (1980) *The International News Agencies* (London: Constable).

Braudy, L. (1992) 'Genre: The Conventions of Connection', in M. Mast, M. Cohen and L. Braudy (eds) *Film Theory and Criticism: Introductory Readings*, 4th edn, pp. 435–52 (Oxford University Press).

Buscombe, E. (1970) 'The Idea of Genre in the American Cinema', *Screen* **11**(2).

Butler, D. (1995) *The Trouble With Reporting Northern Ireland* (Aldershot: Avebury).

Cook, P. (ed.) (1985) *The Cinema Book* (London: BFI).
Feuer, J. (1992) 'Genre study and television', in R. C. Allen (ed.) *Channels of Discourse, Reassambled: Television and Contemporary Criticism*, 2nd edn, pp. 138–60 (London: Routledge).
Focillon, H. (1942) *The Life of Forms in Art* (pub. details unknown).
Gans, H. (1979) *Deciding What's News* (New York: Vintage Books).
Glasgow Media Group (1976) *Bad News* (London: Routledge & Kegan Paul).
Glasgow University Media Group (1980) *More Bad News* (London: Routledge & Kegan Paul).
Glasgow University Media Group (1982) *Really Bad News* (London: Routledge & Kegan Paul).
Gurevitch, M. (1991) 'The Globalisation of Electronic Journalism', in J. Curran and M. Gurevitch (eds) *Mass Media and Society*, pp. 178–93 (London: Edward Arnold).
Helland, K. (1995) *Public Service and Commercial News: Contexts of Production, Genre Conventions and Textual Claims in Television*, Report no. 18 (University Of Bergen).
Katz, E. (1992) 'The End of Journalism? Notes on Watching the War', *Journal of Communication*, **42** (3) 5–13.
Metz, C. (1974) *Language and Cinema* (The Hague: Mouton).
Ryall, T. (1987) *The Gangster Film*, rev. and rep. (London: BFI).
Schatz, T. (1981) *Hollywood Genres: Formulas, Filmmaking, and the Studio System* (Philadelphia: Temple University Press).
Sobchack, T. (1986) 'Genre Film: A Classical Experience', in B. K. Grant (ed.) *Film Genre Reader*, pp. 102–13 (Austin: University of Texas Press).
Solomon, S. J. (1976) *Beyond Formula: American Film Genres* (New York: Harcourt Brace Jovanovich).
Sreberny-Mohammadi, A., Nordenstreng, K., Stevenson, R., and Ugboajah, F. (1984) *Foreign News in the Media: International Reporting in 29 Countries*. (Reports and Papers on Mass Communication No. 93) Paris: UNESCO.
Todorov, T. (1977) *The Poetics of Prose*, trans. by Richard Howard (Ithaca, NY: Cornell University Press).
Tudor, A. (1974) *Theories of Film* (London: Secker & Warburg).
Wright, W. (1979) *Six-guns and Society: A Structural Study of the Western* (Berkeley, Calif.: University of California Press).

8

Analysing Visuals: Still and Moving Images

8.1 Introduction

Visual analysis is possibly the 'poor relation' in mass communication research. With the exception of advertising and film studies,[1] relatively little analytical labour and discussion has been directed at the major media of television and newspapers in regard to their visual dimensions. This is all the more surprising when considering the obvious visuality of the television medium as well as the use and role of photojournalism in and across the press. Of course, a few exceptions can be found and these will be discussed below, but the fact remains that when focusing upon news media mass communication researchers output have tended to concentrate upon properties of written and verbal language while paying little, if any, attention to accompanying visuals. It is in language that messages and meanings are thought principally to reside. In consequence, the analytical tools deployed in visual analysis remain relatively unused and undeveloped in comparison to the repertoire of methods and techniques deployed in relation to written and spoken language. Even major studies whose titles might suggest otherwise, such as *Images of Welfare* (Golding and Middleton, 1982), *Visualising Deviance* (Ericson, Baranek and Chan, 1987) *Triumph of the Image* (Mowlana, Gerbner and Schiller, 1992), fail to pursue in any detail or with any methodological sophistication visual news representations, whether those of welfare, deviance or war. None of them, for example, reproduce news images for analysis and discussion. This is not to single these studies out for criticism but simply to make the point that these, like so many others, have generally failed to attend in any systematic and detailed way to questions of visual representation and analysis. A number of factors are responsible.

Certainly the dominant traditions of mass communication research have played their part in this; a charge which could be laid at the door of the major theoretical traditions of social science more generally (Ball and Smith, 1992). The specific research interests pursued within different paradigms, each underpinned by differing theoretical allegiances and methodological commitments have, until recently at least, tended to ignore issues of 'textuality' as well as the problematic nature of visual representation – concerns brought to the fore in more recent years by structuralist and culturalist theorists (Hall *et al.*, 1980; Turner, 1990). To state the obvious, the behaviourist's pursuit of media effects by laboratory experiments, the positivist's search for opinion change by large-scale surveys, or the political economist's concern with market forces and media ownership are all unlikely to engage with concerns of visual textuality and analysis.

But what about researchers who have attended to media output? Here the influence of positivism, with its faith in value-free observation and measurement, has no doubt contributed to a widespread tendency to approach visual images in relatively transparent and unproblematic terms. Visuals are all too often taken at face-value and simply assumed to 'reflect' or 'mirror' the events and people captured on film. This naïve realism has failed to interrogate the productive contribution of visuals to the construction of social meaning. Two further explanations can also be noted. First, mass communications researchers have, until recently at least, been dependent upon a limited toolbox of methods. Principal among these was, and probably remains, content analysis (see Chapter 5). Though useful and even insightful when deployed in theoretically focused ways, the method can none the less also be a fairly blunt instrument. It tends to disaggregate the coherence of visual images and confronts further problems when used in the analysis of moving film or television news video. Moving film has an analogic or relatively continuous nature, and does not necessarily render down into discrete or digital units and categories for coding and subsequent quantification. This is not to say that content analysis cannot be deployed successfully in relation to visual pictures, whether still or moving, but rather that as an available method it has its limitations.

Most critical studies of news output, for example, are keen to base their interpretations and analysis upon a representative and, therefore, large-scale sample of news output. Studies which have sought to interrogate in detail the visual dimension of news broadcasts shot by shot and/or the interaction between verbal and visual tracks are limited on grounds of practicality to a few news items at most – while most rely on one news item alone for such detailed treatment (Davis and Walton, 1983; GUMG, 1980; Graddol, 1994; Meinhof 1994). Difficulties of conducting visual forms of content analysis, as much as the lack of a suitable alternative method, therefore, have further contributed to the neglect of the visual dimension.

Second, in more general terms, social scientists have tended to approach the social world through an overly rationalist view of social processes and social interactions. The word has been privileged over the image; the rational argument has been preferred over the appeal to the emotions. Social scientists have rarely, for example, sought to incorporate images into their own discourses, and they have approached the world of others with similar visual neglect. The critical study of ideology in media studies has generally proved no exception, with ideology – how ever conceptualised – typically pursued in terms of language-based transmission, with relatively little attention devoted to the symbolic and ritual qualities of news output – a dimension more readily approached via visuals (Elliott, 1980; Carey, 1989). Also, the recent 'linguistic turn' in philosophy now influencing the social sciences (Giddens, 1979), though sensitising many to the discursive, linguistic, performative and social constructivist nature of language, has not been matched with a corresponding interest in visual representations. Even the postmodernists, with their championing of radical indeterminism and view of society as bombarded by media images and signs, have surprisingly little to say about actual images or the methods used to interrogate them. Too often the (totalising) postmodern view of society awash with signs, itself floats above any grounded analysis of actual signs produced, circulated and consumed in particular social-historical circumstances (Baudrillard, 1983, 1988).[2]

The explanations for the relative neglect of visual analysis in mass communication research are therefore complex and relate to deep-seated positions of mass communication theory and methodology, social scientific paradigms and informing positions of epistemology, as well as the more straightforward and practical difficulties of carrying out applied visual analysis. But does visual analysis matter? If written and verbal language is the principal medium for communicating messages and meanings, why bother with visual analysis at all? Though there is still much to fathom about the contribution of visuals to human communication and understanding, there is no doubting the visuality of certain media and the special role that visuals play in imparting information and inviting affective and aesthetic forms of engagement. The visual dimension can operate either independently from, or in combination with, the written and verbal dimension to produce enriched and potentially potent messages. Also, though the study of visuals in comparison with the study of language remains in its infancy, we should not underplay the analytical advances and substantive insights already won.

As intimated above, there is no single method of visual analysis. For this reason the discussion departs from most of the other chapters in this book and their focus upon a principal method. Rather, this discussion identifies *four* general approaches to visual analysis. It deliberately confines its sights to studies of press and television visuals, though the approaches are of wider relevance and can be applied to other media and genres. It reviews the types of findings secured by each and, with use of examples, demonstrates how they can be put into practice. Though actual studies may involve one or more of these four approaches, for analytical purposes it is useful here to consider them separately. The discussion now considers the four approaches, in turn, under the following:

(i) News Visuals as Distortion
(ii) News Visuals as Symbolism
(iii) News Visuals as Semiotic Systems, and
(iv) News Visuals as Epistemological Guarantee.

In conclusion, the discussion briefly considers future avenues for news visual analysis.

8.2 Analysing News Visuals as Distortion

'Seeing is believing', 'the camera never lies' and 'a picture is worth a thousand words' are just some of the many clichés in our culture which draw attention to popular 'views' of, and apparent faith in, observation and visual representations. Of course, as with most clichés, things are not always so clear cut: social beliefs and values are known to influence perception and processes of audience reception – 'believing is seeing'. Initial camera positioning and angle, picture framing and lighting as well as subsequent image selection, photographic retouching, digital image manipulation, editorial cropping and final juxtapositioning can all radically change or even invert the sense of depicted scenes – 'the camera can lie'. And the polysemic quality of visual images, that is, their relative openness to differing interpretations, as well as tendency towards redundancy or high predictabity of content and, in consequence, low information value, suggest that on their own visuals often require the 'anchorage' of words, and do not substitute for them – 'a picture requires a thousand words'.

What is perhaps interesting about such clichés, then, is not so much their contestable claims, but rather the apparently widespread faith in the transparent truthfulness of observation and visual representation. It is generally acknowledged, for example, that television news enjoys enhanced credibility over the press, in part because of its increased use of 'authenticating' visuals. If a faith in the power of news pictures simply to record and document reality is widely held within our culture, so the professional journalists' projected stance of impartial, objective reporting also invests news visuals with a particular responsibility in this regard. Exactly how news visuals help construct a sense of factuality and represented reality is explored later when discussing 'News Visuals as Epistemological Guarantee'. Here the concern is with those more obvious and deliberate attempts to falsify and distort images in line with political interests or professional journalists' views of a story and its requirements.

It is perhaps testimony to the power of the professional journalist's claim to impartiality and/or pursuit of public credibility that examples of gross falsification and image manipulation are rare. Politically motivated doctoring of visual images has been practised elsewhere for some considerable time, however. When in 1920 Stalin had Leon Trotsky carefully removed from a famous 1917 photograph of Lenin addressing the Moscow proletariat, such historical disappearance was a fairly crude attempt to consolidate Stalin's power in the present. In the context of British news reporting, the nearest example of such deliberate faking is provided by the *Sun* (30 June 1993) newspaper when it recently published a front page photograph of a monk dressed in a monk's habit walking with his alleged lover. Unbeknown to its nine million or so readers, however, the *Sun* could not find a picture of the monk with his younger girlfriend, nor could it find a picture of him dressed in that all-important signifying monk's habit. No matter, the *Sun* simply superimposed a habit upon the image of the monk, taken from another picture, and digitally combined this with one of the young woman. The picture, in other words, was a complete fake – a revelation that evidently proved embarrassing for the *Sun* and accounts, no doubt, for its editor's refusal to grant us permission to reproduce a copy in this book. Ironically, the *Sun* evidently felt it necessary to alter an image in order to provide visual authentication for its sex story. Arguably the *Sun*'s offence was not its departure from the 'truth' of the story, but rather its flouting of the journalistic conviction that the public's faith in the veracity of photojournalism should remain inviolate.

In contrast to Stalin and his attempt to falsify the historical record for his own political purposes, the *Sun* was attempting to capitalise visually upon the news values of sexual deviance – a key ingredient to its particular brand of populism with its mutually exclusive ideas about sexuality and religion. Though deliberately altering the photographic record, this was done in line with an editorial view of 'the story' and its news value for its sought readership. Clearly, at this point questions of deliberate visual falsification and alteration begin to merge with considerations of journalistic story selection and framing.

A basic prerequisite for 'distortion analysis' is an alternative source of visual information from which news visuals are thought to depart. Only then can journalistic visual manipulation, misleading selections, significant omissions and sense-changing croppings be identified. Comparative analysis of news images across press or TV news can reveal interesting differences of news differentiation and partisanship, as demonstrated below, but what it cannot do is make claims about the distorted nature of such images with reference to a presumed reality beyond the visual representations, since no alternative representational view is brought into play.

Here production-based studies provide a useful vantage point on issues of news visual 'distortion', as well as general processes of news visualisation (see Chapter 3). Specifically, insights and understanding can be gained from observing two key moments in the production of news images. The first involves the researcher in accompanying and observing reporters, camera crews or photojournalists in the field as they select and film likely news visuals – an opportunity which also provides the researcher with first-hand knowledge of the available news scenes witnessed. Second, it also proves useful to observe newsroom follow-up production processes, including the final selection, editing decisions and discarding of visual scenes into the waste bin. The extract below, taken from a participant-observer study of a news-reported public demonstration against Salman Rushdie's *The Satanic Verses*, makes use of first-hand observations of the demonstration as well as the complete ENG (electronic newsgathering) 'rushes', and demonstrates the sorts of findings that can be gained.

[T]he scenes noticeably dominating this aspect of the news item are close-up scenes of an evident dispute between two demonstrators surrounded by onlookers and juxtaposed with shots of the police. The close-up on the faces and shoulders of the disputants conveys the impression that the wider crowd was itself similarly locked in dispute, despite the fact that this was an isolated, and highly insignificant incident at the fringe of the loosely assembled demonstrators. It is all the more interesting, therefore, that this visual image should dominate the opening scenes. And, when this scene is compared with another – the isolated burning of a flag by a demonstrator at the march destination point – it is apparent that such shots have been selected according to their perceived contribution to the 'news story' as conceptualised by the reporter. Only one flag was seen to have been burnt on that day, as was only one disagreement witnessed within the crowd. Both incidents, however, dominate the imagery and are juxtaposed alongside the sights and sounds of chanting youths holding aloft Khomeini posters, and police marshalling the crowds on their way to the Council House.

Arriving at the rally separately from the ENG crew and witnessing the internal disagreement within the crowd, the reporter asked 'Where's the crew? We need some pictures of this'. When the crew was asked later what scenes they were after, they candidly stated, 'We're after shots of the march, the banners, any trouble that there might be'. Relying on the news sense of the film crew, in terms of both visuals and sound recording of Islamic chants and choruses of shouts, the pursuit of conflict finds a visual and vocal reference notwithstanding its marginal nature during the events of the day [. . .] it is also interesting to note that a conscious editing decision was taken which increased visually the sense of urgency and possible threat conveyed in the images selected. A selected front-view shot showing the first arrivals, in small groups, of demonstrators ambling into the city square was abandoned and replaced by a side shot of groups entering the square, thereby introducing a considerable sense of movement and pace. When combined with the voiced-over commentary of: 'an estimated four thousand converged on the Council House, police flanking the demonstrators throughout', the impression given is that the march constituted a massive presence purposefully taking up position outside the Council House. (Cottle, 1991, pp. 51–2)

Attending to the production of news visuals from the producers' domain proves instructive, and typically reveals a complex of selection and editing decisions which combine to create a particular scene and supporting interpretation of the news event. In the case of the anti-Rushdie demonstration the visual component appeared to emphasise unduly the degree of conflict involved and presented both the demonstrators and demonstration as an irrational threat to white civil society and its presumed collective opposition to the proposed banning of the book *The Satanic Verses*. This construction was built, in part, upon the selective focus, use and juxtapositioning of certain visual scenes and the omission of others. The tendency of news visuals to emphasise drama and conflict through selection and the use of close-up shots on crowd members engaged in some form of dramatic action has been noted for some time (Lang and Lang, 1953; Halloran, Elliott and Murdock, 1970; Murdock, 1981).

Following the introductory comments about 'naïve realism', it is perhaps as well to be clear about what such production-focused studies permit, and do not permit, in the context of a discussion about visual distortion. While participant-observers cannot, on the basis of their own observations of visual scenes or comprehensive viewings of all available news visuals, claim to have an 'objective' understanding of the situation witnessed, they can none the less identify the selective and partial use of news images and how they depart from alternative available scenes. In this sense, researchers can indeed make a case that news visuals are 'distorted', especially when highly unrepresentative scenes are found to be put to work in the service of a particular news frame and/or social perspective on the event in question (cf. Hackett, 1985).

Camera angle, selectivity and omissions are unavoidably a part of news visual production, they are not thereby beyond criticism as distorting and ideological in their presentation however. It has frequently been noted how cameras positioned behind police lines in conflict situations – riots, demonstrations, strikes, – provide a point of view conforming to the literal police perspective (Hansen and Murdock, 1985; Cumberbatch *et al*., 1986). The selective use of visual images from the Gulf War also demonstrates how images helped to construct a view of high-technology and so-called 'smart' bombs which could apparently win the war without inflicting massive 'collateral damage' (that is, civilian deaths or casualties), a picture we now know to have been far from the truth. The consistent omission of pictures of the military and civilian wounded, the maimed and the dying, and above all the bodies of the estimated 40 000 to 200 000 Iraqis killed in the military 'theatre' did little to convey anything of the horror or real consequences of the war (Jowett, 1993; Taylor, 1994). The news imagery of the war and its omissions were arguably part of a powerful 'system of representations which marginalizes the presence of the body in war, fetishizes machines, and personalises international conflicts while depersonalising the people who die in them' (Gusterson quoted in Taylor, 1994, p. 295).

Of course, some readers and viewers may still interpret such scenes in ways that challenge the informing narrative and journalistic use of visuals, but it remains the case that accompanying visuals often invite, in combination with the verbal and narrative elements, a particular interpretation of the news event or issue. How images are cropped can also radically alter the meaning of visuals. A recent press photograph, widely used within the British press, illustrates the point (see Image 8.1). This front-page photograph apparently gives visual and written expression to the wide-spread hope for peace in Northern Ireland in expectation of the IRA's 1994 declaration of a cessation of violence. A young boy throws a tennis ball up against a wall on which the slogan 'Time for Peace' has been written. The *Daily Mirror's* subheading states 'The Writing's on the Wall' and 'Peace with no strings' (31.8.94) while the *Independent* subheaded the same photograph on its front page with 'A boy plays against a wall daubed with a message of hope rather than hatred in North Belfast yesterday' (31.8.94). Only subsequently did it become apparent that the full slogan painted across the wall read 'Time for Peace: Time to Go'! The decision to crop the photograph omitting those final words prompts a very different understanding. Whereas 'Time for Peace' invites an interpretation of a general, perhaps liberal humanist, concern for peace, the cropped words raise a more conditional prospect for peace based upon the particular political viewpoint of Northern Ireland's nationalist and republican communities – 'Time to Go' indicates that for some peace may indeed be conditional upon the withdrawal of the British from the six counties of Northern Ireland.

The example illustrates again how news visuals can distort in line with journalistic story requirements and framing. Unfortunately the relatively few news production studies, and the limited attention within most of them to visual news processes, has led to too few studies of this important aspect of news visualisation.

DAILY Mirror

Wednesday, August 31, 1994 HONESTY, QUALITY, EXCELLENCE July daily sale: 3,253,123 (INCORPORATING THE DAILY RECORD) 27p

After 25 bloody years, IRA lay down the gun

THE WRITING'S ON THE WALL

PEACE WITH NO STRINGS - SEE PAGE 2

Image 8.1 *Daily Mirror*, 31.8.94

8.3 Analysing News Visuals as Symbolism

The cropped 'Time for Peace: Time to Go' news photograph, as well as revealing a form of news distortion, also reveals the symbolic nature of many news images. A young boy playfully throwing a ball up against the sloganned wall, arm outstretched, feet slightly in mid-air, can become an effective symbol of peace, hope and the future. Children, and the idea of childhood, it is well known, can become invested with historically variant meanings, values and societal aspirations and fears. They have a symbolic capacity, in other words, to condense and give visual expression to abstract ideas. Analysing news visuals in terms of their symbolism or capacity to combine, condense and convey social meaning, begins to move us beyond the pursuit of direct news distortion. Approached symbolically, news images are here not strictly speaking referential but affirmational or, even, aspirational. That is, questions of visual 'documentation' or strict authenticity may be less important now than questions of political or emotional 'realism'. The power of an image to appeal to, mobilise, or engage with deep-seated feelings, hopes and fears may be what really counts. Keeping to the press coverage of the Northern Ireland peace process, a further image, also used by many of the British national newspapers including the *Guardian* (1.9.94), *Today* (1.9.94) and *Daily Express* (1.9.94), helps illustrate the point (see Image 8.2).

This news picture also depends for its effect upon the symbolic value of the image. A young Catholic boy embraces an armed British soldier. The innocence and hope for the future invested in the image of the child, contrasts with the image of the British soldier fully-equipped in battledress, prominently holding his gun. The boy, raising himself up just above the soldier's eye-level, holds on to his battle-dress straps and captivates an engaged smile from him. Symbolically the image is not difficult to fathom, indeed at one level its effective-ness depends upon it. In the context of the particular news story the image works metaphorically, it stands for something else. The young boy, the soldier, the embrace, all work to symbolise the abstract process of past conflict, reconciliation and hope for the future. It also works at a metonymic level. That is, helping to secure this abstract reading in more concrete terms, the part stands for the whole. The young boy *is* part of a community locked in past conflict, the soldier *is* part of the British army, and the embrace *is* an example of improved relations brought about by the peace process. The symbolic, or

In the broadsheet: Gerry Adams on peace and the IRA | Guardian 2 tabloid: Stories from the Streets

45p
Thursday
September 1
1994
Published in London and Manchester

The Guardian

NEWSPAPER OF THE YEAR

After 25 years, 3,169 dead, 38,680 injured, 10,001 bombings . . .

The promise of peace

'There is now the historic opportunity to take the gun out of Irish politics for ever' — Albert Reynolds

'Nobody can be in any doubt that it will be immensely difficult for the IRA to return to the armed struggle'

Commentary

Martin Woollacott

Objecting to the form of the announcement is a struggle over symbols

Party mood in the streets of grief, pain and hatred

David Sharrock finds Catholics claiming victory and looking forward to freedom

IRA statement

Inside

News in brief

Lady Archer had takeover notice

World exclusive

Brando

"This book is my declaration of liberty. I finally feel free and don't give a damn any more what people think of me."
Marlon Brando in his own words. World exclusive serialisation begins this Saturday.

Image 8.2 *Guardian*, 1.9.94

abstract, meaning of the photograph is thus reinforced by its iconic, or concrete, reference to an actual scene.

To make such distinctions is to refer to two of Charles Saunders Pierce's influential tripartite view of signs. Whereas, for Pierce, the abstract meaning of a symbol becomes known through social and cultural conventions, an icon can be understood through its likeness to that which it depicts. Photographs at the level of direct resemblance or likeness are therefore heavily iconic. It is this which enables news photos to play such a powerful authenticating role when placed in the service of news reports. However, as the examples above indicate, news photographs can work in multi-layered and mutually reinforcing ways with images carrying both iconic and symbolic charge. The third, indexical, aspect of Pierce's understanding of signs is also of relevance to an understanding of news visuals. The indexical aspect of a sign is understood by its relationship to that to which it refers. Thus, it is neither a direct resemblance (icon) or a total convention (symbol), but works in terms of a relationship with, or causal connection to, that to which it refers (index). A useful illustration of Pierce's indexical sign is found in a further newspaper front page reporting the expected IRA cease-fire (*Daily Mirror* 1.9.94) (see Image 8.3).

Here we see not an iconic photograph but an indexical drawing, in which various elements help visualise, indexically, the accompanying IRA statement – the armalite rifle put down to rest, the coffin draped in the flag/shadow of the bird of peace, and the summary statistics of deaths from the Troubles up to 1994 on the coffin's lid. These elements are causally related to the IRA and its statement in a fairly obvious and direct way. It is also obvious that the indexical image is overlaid with a further ironic level of meaning. The symbolic dove of peace replete with olive branch is coloured-in with black, not white: the bird of peace is transformed into the shadow of death. Its shadow falls across the coffin in the manner of a draped flag, and suggests ambiguously either past deaths, or the possibility of future deaths to come, or perhaps both: the dove of peace may not be what it seems. The image works principally at an indexical level, though again conventionalised symbolic elements are also at work – the colour black, the dove of peace and the olive branch, the language used in the drawing. Again the example illustrates the complex and multi-layered nature of visual news images and the way in which they can contain, simultaneously, iconic, indexical and symbolic aspects.

Charles Saunders Pierce is generally acknowledged, along with Ferdinand De Saussure, to be one of the founding theorists of modern

DAILY Mirror

Thursday, September 1, 1994 HONESTY, QUALITY, EXCELLENCE July daily sale: 3,253,123 (INCORPORATING THE DAILY RECORD) 27p

'The IRA have decided that as of midnight, 31 August, there will be a complete cessation of military operations. All our units have been instructed accordingly'

IRA STATEMENT, 11am, AUGUST 31, 1994

GIVE PEACE A CHANCE -PAGES 2, 3, 4, 5, 6 AND 7

Image 8.3 *Daily Mirror*, 1.9.94

semiology. As such, it could be suggested his ideas ought to be discussed under semiological, not symbolic, approaches to the analysis of news analysis. As the illustration above indicates his ideas are none the less of particular relevance for the analysis of news symbols. Two distinctions between symbolic and semiotic analysis can be usefully drawn, however. Whereas semiotic analyses, as discussed below, are apt to provide more comprehensive and detailed readings of news images using the full arsenal of semiotic concepts and techniques, symbolic analyses have tended to be more focused on the central symbolism found within particular news images. Though going deeper into the visual textual qualities of news images than forms of distortion analysis, applied analyses of news symbolism have not generally pursued the more detailed relationship of such symbols to wider systems of signs. Also such analyses have tended to focus selectively on key visual images, those which are thought to crystallise news interpretations of important events.

A point of possible confusion also needs to be recognised. Not all theorists, or even semioticians, share the same understanding of 'symbol'. Pierce's designation of 'symbol' as purely abstract and conventionalised can be contrasted, for example, to Saussure's where the 'characteristic of the symbol is that it is never wholly empty, for there is a rudiment of a natural bond between the signifier and the signified. The symbol of justice, a pair of scales, could not be replaced by just another symbol, such as a chariot' (Saussure, 1966, p. 68). Here Saussure's 'symbol' sounds remarkably akin to Pierce's 'indexical' sign. Raymond Firth's summary definition is also of interest: 'symbolisation is a universal process' in which 'the essence of symbolism lies in the recognition of one thing as standing for (re-presenting) another, the relation between them normally being that of concrete to abstract, particular to general' (Firth, 1973, p. 15). With no settled definition of symbol, it is as well to be aware of different usages. In the context of press photographs, however, it would appear that all three of Pierce's aspects of signs – iconic, indexical, symbolic – are often found at work helping to support particular news story interpretations and framings. Two further examples help draw attention to the often heavy symbolism within, and ideological nature of, press photos.

In their study of the news reporting of a anti-Vietnam war protest in 1968, James Halloran and his team observed how a particular news photo was used across the front pages of most of the British press. This so-called 'Kick Photo' provides a good example of how a single image can come to symbolise an important news story in line with a particular definition of the situation (Halloran, Elliott and Murdock, 1970; Murdock, 1981; Hall, 1981). The photo, depicting a police officer being kicked in the head by a demonstrator, helped to construct a view of this major protest as a violent attack upon the political order. Though an isolated incident, it served to devalue and delegitimise the protesters as well as their legitimate concerns and democratic right to protest. Similarly, in their analysis of press coverage of inner city riots, Hansen and Murdock (1985) note how the use of a picture by the *Daily Mail* (7.7.81) of a masked man, subtitled 'The Masked Face of Violence' invoked 'two established sets of popular imagery: violent crime and terrorism'. They suggest '[B]oth of these connotations reinforce the populist construction of the Toxteth riots as an outbreak of criminal violence fermented by political extremists' and note how this symbolic image was then available for use in subsequent reports of riots (pp. 254–5).

The discussion so far has highlighted the role of visuals in providing symbolic form and definition to particular news events. The role of written or verbal language in this process, in combination with visuals, must also be taken into account. This concerns the evident tendency for news visuals to be 'anchored' by surrounding words – whether verbal or written. Roland Barthes, when discussing visual images, has observed how meaning is either 'anchored' by accompanying text, which helps to limit the possibility of different interpretations, or is 'relayed', that is, developed and moved on at the level of the visual dimension alone. On the basis of the various studies and examples discussed above, a strong case can be made that news visuals tend to be anchored by words, and rarely involve aspects of visual relay; it is words that constitute 'a kind of vice' and stop the possible meanings from proliferating (Barthes, 1977, p. 39). Consider, for example, the three press front pages reporting and symbolising the IRA cease-fire (Images 8.1–8.3); without exception all three depend upon the linguistic message to guide interpretation. Surrounding headlines, subheadings and, in the case of two of them, linguistic statements within the images themselves, steer the reader to interpret the images in 'relevant' and symbolically charged ways. While this should not be taken to lessen the importance of the visual contribution which, as has been illustrated, can often play an important role in providing symbolic form and emotional charge to news framing and its ideological construction, it draws attention none the less to the complex interplay between linguistic and visual elements.

8.4 Analysing News Visuals as Semiotic Systems

> We can therefore imagine a science which would study the life of signs within society . . . we call it semiology, from the Greek semeion('sign'). It would teach us what signs consist of, what laws govern them. Since it does not yet exist we cannot say what it will be: but it has a right to existence; its place is assured in advance. Linguistics is only a part of this general science . . . (Ferdinand de Saussure, quoted in Fiske, 1991, pp. 51–2)

Semiotics, or the 'science of signs', is primarily concerned with how meaning is generated at the level of signs and their relationship to other signs within sign-systems. This approach therefore seeks to go deeper into the actual mechanisms of meaning generation than either of the two approaches above. *How* representations mean, as much as what representations mean, becomes the principal analytical interest. Though originally conceptualised in relation to written and spoken language, semiotics has subsequently been developed and applied to diverse social objects and practices, including news images (Hartley, 1982; Webster, 1985; Fiske, 1991). Before demonstrating how semiotic analyses of news visuals can be carried out, a few summary words are in order concerning the wider theoretical framework informing semiotics and some of its key concepts.

Four fundamental features of Saussure's view of language can be noted at the outset.

(1) His structuralist view of language challenges common-sense views of language as simply referential, or as naming objects out there in the world. He argues that language is, in fact, relational, not referential.
(2) Language is organised on an internal system of signs which exist in a system of relationships and differences which help give meaning to individual and social experience.
(3) The relationship between language and meaning is arbitrary; different words could serve equally well to convey the same meanings.

(4) The system of language pre-exists the individual and his or her entry into society, providing the necessary and inescapable means by which the world can be made sense of and known.

The 'sign' is the smallest unit within language capable of signification, or the discharge of meaning. In the context of language, Saussure breaks it down into two aspects, the sound-image (signifier) and the concept (signified). Importantly, he argues that the relation between the signifier and the signified is arbitrary, purely a matter of convention. Signs exist in a system of networks and relationships internal to language itself. Two dimensions, the *paradigmatic* and the *syntagmatic*, help structure language choice and use.

- On a vertical axis, different repertoires of related terms are available within a language for selection and use, each capable of carrying distinct meanings defined in relation to other paradigmatic terms – for example, 'soldier', 'commando', 'insurgent', 'terrorist', 'guerrilla', 'freedom fighter'. Choice of words, in this example, is clearly not unlimited, and yet selection choices can convey very different associated meanings.
- How these words are then used in combination with others, in sequence along the horizontal chain of language use, or the syntagmatic plane, introduces further opportunities to make associations and meanings.

These features of language represent for Saussure the deep structures of language or 'langue', both facilitating and limiting actual instances of language use or 'parole'. How 'signs' come together and work as 'codes', communicating particular cultural views of the social and natural world, and assume the position of contemporary 'myths' (which is not to imply they are distorted or false) has subsequently been developed in relation to diverse areas of social and cultural interest (Eco, 1965; Barthes, 1972; Williamson, 1978; Turner, 1988).

Saussure's contribution to the 'traditional' view of semiotics developed in relation to his view of language, has not gone without criticism. The emphasis upon the 'internal' structural properties of language as system or 'langue', in contrast to the actual instance of language use or 'parole' within 'external' contexts has tended to provide a relatively fixed and impersonal view of meaning buried within texts and universal codes. The social nature of semiotic processes, in other words, involving the cultural and social generation of meanings which themselves become subject to processes of semiotic negotiation and contestation has been, until recently, insufficiently developed (Hodge and Kress, 1988, pp. 13–36). Saussure's achievement is none the less generally acknowledged to be profound, and has opened the way to serious analysis of the realm of social and cultural meanings. Roland Barthes, perhaps more than any other semiotician, has demonstrated how signs which appear simply to denote in the first order of signification, that is, refer in some obvious and commonly understood way to an object, in fact connote in a second order of signification and contribute to the circulation of social and cultural meanings (Barthes, 1972). It is the facility of signs to work at the level of connotation that produces such a rich pasture for semiotic grazing.

Returning to our focus on news visuals, a number of theorists have provided an attempt to map and decode the 'grammar' of film language and how film conventions connote certain meanings (Tuchman, 1978; Turner, 1988; Berger, 1991). Clearly, this is of some relevance to the use of still and video or film pictures in TV news. Berger provides a useful summary of some of the visual signs of the TV medium and their conventionalised social meanings (Figure 8.1).

Signifier (shot)	*Definition*	*Signified (meaning)*
close-up	face only	intimacy
medium shot	most of body	personal relationship
long shot	setting and characters	context, scope, public distance
full shot	full body of person	social relationship
Signifier (film)	*Definition*	*Signified (meaning)*
pan down	camera looks down	power, authority
pan up	camera looks up	smallness, weakness
zoom in	camera moves in	observation, focus
fade in	image appears on blank screen	beginning
fade out	image screen goes blank	ending
cut	switch from one image to another	simultaneity, excitement
wipe	image wiped off screen	imposed conclusion

Source: Berger, 1991, pp. 26–7

Figure 8.1 Asa Berger's semiotic film conventions

Interestingly, while some of these visual signs may be thought to be entirely arbitrary, there are at least some grounds for assuming that some of them relate to principles of real-world perception (Messaris, 1994), and some may also convey different meanings according to the medium, whether television or cinema (Ellis, 1982).

Hodge and Kress take some of these visual cues further in their discussion of 'proxemics'. This refers to the set of meanings carried by physical relationships in space, specifically by closeness ('proximity', hence the name for the codes) and distance (Hodge and Kress, 1988, pp. 52–78). Before accepting that 'closeness' signifies intimacy, or distance 'social remoteness' however, the authors point to further levels of complexity, involving different cultural readings and the complicating dimension of social power. The discussion alerts us, in other words, to the possible complexities of semiotic decoding, and the necessity for the semiotician to be both aware of, and sensitive to, the complex cultural codes operative in a visual image and their meanings for different audiences.

A similar case could be made in relation to the assumed status-conferring attributes and props of television interviews. Managers dressed in formal suits, interviewed behind polished oak desks or high-tech office stations, may or may not signify higher status and associated credibility than workers dressed in boiler-suits, interviewed in front of factory gates. Much will depend upon prevalent cultural codes and the anchoring effect of language; the role of such props in connoting 'management', for example, can also sustain meanings of archaic social power and/or bureaucratic remoteness and uncaringness.

To help demonstrate some of the semiotic concepts and techniques introduced, two front page press photographs are now subjected to semiotic analysis. Both concern the reporting of the same demonstration (against the British Criminal Justice Bill) and, incidentally, also serve to illustrate something of the possible press variances at the level of visual representation (see Images 8.4 and 8.5). For the purposes of illustration, the analysis confines its observations to just a few of the many semiotic features of interest. Image 8.4 is a reproduction of a front-page article and photograph taken from the *Daily Mail* (10.10.94). At a denotative level, what do we see? We see a picture of three crowd members, one of whom is a man positioned centre stage with another, possibly a woman, bending over in front of heavily protected police officers. The picture depicts prominent crowd members in dynamic movement towards the police line at the rear of the photograph. The character positioned in the middle of the photograph is a young bald man who appears to be shouting and holding a can of beer.

The *Guardian* (10.10.94) front page photograph, in comparison, depicts at a denotative level two young men sitting on the ground, heads bowed, their backs to a row of standing police holding riot shields; in the foreground, resting on the floor, are two crumpled posters proclaiming 'Kill the Criminal Justice Bill' and a can of beer. Paradigmatically these two photographs illustrate two differing selections available to photographers attending the protest. Syntagmatically the different sets of visual elements combine to connote different meanings, and activate different social codes. Each image, discussed below, is composed of an ensemble of signs, each of which contributes to further layers of meaning by juxtaposition and association.

The prominent headline of the *Daily Mail* picture – both in terms of its overall proportion to the photograph and its white type-face set against a bold black background – proclaims 'Return of Rent-a-Mob'.

Return of Rent-a-Mob

Flashpoint: Chanting protesters clash with riot police at Hyde Park yesterday

A VICIOUS explosion of hatred left police nursing their wounds last night.

At least 11 officers were injured in clashes with a ragtag army of demonstrators in Hyde Park.

At one point police, who had struggled all day to contain a 20,000-strong march in protest against the Criminal Justice Bill, faced being overwhelmed by attacks from a combination of groups including squatters, New Age travellers and motorway protesters.

Police said many had been seen defying police in incidents across the country in recent months and were the very groups whose activities would be curtailed by the Bill.

Near Speakers' Corner, police were forced to form a protective square as a mob inside the railings, and a breakaway group spilling out of the park, pelted them with bottles, cans and wooden placards.

When a firecracker exploded on the shield of one riot policeman, and a teargas canister was let off, the 200

Turn to Page 2, Col. 6

Image 8.4 *Daily Mail*, 10.10.94

The **Guardian**

NEWSPAPER OF THE YEAR

Protest against justice bill leads to violence

DEMONSTRATORS make a point to police in a clash at the end of a rally in Hyde Park, central London, in protest against the Criminal Justice Bill, which reaches the statute book later this month, *write Alan Travis and Duncan Campbell.*

The rally, which followed a march by some 50,000 people through central London, heard the veteran Labour MP Tony Benn say: "There may be a legal obligation to obey but there will be no moral obligation to obey. When it comes to history, it will be the people who broke the law for freedom who will be remembered and honoured." His comments were echoed by Arthur Scargill, the miners' leader, and by Andrew Puddephatt, general secretary of Liberty. Mr Puddephatt said the legislation would give police new powers to clamp down on raves, unlicensed parties, protests and new age travellers, as well as restricting the right to silence and to assembly.

The end of the march was marred by clashes between mounted police with riot shields and a small group of protesters.

Litter bins, bottles and sticks were thrown at officers, who responded with a series of charges. The incidents occurred after police tried to clear a lorry with a sound system from the roadway.

A CS gas cannister was thrown at police. Eleven officers and two protesters were injured.

Chief Superintendent Richard Cullen, the officer in charge, said that most of the demonstrators behaved quietly and peacefully.

Weyman Bennett, one of the organisers of the march, said: "All this trouble could have been avoided if the police had allowed people to get to their coaches."

PHOTOGRAPH GRAHAM TURNER

Image 8.5 *Guardian*, 10.10.94

The headline invites a particular set of meanings and interpretative framework for the picture below. 'Rent-a-Mob' makes reference to a wider 'mythic' view of society established in past reporting of conflict situations, including riots, demonstrations and strikes, in which organised groups of politically motivated extremists, anarchists and general 'trouble-makers' are said to travel the country in pursuit of violent confrontation. The label implies that such 'mob' members may be motivated by less than political ideals. The central image of the young white man, dressed in a white hooded top, appears to personify the white headline proclaiming 'Return of Rent-a-Mob'.

With no head hair he readily becomes assimilable to a public perception of skinheads – a group widely identified with anti-social behaviour and thoughtless violence – an image further reinforced by the can of beer connoting public drunkenness, lack of self-control and disorderliness. Mouth open, he appears to be shouting in anger, a further form of public behaviour often associated with 'yobbish' activity. A series of cultural 'binary oppositions' thus appears to inform the news report, including: 'them' versus 'us'; 'order versus disorder'; 'legitimate force' versus 'illegitimate violence'; and 'civilised norms' versus 'deviant behaviour'.

With these powerful connotations now in play, an ambiguity in the picture could well be overlooked. A first glance at the picture is likely to position the young man with no hair as engaged in some act of violence towards the police, or perhaps he is responsible for the person falling towards the ground? Only on closer inspection does it become apparent that one of the riot officers has a drawn truncheon and that he could have been responsible for the person's fall through a previous act of violence. Perhaps the 'skinhead' is in fact not acting in an aggressive manner but trying to prevent the fall of the person to his left? If the headline fails to clinch the preferred interpretation without any visual ambiguity, there is always the cultural typification of anarchy, mayhem and general confusion surrounding 'mob violence', as well as invited views of 'reasonable force', to help remove any remaining doubt.

The photo on close reading therefore remains ambiguous; as such it requires a strong anchorage from both the headline and subsequent news report. This is provided in both, as well as a further sub-heading of 'Flashpoint: Chanting protesters clash with riot police at Hyde Park yesterday' and the news report's opening words: 'A vicious explosion of hatred left police nursing their wounds last night. At least 11 officers were injured in clashes with a ragtag army of demonstrators in Hyde Park'. While the words 'ragtag army' may find at least some visual support in the depiction of variously attired demonstrators, the 'vicious explosion of hatred' has to be read into the picture in line with the linguistic message, possible readership expectations and informing political views.

The *Guardian*, in contrast, does not display such a prominent headline either in proportion to the overall visual image or in its choice of type-face. 'Protest against justice bill leads to violence', all written, with the exception of the first letter, in lower case, is much less obtrusive. The picture has no accompanying sub-heading, and appears not to relate directly to the lead headline at all. Instead we see two relatively inert, individuated young men sitting with their backs to a row of heavily equipped riot police. Proxemically and dispositionally they connote no sense of threat, the camera angle looks down at them, they are sitting on the ground, their heads are bowed, they look at their hands while the anonymous row of police (we cannot see their faces), appear to dominate the situation powerfully – connoted by force of numbers, riot equipment, their standing and seried position as well as by their impersonal collective presence. This picture also works to invoke a number of wider cultural codes and 'myths' associated with Britain in the 1990s. These organising 'codes', or available ways of understanding, are signified in part by the close-up shots of the two young men and their associated signs, both literal and semiotic – badges, posters, hair-style, drinking, demeanour – connoting ideas of social marginality, political disaffection and, possibly, youth unemployment. This chain of syntagmatic associations and meanings is held in place by a third order of connotation signifying political and personal defeat; the depiction of two politically motivated but hapless young men literally 'down on their luck'.

The opening lines of the news report begins by stating 'DEMONSTRATORS' (in upper case) 'make a point to police in a clash at the end of a rally in Hyde Park, central London in a protest against the Criminal Justice Bill, which reaches the statute book later this month'. Here at least appears to be some support to the lead headline and its postulated 'protest' and 'violence', though again the image does little to endorse such a view. Unlike the *Daily Mail*, the report does not focus on the effects of violence nor seek to submerge the informing politics at the core of the protest within a generalised concept of anti-social 'mob violence'. Rather, in line with the *Guardian*'s editorial stance, readership expectations and general liberal political viewpoint, the image and text tend to support a less-reactionary set of concerns and values. This is achieved through a combination of word and image, with each mobilising extant cultural 'myths' through particular chains of signification.

The above, for reasons of space, has barely begun to unpack semiotically all the complexity and detail presented in these two different uses of news photographs. In self-criticism the analysis has wandered at times from a strict analysis of the textual and photographic elements into a more interpretative mode. While a 'social semiotic' analysis, in contrast to a more 'traditional' text-bound semiotic analysis, is bound to draw upon the analyst's own understanding of surrounding cultural codes and myths, it is as well to remind oneself that to read too much into an image without identifying the exact textual mechanisms and referents by which the seeming proliferation of connotations is sustained can lead, on occasion, to highly speculative readings. The analysis has, we hope, also demonstrated how both sets of news reports and visuals, though clearly working to different news frames and preferred interpretations, contain elements of ambiguity, inconsistency and possible contradiction. Such are often part and parcel of complex news stories compiled and produced under pressurised conditions; these, as much as the textual tendencies towards closure, need to be revealed. Beware, in other words, the semiotic analysis which proclaims a 'watertight' ideological reading. Finally, a useful technique to check out the semiotic value of certain signs within an image is to deploy the 'commutation test'. By substituting various elements in your mind's eye, whether colour, proxemics, dynamics, age, gender, ethnicity, attire, expression, hair style, accessories, aspects of accompanying language, and so on, it is possible to build a more nuanced and detailed understanding of the exact contribution of each to the overall meaning of the image and its dependence upon wider cultural codes and myths.

8.5 Analysing News Visuals as Epistemological Guarantee

One last approach to visual analysis is evident across a number of news studies. This concerns the way in which the use of news visuals are thought to help secure both the authoritative status and knowledge claims of news (Brunsdon and Morley, 1978; GUMG, 1980; Davis and Walton, 1983; Graddol, 1994; Meinhof, 1994). The approach is most clearly associated with the semiotic approach above but can be differentiated in two important respects. In relation to particular news stories, whether TV or press, the tools of semiotic analysis are specifically set to work in recovering or decoding the way in which the visual component helps authenticate the news report and its projected status as a provider of knowledge.

In other words, attention focuses upon exactly how visuals perform a function of epistemological guarantee. The analytical focus and interest is not on the veracity or 'truthfulness' of certain images, as with forms of distortion analysis, nor on the symbolism of images and their role in the construction of particular story-related meanings, but rather the way in which such images help construct a sense of news as a distinct, and trustworthy, form of knowledge. Typically the projected news epistemology, or 'way of knowing', pursued by news analysts concerns the generalised 'objectivity' claims of news. How visuals are selected and positioned in an evidential way, how they are used apparently to 'document' or 'record' historical events and happenings, and how they are deployed to authenticate verbal claims, and underwrite the general 'meta-discourse' or the constructed news package of the news producers, becomes a key area of interest.

Also differentiating this approach from those above, is the way in which it addresses general visual or presentational properties of news programmes and forms. Here questions of visuality merge into general codes of programme presentation and their contribution to maintaining the boundaries and conventions of differentiated genres, and the authoritative 'factuality' claims of the news genre in particular.

A third area of interest, which can be discussed under this approach, is the possibility of differing news epistemologies and their use of visuals. While attention, to date, has tended to focus upon the role of visuals and their contribution to an 'objectivist' news epistemology, news visuals may also be implicated in a 'subjectivist' news epistemology – most often associated with popular and tabloid forms of journalism, though not exclusive to these (Cottle, 1993a, 1993b). Here a different 'way of knowing', a different 'regime of truth' appears to underpin tabloid appeals and forms of news presentation. Each of these themes – visuals and news story epistemology, considerations of programme visualisation, and use of visuals in 'objectivist' and 'subjectivist' epistemologies – can now be discussed in turn along with considerations of method.

An early study of *Nationwide*, a former BBC television news and current affairs programme, makes reference to the possible ideological effects of visuals when dependent upon news commentary:

> But the dominant tendency – which the specific work of combination accomplishes here – is for the visual images to be 'resolved' into those dominant meanings and interpretations which the commentary is providing. This interpretative work is, however, repressed or occluded by the synchronisation of voice-over with images, which makes it appear as if the 'images speak for themselves' – declare their own transparent meaning, without exterior intervention. This synchronisation of discourses is the work of

> coupling – the accomplishment of a particular combination of discourses which has the effect of fixing certain privileged meanings to the images, binding the two signifying chains together in a 'specific relation of dominance'. (Brunsdon and Morley, 1978, p. 62)

The claim here is that TV news visuals, in line with current thinking about common sense as the terrain of ideology, provided a seemingly neutral or transparent view of reality, a view which in actuality was dependent upon the work of ideological interpretation and labour. Both the moments of producer 'encoding' and audience 'decoding' involve active interpretation and sense-making processes (Hall, 1980), but in so far as visual images appear simply to record and document independently of considerations of accompanying commentary and interpretation, so the reader is vulnerable to the particular constructions provided by news producers. Interestingly, and contrary to professional TV journalist's claims about the centrality of images to TV news stories, research has tended to find that not only are TV images highly dependent upon accompanying news commentary but also, for the most part, provide relatively few iconic pictures at all (GUMG, 1980; Davis and Walton, 1983).

> In television news, in fact, a relatively small proportion of the total number of shots is iconic or directly representative of the people, places and events which are the subjects of the news text. A far greater proportion of shots has an oblique relationship to the text; they 'stand for' the subject matter indexically or symbolically. (Davis and Walton, 1983, p. 45)

To what extent this, and similar findings, may reflect on the particular news form, news issue and continuity of news story under consideration could all be raised, however. Is it the case that different types of news programmes, including populist regional and breakfast news programmes, deliver a comparable visual dimension? If some news stories are event-orientated, are these more likely, given the absence of event pictures, to be dependent upon aftermath and other indexical shots, whereas feature type news stories are not? And does the running story, in contrast to the one-off, provide more iconic images? (Cottle, 1993b). These questions must also be addressed in relation to the verbal track. In her study, Meinhof identifies three types of interrelations between news text and pictures:

(1) Overlap – where the film footage and the text share the same action component though the relationship may be direct or metonymic;
(2) Displacement – where the film footage and text represent different action components of the same event, for example, the news report of the event of an earthquake provides images of the effects of the earthquake; and
(3) Dichotomy – where the film footage and text represent action components of different events, that is, scenes may be shown which bear no direct or even indexical relationship to the verbal track.

Interestingly, she concludes that news texts at the level of visual and verbal interrelations may be more open to differing interpretations than once assumed (Meinhof, 1994). The reported study remains dependent upon a partial analysis of a single news report, however.

All the studies above have had to grapple with the difficulties of applied visual analysis. The difficulties and complexities of pursuing a representative sample of news stories and their visuals, examining visual composition as well as forms of interaction with the verbal track, have proved enormously time-consuming. Davis and Walton (1983) have outlined the basic procedure for conducting this type of analysis. A full transcript of the news item, indicating details of presentational format, is set alongside the visual unit of analysis, which is taken to be the shot. A still image is reproduced from the moving film and subsequent movements within the shot are indicated with reference to pan, zoom, close-up and so on. With the next shot, the procedure is repeated until a complete verbal and visual transcript is achieved. Only then can the actual detail of the image be 'read' and analysed in synchrony with the accompanying verbal commentary as broadcast. Clearly this is a cumbersome process, but a necessary one if the interactions between verbal and visual dimensions are to be examined in detail.

A slightly different methodological approach allowed similar scrutiny of the visual track in interaction with the verbal, but was assisted by a form of computer-assisted content analysis, thereby permitting a much-increased sample of news reports. In this case, a detailed study of news portrayal of a major riot across one year of 153 follow-up news items was carried out, in which all 153 news items and accompanying visuals were subject to systematic and quantitative review based upon a comprehensive coding schedule of riot themes and issues. On the basis of this much-expanded sample of news reports, the study found the news portrayal to be heavily iconic and concluded:

> The extent to which the event and its immediate aftermath have found pronounced visual reference, denoting destruction and violence, and repeatedly resurrected across the extended portrayal, may be taken once again as preferring the conservative discourse . . . The prevalence of iconic images may be thought to be all the more authenticating here, to the extent that they appear to provide an independent source of confirmation of unfolding events. (Cottle, 1993b, p. 195).

Clearly, both quantitative and qualitative techniques can usefully address issues of news visual composition and interaction with verbal tracks, and much work remains to be done even on the basic questions of visual composition and text–visual interaction. Recently Graddol has made promising headway on the 'epistemological guarantee' front and suggests:

> TV news is both a knowledge system and a genre. That is, the news system represents a particular way of collecting and establishing 'facts' which are different from, say, the institutions of science or the courts, and there are conventional ways of organising and presenting these facts on television . . . In order to accomplish factuality, TV news must work hard to maintain the security of its knowledge-system, must establish the distinctiveness of the genre, and must use all the resources at its disposal for achieving high modality in its presentation. The visual component of TV news provides crucial resources in all three areas. (Graddol, 1994, pp. 138–9)

At the heart of the analysis is an identification of a form of 'realism', in which the omniscient camera/narrator provides the viewer with a privileged view of the 'objective' world, and steers him or her through competing partial accounts. The news account proclaims itself visually, however, to be above the fray. Furthermore, this visual accomplishment of 'realism' combines with a form of news 'naturalism', typically found in actuality reports filmed in the field, where the camera now appears to provide a vicarious experience of the scene, as if we were there witnessing it in person. This combination of realist and naturalist film modes, though not without some tension, acts visually to produce a sense of news factuality.

The way in which the news is presented and visualised, not simply within news reports, but across the programme as a whole, is also thought to be extremely important in constructing an overall stance of news authority and 'factuality'. Here Graddol notes, for example, the use of distinctive genre boundaries and opening sequences involving dramatic and fast-moving images, the appearance of hi-tech news studios, studio lighting and camera angles, and the dress codes of newsreaders. All of these help to establish visually the sense of news as a distinctive genre and authoritative provider of factuality: 'factuality is not merely a question of truth or lies, but a more complex semiotic system which provides for varying authority, certainty and appropriateness to be allocated to particular representations of the world' (Graddol, 1994, p. 137).

This last statement finally draws attention to the possibly differentiated nature of news forms, each characterised by particular conventions and appeals, modes of address and use of visual imagery. The question of differing functions and forms of news visuals across the news spectrum is an area which has yet to be fully explored and theorised. There are certainly sufficient grounds to suggest that press visuals can indeed be differentiated in important respects (Cottle, 1993a; Fiske, 1992; Becker, 1992). Just to state a few obvious differences, the tabloid press is much more visual than its so-called 'quality' neighbours; more overall space is devoted to news pictures, more copy-space of individual stories is taken up by news pictures, and more space is given over to visually bold headlines. In part, this sustains a more subjectivist news epistemology. Tabloid newspapers are orientated less towards the public sphere of rational engaged debate and authoritative and expert comment, and more towards the private sphere of experiential accounts and affective, often morally informed, emotional response. Rather than proclaiming a stance of 'objective', independent reporting, coolly presenting facts and opinion, tabloids often seek to champion causes and police moral boundaries in a deliberate display of emotional partisanship. Pictures within such a heady brew play a complementary role (Cottle, 1993a).

John Fiske (1992), examining one such picture, has gone further, however. Noting the sensationalist claims of many tabloids he lights upon a front-page picture taken from *Weekly World News*. Under the headline 'Wife Meets Dead Husband in the Devil's Triangle!' and 'Astonishing photo is PROOF of life after death!', the newspaper provides a photograph of a middle-aged woman apparently about to hug her long-dead husband dressed in a 1920s suit. Fiske argues that the tabloids' penchant for the superstitious and supernatural present an alternative reality to official reality.

In this instance the tabloid article and photograph implicitly challenge, he suggests, the official epistemology based on scientific rationalism, the power of Christianity to define and control the meaning of life and death, and the normalising practice of journalism and its distinguishing of fact and fiction. For Fiske such tabloid excesses can be interpreted not only as a challenge to official epistemology but to the power-bloc of society, arguing: 'if the power of the norms to explain is inadequate, so too is their power to rule and discipline our lives' (Fiske, 1992, pp. 51–2). While there is much to contest here, not least of which is Fiske's failure to consider the more material underpinnings to tabloid forms, as well as the less than 'radical' interpretations sustained in actual readership decodings – either of which may puncture his flight into celebratory fancy – there is no doubting the fact that tabloid photojournalism may well service a different form of news epistemology which, in turn, informs a distinctively different form of news journalism.

8.6 Conclusion

This chapter has identified and sought to introduce four principal approaches to the analysis of news visuals. Space permitting, other approaches could also have been discussed. Experimental work on visual imagery and news retention and memory, for example, is clearly of interest (Adams, 1978; Graber, 1990; Newhagen, 1992), as is the recent and very promising involvement of news visuals in studies of audience beliefs (Philo, 1990; Miller, 1994), and the development of the method of so-called 'Editing groups', in which participants assemble news items and discuss the nuances of meaning associated with visual choices and selections and so on (MacGregor and Morrison, 1995). Here, however, the focus has been confined deliberately to those studies which have sought to engage directly with news visuals and the range of methods and techniques used in their analysis.

For analytical purposes the four approaches subject to review have been separated out. While many studies appear to fall neatly under one or other of the four approaches, others have a foot in one or more camps. The fact remains, however, that the four means of analysis labelled for convenience 'distortion', 'symbolic', 'semiotic' and 'epistemological' approaches have each deployed a number of methods and techniques, some quantitative some qualitative, in their search for improved understanding of the visual dimension and its contribution to news processes and understanding. On the basis of the review and discussion there is clearly a case to be made for improved methods and refined forms of visual analysis across all four.

The news production domain remains a rich vein for forms of distortion analysis, notwithstanding the relativist's concerns about the abstract impossibility of 'objectivity'. Confronted with professional processes of news visualisation, the participant observer can indeed observe alternative visualisations and the partial (often partisan) nature of those finally enacted. There is much work to be done here. The symbolic nature of news visuals is also in need of further work; studies of news symbolism remain in a minority despite the evident ritualistic and symbolic appeal of much news imagery, a theme readily confirmed via public memories of mediated important events. Semiotic analyses of news visuals, though more numerous, could nevertheless be developed with heightened sensitivity to the contexts of reading, changing nature of surrounding cultural codes and discourses as well as the often 'contradictory' or less than unitary meanings found within actual instances of news visualisation. Lastly, studies of news visualisation and epistemology generally, and contrasting 'objectivist' and 'subjectivist' epistemologies particularly, promise a further rich vein for future news visual analysis and research. Enough has been indicated that on all four fronts, methods and techniques have been developed and deployed to some effect, they now need to be refined and put into practice within a more concerted approach to the study of news visuals as an integral part of mainstream news studies. They also, of course, hold much relevance for the applied analysis of non-news visuals.

8.7 Summary

- Approaches to visual analysis within mass communication research remain relatively undeveloped in comparison to the study of language and linguistic-based approaches. This situation is beginning to be redressed, though much work remains to be done.
- A widespread faith in the power of photography and television images to simply record and 'mirror' reality invests images with possible potent effects. Many mass communication researchers appear to have also been 'blinded' by this 'naïve realism' and failed

to appreciate or inquire into the active role of images in processes of representation and communicated meanings.

- None the less, four analytically distinct approaches to the analysis of visuals can be identified as informing some mass communication studies; approaches that promise to provide important findings and insights in applied discussion of media representations. These have been identified and discussed here as 'distortion', 'symbolic', 'semiotic' and 'epistemological' approaches to visual analysis.
- With the partial exception of the 'distortion' approach which has, occasionally, pursued its inquiries in relation to professional media practices and the production domain, these approaches have tended to be text-based methodologies. As such, though they undoubtedly provide insight into the mechanisms and processes of meaning generation *within* the text, they nonetheless sometimes tend theoretically towards a position of textual determinism, paying insufficient attention to considerations of production and audience involvement in the social processes of communicated meaning.
- Distortion approaches actively seek alternative sources of visual evidence in order to critically appraise the authenticity or representativeness of the selected scene and images. On occasion the approach can detect visual falsifications and fabrications. This position can, on occasion, be criticised for being informed by 'naïve realism', where the researcher assumes he or she is in possession of an objective visual understanding. Gross falsifications tend, for reasons discussed, to be rare in the British news media. When informed by a more relative appreciation of how selected available scenes are textually put to work in support of particular social viewpoints and interpretation of events, the distortion approach escapes the charge of naïve realism and can provide important insight into the influence of professional decision-making and practices upon the framing of news events and issues. Such studies provide invaluable evidence to support the contention that available visual scenes and images could have framed the news differently.
- Symbolic approaches to news have helped identify the way in which images can condense and crystallise social values, aspirations or fears in visual form, and serve in consequence as potent signs in the discharge of meaning.
- Semiotics has helped to develop the means by which visual images can be interrogated and *how* the ensemble of signs within an image work to generate particular meanings. When applied to news images the technique proves illuminating, though examples of the technique in use have also revealed the 'leaky' nature of some

images and the role of surrounding language in 'fixing' meanings to preferred news interpretations. In the context of news, the leaky quality of visual images draws attention to the conditions and contingencies of production as well as the differentiated audience and its active role in activating particular social meanings.

- Developing upon semiotic techniques, the epistemological approach goes deeper into the visual contribution of images to the construction of 'knowledge', not simply in relation to particular news items or stories but generically and conventionally in relation to the news form now approached as a socially and discursively differentiated 'way of knowing'. Visual images are implicated, it would seem, in establishing our deepest and often taken-for-granted ways of knowing about the world.
- There is much work to be done on the development of visual-based methodologies. Wherever possible this should be carried out with due regard to the known complexities of mass communication processes involving 'moments' of institutionalised and professionalised production, textual complexities of medium and form, and contexts and processes of audience reception.

Notes

1. This chapter confines its analytical sights to news visual analysis. This is not to suggest, however, that the approaches discussed cannot or have not been applied usefully to the visual dimensions of other media genres. Semiotics, for example, has been used extensively in both film and advertising studies (cf. Barthes, 1972; Williamson, 1978; Turner, 1988).
2. Perhaps the most promising attempt to address the changing nature and role of visual images within contemporary society has been elaborated by Lash (1990, p. 174) with his distinction between 'discursive' and 'figural regimes of signification'. As with most 'postmodern' statements in this regard, however, the value of his schema has yet to be established or demonstrated in applied empirical analysis.

References

Adams, W. (1978) 'Visual Analysis of Newscasts: Issues in Social Science Research' in A. Adams and F. Schreibman (eds) *Television Network News – Issues in Content Research*, pp. 155–73 (George Washington University).

Ball, M.S. and G.W.H. Smith (1992) *Analysing Visual Data*, Qualitative Research Methods Series 24 (London: Sage).

Barthes, R. (1972) *Mythologies* (London: Cape).

Barthes, R. (1977) 'The Rhetoric of the Image' in R. Barthes, *Image-Music-Text* (essays trans. S. Heath), pp. 32–51, (London: Fontana).

Baudrillard, J. (1983) *In the Shadow of the Silent Majorities . . . Or The End of the Social* (New York: Semiotext).
Baudrillard, J. (1988) 'Simularcar and Simulations', in M. Poster (ed.) *Jean Baudrillard: Selected Writings* (London: Blackwell).
Becker, K. E. (1992) 'Photojournalism and the Popular Press' in P. Dahlgren and C. Sparks (eds) *Journalism and Popular Culture* (London: Sage).
Berger, A. A. (1991) *Media Analysis Techniques* (London: Sage).
Brunsdon, C. and D. Morley (1978) *Everyday Television: 'Nationwide'* (London: BFI).
Carey, J. (1989) *Communication as Culture–Essays on Media and Society* (London: Unwin Hyman).
Cottle, S. (1991) 'Reporting the Rushdie Affair: A Case Study in the Orchestration of Public Opinion', *Race and Class*, vol. 32, no. 4, pp. 45–64.
Cottle, S. (1993a) 'Taking the Popular Seriously: A Typology for the Analysis of The Tabloid Press' *Social Science Teacher* Journal of the Association of Social Science Teachers vol. 22. no. 3. pp. 20–23.
Cottle, S. (1993b) *TV News, Urban Conflict and the Inner City* (Leicester: LeicesterUniversity Press).
Cumberbatch, G., R. McGregor, J. Brown and D. Morrison (1986) *Television and the Miners Strike* (London: Broadcasting Research Unit).
Davis, H. and P. Walton (1983) 'Death of a Premier: Consensus and Closure in International News' in H. Davis and P. Walton (eds) *Language, Image, Media*, pp. 8–49, (London: Blackwell).
Eco, U. (1965) 'Towards a Semiotic Inquiry into the TV Message' (trans.), in *Working Papers in Cultural Studies* (University of Birmingham) no. 3 (1972) pp. 103–21.
Elliott, P. (1980) 'Press Performance as Political Ritual', in H. Christian (ed) *The Sociology of Journalism and the Press*, pp. 141–77 (University of Keele, Sociological Review monograph no. 29).
Ellis, J. (1982) *Visible Fictions* (London: Routledge & Kegan Paul).
Ericson, R. V., Baranek, P. M. and Chan, J. B. L. (1987) *Visualizing Deviance: A study of news organization* (Milton Keynes: Open University Press).
Firth, R. (1973) *Symbols – Public and Private* (London: George Allen & Unwin).
Fiske, J. (1991) *Introduction to Communication Studies*, 2nd edn (London: Routledge).
Fiske, J. (1992) 'Popularity and the Politics of Information', in P. Dahlgren and C. Sparks (eds) *Journalism and Popular Culture* (London: Sage).
Giddens, A. (1979) *Central Problems in Social Theory* (London: Macmillan).
Glasgow University Media Group (1980) *More Bad News* (London: Routledge & Kegan Paul).
Golding, P. and Middleton, S. (1982) *Images of welfare* (Oxford: Basil Blackwell).
Graber, D. A. (1990) 'Seeing is Remembering: How Visuals Contribute to Learning from Television News', *Journal of Communication* vol. 40. no.(3), pp. 134–55.
Graddol, D. (1994) 'The Visual Accomplishment of Factuality', in D. Graddol and O. Boyd-Barrett (eds) *Media Texts: Authors and Readers* (Clevedon: Multilingual Matters in Association with The Open University).

Hackett, R. A. (1985) 'Decline of a Paradigm? Bias and Objectivity in News Media Studies', in M. Gurevitch and M. R. Levy (eds) *Mass Communication Review Yearbook*, pp. 251–74 (London: Sage).
Hall, S., D. Hobson, A. Lowe and P. Willis (eds) (1980) *Culture, Media Language* (London: Hutchinson).
Hall, S. (1980) 'Decoding/Encoding', in S. Hall, D. Hobson, A. Lowe and P. Willis (eds) *Culture, Media Language* (London: Hutchinson).
Hall, S. (1981) 'The Determination of News Photographs' in S. Cohen and J. Young (eds) *The Manufacture of News*, pp. 226–43 (London: Constable).
Halloran, J. D., Elliott, P. and Murdock, G. (1970) Demonstrations and Communication (Harmondsworth: Penguin).
Hansen, A. and Murdock, G. (1985) 'Constructing the crowd: populist discourse and press presentation', in V. Mosco and J. Wasko (eds) *Popular culture and media events*, vol. III, pp. 227–57 (Norwood, NJ: Ablex)
Hartley, J. (1982) *Understanding News* (London: Methuen).
Hodge, R. and Kress, G. (1988) *Social Semiotics* (Oxford: Polity Press).
Jowett, G. S. (1993) 'Propaganda and the Gulf War', *Critical Studies in Mass Communication* **10**(3) 287–300.
Lang, K. and G. Lang (1953) 'The Unique Perspective of Television and Its Effects', *American Sociological Review*, **18**(1) 3–12.
Lash, S. (1990) *The Sociology of Postmodernism* (London: Routledge).
MacGregor, B. and D. E. Morrison (1995) 'From Focus Groups to Editing Groups: A New Method of Reception Analysis', *Media, Culture and Society*, **17**(1) 141–50.
Messaris, P. (1994) *Visual Literacy* (Oxford: Westview Press).
Meinhof, U. H. (1994) 'Double Talk in News Broadcasts', in D. Graddol and O. Boyd-Barrett (eds) *Media Texts: Authors and Readers* (Clevedon: Multilingual Matters in Association with The Open University).
Miller, D. (1994) *Don't Mention the War: Northern Ireland, The Propaganda War and the Media* (London: Pluto).
Mowlana, H., G. Gerbner and H. Schiller (eds) (1992) *Triumph of the Image* (Oxford: Westview).
Murdock, G. (1981) 'Political Deviance: The Press Presentation of a Militant Mass Demonstration', in S. Cohen and J. Young (eds) *The Manufacture of News* (London: Constable).
Newhagen, J. E. (1992) 'The Evening's Bad News: Effects of Compelling Negative Television News Images on Memory', *Journal of Communication* **42**(2) 25–41.
Philo. G. (1990) *Seeing and Believing* (London: Routledge).
Saussure, F. de (1966) *Course in General Linguistics* (New York: McGraw-Hill).
Taylor, J. (1994) 'The Body Vanishes – Photojournalism in the Gulf War', *Contemporary Record*, **8**(2) 289–304.
Tuchman, G. (1978) *Making news: A study in the construction of reality* (New York: The Free Press).
Turner, G. (1988) *Film as social practice* (London: Routledge).
Turner, G. (1990) *British Cultural Studies* (London: Unwin Hyman).
Webster, F. (1985) *The New Photography* (London: John Calder).
Williamson. J. (1978) *Decoding Advertisements* (London: Marion Bowers).

9

Media Audiences: Survey Research

9.1 Introduction

Survey research usually seeks to provide empirical data collected from a population of respondents on a whole number of topics or issues. Sometimes, the data is used to lend support to, or to negate, hypotheses or propositions, but at other times it can simply provide basic information on existing or changing patterns of behaviour. One such area would be the adoption of 'new' media of cable and satellite broadcasting: surveys could identify not only who takes up these media but also why. Surveys can be used to collect data about current attitudes and opinions as well. They are not simply restricted to the collection of information about things, and this makes them a useful method for finding out about individual opinions, attitudes, behaviour and so on towards a whole range of topics and issues.

The basic tool for this kind of research is the questionnaire. It standardises and organises the collection and processing of information. In this way, identical or very similar questions can be asked of a large number of people. But if questionnaires offer a good way of organising the collection of information, they are by no means all of a standard format and they can vary depending on who is being surveyed and in what settings. Questionnaires can be used in a face-to-face situation either in the home or in some public space, usually a street corner. These are the most common types of questionnaire that people come across and they require an interviewer to ask the questions and complete the form. However, questionnaires for surveys can also be handed out, or posted, to individuals or individual addressees for self-completion. Such questionnaires are usually known as 'self-completion' questionnaires because, as their name suggests, they require respondents to complete the questionnaire on their own and in their own time. In addition to these types of questionnaires, some questionnaires are designed to be completed by phone, with the respondent answering questions read out over the phone by the interviewer (see, for example, Lavrakos, 1995). These too are organised around the asking of a standard set of questions.

The type of questionnaire to be used will, in part, be determined by the nature of the investigation and the availability of resources. These factors will also determine the types of questions that will be asked: some simply seek out factual information, others may seek out opinions or attitudes. It follows, therefore, that different types of questions may be needed: closed questions for the factual data, say, and open-ended questions for those instances when the respondent's opinions are sought at length.

In the course of this chapter, we shall see the way that different types of questions can be used in some typical examples from a collection of recent surveys. Figure 9.1 shows part of such a survey.

How such surveys and questionnaires can be organized to maximum effect will be discussed more fully below. It is important though at this point also to bear in mind that in order to obtain useful, and meaningful, information about any of the areas listed above, some consideration must be paid to the question of 'sampling', that is, to the question of just how many respondents to survey. In an ideal situation, it is obviously advisable to survey as many people as possible so that one can say something about not only specific behaviour (or opinions, or whatever) but behaviour that can be generalised to populations as a whole. If that is not done, the information collected will be of limited value, since it can only reflect

1. On average, how many hours a day do you spend watching television?
   _____
2. On a typical day, how many hours do you spend watching:

   Sky News _____
   BBC 1 _____
   BBC 2 _____
   ITV _____
   Channel 4 _____
3. On a typical day, how many hours do you spend watching a cable service such as Leicester Cable? _____
4. Do you think that the licence fee is good value for money? _____

Figure 9.1 Questionnaire design: Example 1

the views or the behaviour of a small number of people, or of collection of people which is not representative or typical of the population under investigation. Techniques of sampling help ensure that an appropriate mix of respondents is surveyed so that the results are seen to reflect more accurately the population at large. (For a detailed discussion of sampling see Moser and Kalton, 1993.)

All these issues: of the type of questionnaire to use, the sorts of questions to ask, how to sample, of resource availability, how to analyse the data, and many others, are bound together in a complicated way. Yet they all concern the researcher before he or she embarks on a piece of research. How to disentangle these issues and to proceed to conduct meaningful research using the survey method will be explored in the following sections.

9.2 Why Conduct a Survey and How to Go About it

The introduction identified some of the key issues that concern any researcher. Despite their connections, it is possible to identify a certain order to them and, hence, to the research itself.

9.2.1 The Development of a Hypothesis

In most circumstances, the first step is to familiarise oneself with the particular subject matter to be investigated. This could involve reading around the subject, becoming familiar with previous research into the specific area of research, and generally gaining an overview of the subject area. This is a crucial preliminary stage and it allows the researcher to begin to define what it is that the survey intends to find out, what new information is to be sought, what sort of gaps in the literature are apparent.

For example, in order to study the diffusion of cable and satellite broadcasting, it is only reasonable to become aware of previous work in this area and of other surveys. Yet, and at the same time, one needs to define more precisely what one's own survey's aims and objectives are and how these differ (or not) from others in the literature. So that if one wanted to explore whether or not those who adopted the 'new' media first came from certain social classes and/or lived in larger households, one would need to seek out previous research into this question at the same time as formulating one's own newer or more up-to-date or contemporary research.

In this example, there are two main hypotheses:

- the 'new' media are first adopted by, say, families in social classes C and D;
- the larger the family, the more likely it is that it will take up the 'new' media.

These hypotheses themselves suggest the sort of questions that need to be asked of cable and satellite households. At the same time, the hypotheses also introduce the idea of obtaining information from as wide a population as possible so as to be able to compare, in the first instance, different types of households: are cable and satellite households different from non-cable and non-satellite households? Are all cable and satellite households the same or are there differences in cable and satellite use between different households? Are cable and satellite households the same in different localities? and so on.

These sorts of questions – and they roll off with alarming rapidity – all relate to the original hypotheses because they all seek to provide information which will enable us, as researchers, to understand and explain similarities and differences. Unless we are able to compare households, for example, we will not be able to say whether our original hypotheses are confirmed or not. Similarly, unless we have collected information from a sufficient number, and different types, of households we cannot say whether what we find out is due to our restricted sources of information. We are not able, in other words, to generalise to the wider population as a whole unless we are confident that our information is obtained from a representative number of households. How one can obtain a representative number of households is briefly discussed in Section 9.4 below.

9.2.2 How to Proceed?

Much of what has been discussed above is perhaps little more than 'common sense' – it provides no more than a general background for the inexperienced researcher. Nor does it provide an insight into the mechanics of embarking on such data collection. How, then, does one proceed?

If the development of a hypothesis was described as the first stage in the research process, the next two stages are

(2) to consider *what* information to collect, and
(3) to consider *who* to collect that information from.

To return briefly to the example of cable and satellite households, it is clear that one will need to collect information *about* cable and satellite households – income, size of households, leisure patterns, and so on – and *from* a variety of cable and satellite and non-cable and non-satellite households. These two stages represent two almost distinct stages in the research process:

- the first focuses on the sorts of questions one would need to ask in order to get hold of the necessary and relevant information;
- the second on the sorts of households that need to be surveyed.

More precisely, the first stage represents the *designing* of the questionnaire, whilst the second refers to the *use* of the questionnaire in an appropriate setting. These two stages will be dealt with separately for convenience, although it will become abundantly clear that in practice they are very closely related: the design of the questionnaire itself takes into account the numbers of householders one will seek to survey. The difficult relationship between these two stages is explored at greater length in the next section.

9.3 What to Ask? Who to Ask?

The basic tool of survey research is the questionnaire. In practice, this will contain all the questions which the researcher seeks to ask of respondents, and it will be organised in such a way as to allow for the efficient and speedy collection of the answers. Once the questionnaire has been finalised it can be administered to the chosen population or to the sample of the population under investigation. One key feature of the survey method, then, is that it does provide researchers with the facility to get a considerable amount of information from a great many people quickly and at a relatively low cost per person. Once a survey has been conducted properly, researchers can feel confident that their statements on, say, public attitudes or public opinions are based on data collected from a large number of people who come to represent the much larger population. In this way, a polling organisation can feel confident that the results from its survey of just over

1 000 people can be generalised and made relevant to a country's population as a whole.

9.3.1 Making Compromises

This research method acknowledges, however, two important considerations which play a major part in the way research work is organised.

(1) As it is impossible to ask an infinite number of questions of literally every person, it is necessary to decide upon a selection of a much more limited number of questions which could elicit the required information.
(2) As it is impossible to survey literally every person, it is important to develop a way of selecting a representative sample of the public under investigation.

Both of these points emphasise the extent to which compromises are an essential feature of research: in the case discussed here, there are compromises with respect to the numbers to be questioned, as well as with respect to the types of questions to be included, or excluded, from the questionnaire.

Such compromises do not necessarily devalue the worth of research. In effect all research methods involve some sort of compromise, since researchers rarely have unlimited resources. For the researcher, though, the issue is whether or not the compromises impact on the quality of the information and whether, in spite of the compromises, the method used for obtaining that information is still preferable to or more suitable than other available research methods.

9.3.2 Some Examples

We can observe these trade-offs by looking at some examples of research where surveys have been used extensively. In the mid-1980s, there was widespread concern about the future funding of British broadcasting and of the BBC in particular. The Peacock Committee (1986) had been set up by the Thatcher government to look at radical alternatives to the licence fee, and the possibility of overhauling the existing structures of broadcasting. The political agenda was fairly transparent, but would the public accept this agenda? Would it agree to the suggestions for possible reforms? What, in other words, did the public *think* about these matters?

The simplest way of finding out what members of the public felt, or wanted, was literally to *ask* them. Unless this was done, it would be difficult to gauge their views. As Morrison (1986) points out, the existence of the Peacock Committee generated considerable interest in surveying public opinions about broadcasting. Between December 1984 and December 1985, questions about the BBC were included in nine different opinion polls. In none of these nine polls were questions asked of fewer than 1 000 people. The Broadcasting Research Unit (BRU) which also looked into public attitudes to broadcasting, interviewed 1 061 people (Morrison, 1986, Appendices I and II).

From this example, which will be looked at in more detail below, we can see how the survey method permits a large-scale investigation of public attitudes. Assuming that no one person was interviewed twice, at least 10 000 people were interviewed about broadcasting matters. And this was done in a very short space of time – the BRU study, for instance, was conducted in a period of two weeks (Morrison, 1986, Appendix II). All these surveys also allow for cross-referencing and for comparing data, itself an important activity in determining the consistency and strengths of public attitudes.

9.3.3 Large-scale or In-depth Survey?

One can see the contrast between the use of the large-scale social survey and more qualitative methods of research in the following two examples drawn from studies of the public understanding of political issues. In the first case, having surveyed over 1000 people properly selected, the researchers can make claims to having obtained a representative sample of the population and can then generalise from their specific findings to the population at large. Admittedly, this does not always work: during the 1992 election campaign pollsters were wrong-footed by respondents who did not always reveal their true voting intentions. Consequently, the findings did not accurately predict the outcome of the election (Worcester, 1992).

Nevertheless, the contrast between the large-scale social survey and more limited exercises in finding out about what people think remains, and is instructive. Doris Graber's work on media effects on American public opinion involved examining both 'news content and audience response' but, with respect to the latter, 'she did a long series of intensive, open-ended interviews with *twenty-one* participants over a year.' (Graber, quoted in Gamson, 1992, p. 179; emphasis supplied). Gamson and colleagues who were also interested in similar questions about the public understanding of contemporary political issues employed a different research method, in this case focus or discussion groups (see Chapter 10), but none the less they were only able to talk to 188 people (Gamson, 1992, p. 13) and over a long period of time.

Both Doris Graber and William Gamson would probably claim that the information they obtained through the use of their different research methods allowed them to explore matters in greater detail than could have been done by the use of a questionnaire. And there is some truth in this. A two-to-three hour discussion with one person or a group of people allows for a better appreciation of the ways in which they perceive contemporary issues, the ways in which they link up abstract ideas such as democracy with concrete examples, and so on. A questionnaire does not usually allow space for an on-going, in-depth investigation of attitudes and opinions. On the other hand, it is easier to generalise from the survey than it is from the limited number of interviews conducted by either Graber or Gamson.

The important point to stress here is that the methods described above are all useful within the different research contexts set out. Moreover, they reflect different sets of problems, and different preferences and solutions. It would, for example, have been difficult for Gamson (1992) to get the sorts of information he wanted through a questionnaire, just as it would have been wasteful for Morrison (1986) to conduct focus groups to gauge the nature of public opinion. The compromises made reflect back on these sorts of considerations. The research method which is used may thus depend on what sorts of information one wants, as well as the nature of the available resources. If one wanted a general idea of the nature of public opinion, a survey would be preferable to a small study of, say, two dozen people. On the other hand, if one was interested in finding out how people make sense of their world, in-depth interviews would be of greater use. A related consideration here is that despite the minimal cost per person, large-scale surveys are initially expensive to put into operation, whereas an in-depth analysis of twenty-one people would be relatively cheap, especially if it was undertaken by the researcher on his or her own.

Nevertheless, it should be obvious that the advantages of the survey method do not overcome its limitations: it cannot go deeply into responses given by respondents, and it assumes that the answers given are, more or less, truthful. In contrast, in-depth interviewing can often pick up on contradictions and play around with responses. Nevertheless, these two methods should not be seen as antagonistic, and they can be combined to good effect. To return to the BRU's study of broadcasting conducted by David Morrison (1986), the survey of 1061 people was supplemented by a series of eighteen focus group discussions. In this way, the broad data obtained from the survey could be supported by more qualitative information which would give depth to bold figures. Again, the subject of resources looms large: a combination of methods may be possible and desirable, but is it feasible given the costs of conducting not only one, but two, research exercises?

It would be wrong, however, to give the impression that all surveys are administered to large numbers of people. Again, the research area may determine the nature and the size of the population to be investigated. A survey of public opinion obviously requires a large sample if it is to produce meaningful results, but there are occasions when even a sample of the size used in relation to the issue of broadcasting in the mid-1980s is unnecessary. Jeremy Tunstall, for example, conducted a study of specialist correspondents in the mid-1960s which was partly based on 295 questionnaires posted to individual journalists. This figure represented the bulk of the London-based specialist correspondents in which he was interested (Tunstall, 1971, Appendix, pp. 292–5).

9.3.4 Ways of Administering Questionnaires

In practice, therefore, any researcher has to make a choice between different research methods. But there are also choices to be made *within* each available research method. There are, for instance, choices to be made between *different ways* of administering *different types* of questionnaires. Assuming that the researcher wanted to carry out a fairly large-scale national survey, this could be done by:

- using a questionnaire administered face-to-face by (an) experienced interviewer/s (or by the researcher himself/herself with or without the help of others);
- having the questionnaire completed via the telephone; or,
- mailing self-completion questionnaire to respondents.

Taking Cost into Account

Which route one chooses will depend largely on the availability of resources. Does one have enough resources to conduct a large-scale survey using a face-to-face questionnaire administered by an army of experienced interviewers or would the available resources only stretch to a questionnaire administered over the telephone by a handful of loosely trained students? Each method has different costs attached to it.

- **The large-scale, face-to-face interview** requires a team of trained interviewers in many locations across the country. Although the cost of such a survey may appear incredibly high, say £20 000 for a 1000 respondent survey, this breaks down to only £20 per respondent. Given the nature and quality of the information provided by those conducting the survey, £20 per respondent may not be considered particularly expensive.
- **The telephone survey** is comparatively cheap – there are no transportation costs – but the questionnaires need to be considerably shorter and sensitive to the needs of the telephone respondent. Resources need to be matched to the sorts of information required.
- **A mailed self-completion questionnaire** is comparatively cheap, since the costs are mainly those of postage, but the absence of contact with respondents may affect the quality of the answers and the completion rates.

As a general rule, then, what type of questionnaire is to be used is closely related to the nature of the survey to be carried out. There are ideal questionnaires and ideal methods but in the context of a carefully funded research project of limited duration, the ideal is soon reduced to the practicable and the feasible.

9.3.5 Some Basic Questions

In practical terms, then, at an early stage of research the researcher has to confront some basic questions:

- What is the nature of the research?
- Is it necessary to canvass opinions and attitudes of the public, or a part of the public, or of a specific group in society such as journalists?

- What methods of research are available to the researcher, and what type of questionnaire would be most appropriate?
- What resources are available for canvassing such opinions?
- What is the preferred method of data collection?

If the answers to these questions suggest that many opinions have to be canvassed, or information from a large number of households has to be collected (to return to our example above), then the easiest way to do this would be to design a questionnaire and to administer it to the population in question. The questionnaire itself will simply consist of a series of questions set out in a logical sequence so as to make the respondent's task easy, as well as to enable the interviewer – if one is being used – to collect the information speedily and efficiently.

But, if a questionnaire is going to be used, it is vital for the researcher to be clear about what sort of questionnaire it is going to be (and this relates to the sorts of respondents from whom one is going to collect information – see Section 9.4). To return briefly to the discussion above, it is possible to collect information from a large number of respondents in a number of different ways: these could include face-to-face interviews, telephone surveys, self-completion questionnaires. Face-to-face interviews can last anything from ten minutes to about one hour; telephone surveys cannot be particularly long and involve no face-to-face contact; self-completion questionnaires are simply posted or delivered by hand and left to be completed by the respondent at his or her convenience. As with telephone questionnaires, self-completion questionnaires should not be particularly long if a high response rate is desired. So how does one decide? There are a number of obvious stages in making a particular choice.

Face-to-Face Surveys

Unless the researcher has a large budget and a great deal of assistance – usually bought by a large budget – it is unlikely that a large-scale, face-to-face survey will be a real option. Even a face-to-face survey of 300 members of the public, itself a reasonable size sample, is likely to prove expensive. The major costs would be staff, to administer the questionnaire as well as to input the data. If one estimates that it may take up to two hours to complete a single, one-hour questionnaire, that is, travel time plus finding a willing respondent, then the full survey would be costed at about 600 person hours (minimum).

Assuming interviewer costs are in the region of £10 per hour, a figure of £6000 for a questionnaire administered to 300 people is not out of place.

Interestingly, the issue of physical distances between interview locations does not always significantly increase research costs. For instance, a national survey or one comparing different regions can be organised and administered from a central location with the interviewing in the different locations being carried out by sub-contracted interviewing agencies. In such circumstances, the costs of carrying out the research are not significantly different from what they would be if it was being carried out in a local city. The main differences in costs would involve postage of questionnaires, payments to the person in charge of local teams, and such like. Notwithstanding these points, the costs of such research are still considerable.

Self-Completed Questionnaires

The best alternative to a professionally administered face-to-face questionnaire, or even to a face-to-face questionnaire administered by a single researcher, would clearly be a self-completion questionnaire. This could be posted to the respondent or dropped through the letterbox if the survey was to be conducted in a small geographic area. A variation on the latter theme would be to deliver each questionnaire personally but to ask respondents to return it in an attached self-addressed envelope. One reason for adopting the latter technique would be that the personal approach used to deliver the questionnaire might ensure a higher response rate. If there is no personal approach, a self-completion questionnaire might go the same way as all the other unsolicited literature that comes through the letterbox.

Self-completion questionnaires, however delivered, have certain problems which cannot easily be overcome. The main one is that they must be fairly short, otherwise the respondent, particularly if he or she is 'an ordinary member of the public' may not be inclined to spend hours filling it in. Interested respondents, such as the 207 journalists who were prepared to complete Tunstall's 22-page questionnaire, may have a higher tolerance level and a longer questionnaire may be possible. This, however, cannot be taken for granted, for although Tunstall had a 70.2 per cent successful response rate (Tunstall, 1971, p. 293), Stephen Hess's questionnaire for American correspondents only achieved a 23 per cent success rate (Hess, 1981, p. x).

Telephone Surveys

These are less common than the other two types of surveys and experience with them is thus fairly limited. They have some obvious advantages in that interviewers can simply go through a list of phone numbers calling up individual households. They are easy to administer and cost-effective. The lack of personal contact, and the sense of soliciting responses – is the interviewer really *not* selling anything? is he or she a genuine researcher? – may be significant disadvantages though. Another significant limitation is the possibility of phoning 'at the wrong time'; or being unable to predict when the right time is. In addition, two further points here are:

(1) cultural factors – differences in how telephones are typically used in different societies,
(2) the availability of telephones – such as the greater number of phone lines in the USA than in Europe, which explains their greater use there.

In most of the examples given above, particularly where one knows well in advance which respondent or household is to be interviewed, it may be advisable to forewarn the would-be respondent that they will be approached in a few days or weeks and asked about certain matters which are currently being investigated. This can be done by letter (see Appendix 9.1) and it does have the advantage of both explaining the research and of introducing the interviewer. It also gives the would-be respondent time to react, write back and refuse to be interviewed or simply rearrange the time and date of the interview. Given that surveys are rarely spontaneous affairs, and that the random sample of households or phone numbers can be chosen in advance, this is not an impossible task and it can have benefits. Obviously, this cannot be done if the respondents are to be selected at random either at street corners or elsewhere.

How Long Should a Questionnaire Be?

What guides the researcher in these matters? Part of the answer is to be found in examples of other surveys, and part of the answer lies in personal experiences. As a potential respondent (in someone else's survey), the researcher is unlikely to be persuaded to engage in a lengthy conversation with a stranger at a street corner, or at home. Similar considerations apply when deciding how long the

Appendix 9.1

Centre for Mass Communication Research
University of Leicester
104 Regent Road
Leicester LE1 7LT

Dear Resident,

The Centre for Mass Communication Research is conducting a survey in the local area. The survey asks about the different types of media people come across in everyday life, both at home and at work. It asks about how often people read newspapers, watch television, go to the cinema or listen to the radio.

Within the next few weeks, one of our interviewers will call on you to explain the survey in more detail. The interviewer will show you an official identification card with a photograph, and will ask to interview one person, selected at random by the interviewer, from among the adults in your household. The information you give will be treated in strict confidence.

We rely on people's voluntary co-operation in carrying out such surveys and so we would be very grateful if you would agree to take part in our survey.

For further information about our organisation or the survey, please contact us by telephoning . . . .

If you feel that you do not wish to take part in this survey, please contact us to let us know. In this way, we can ensure that our interviewer will not call at your address.

Yours sincerely

questionnaire ought to be and some sense of what is appropriate is not out of place.

Experience suggests that a face-to-face survey in a respondent's home lasts on average about 45 minutes. Face-to-face interviews in the street are clearly going to be of a much shorter duration. As for self-completion questionnaires, or for that matter telephone surveys, the respondent may be under less obligation to spend time doing something which is only of tangential interest, if any interest at all, to him or her. So questions need to be precise, clear and short, and the completion of the questionnaire should probably take no more than twenty minutes. These approximations are just that, approximations, but they have a serious point behind them and that is that the researcher must not assume that the respondent will be willing to devote large amounts of time to an unfamiliar and uninteresting research topic. Considerations of respondent interest and time mean, in effect, that the researcher has to make yet more compromises: how many questions can one expect a respondent to answer? Which questions to include and which to exclude? And so on.

These points notwithstanding, it is worth bearing in mind that often members of the public do enjoy the opportunity to air their views and to discuss issues seriously. This is an often overlooked feature of survey work, and respondents, if approached correctly and made aware of the value of their contribution, will often participate actively in the survey and will not feel that they are simply being used by the researcher.

These last considerations lead us on to the more practical questions of, on the one hand, sampling, and, on the other, actual questionnaire design. Having made the decision to undertake a survey, and having made a decision about what sort of survey it is going to be, it is then a matter of deciding on the number of respondents that may need to be interviewed and how to design the questionnaire.

9.4 Sampling: How Many and Whom?

9.4.1 How Many Respondents?

One question which cannot be avoided when it comes to survey research is the simple 'how many respondents do I need?' Some of the examples given above begin to answer this questions in that the total population of respondents may be known – all lobby correspondents, all specialist correspondents – and contactable, but in most other circumstances, it is unlikely that the researcher will know all respondents or will be able to make contact with them all. To return to the cable television example, there are over a million such households spread across the country and it will therefore be essential to sample from this larger population in order to obtain enough respondents who, when taken together, could be treated as representative of the population as a whole. In effect, surveys are usually administered to only a sample of the population under investigation.

There are some basic statistical rules for sampling and these provide useful guides (see, for example, Moser and Kalton, 1971, and 1993). Briefly, there are certain differences between sampling techniques which need to be considered. As Hartmann observes, 'if a sample is appropriately drawn, the results can be used to make projections for the population as a whole. In this case the sample would be said to be *representative*' (1987, p. 15) And there are a number of different ways in which this can be achieved.

Random Sampling

This sample is one in which each person (or address, or news item) has an equal chance of being selected. Moser and Kalton, for example, discuss the use of random numbers to arrive at a random sample (1971, pp. 75–6). However, researchers often use lists such as the electoral register for a particular district to arrive at an appropriate sample for a survey. In such cases, the list provides the researcher with all (or nearly all) the population under investigation. This would be true for a survey of voting behaviour, for example, since all those on the list are of voting age. Such a list will not be appropriate if those who are to young to vote are to be surveyed. None the less, lists can be a useful way of obtaining information about the respondents in question and can form the basis for selection. One common way in which a sample can be selected from a list is to determine how many respondents are to be involved in the survey and to select the appropriate number from that list accordingly. If 10 respondents are to be selected from a list of 100, say, this represents a tenth of the population. The researcher can then choose ten respondents by simply selecting a random number less than 10 and use this as the first number for drawing the sample. In this example, the first number can be 9, and the subsequent numbers can be 19, 29, 39, and so on until the full list is exhausted. Moser and Kalton refer to this method of sampling as 'quasi-random sampling' on the grounds that it differs from simple random sampling since not all members of the population have an equal chance of being selected (1971, p. 76). Moser and Kalton also use the phrase 'systematic sampling from lists' to describe this technique (1971, p. 77).

Stratified Random Sampling

The examples of sampling given above touch on some of the ways in which samples can be drawn, and there are techniques which allow for better ways of ensuring that the sample drawn is more representative of the population under investigation. In such cases allowances are made for significant differences which may exist across the population, or between cities, college students, cabled areas as against non-cabled areas, and so on. In such stratified random samples, a selection is thus made prior to a random sample being drawn. This allows for the appropriate representation of different groups in the population, for example, women as against men, employed as against unemployed, and so on.

Quota Sampling

Quota sampling is another commonly used method in survey work. This is described by Moser and Kalton as 'a method of stratified sampling in which the selection within strata is non-random' (1971, p. 101). An example would be a survey in which the interviewer had to interview a quota of fifty female respondents and where the choice of those fifty respondents would be up to the the interviewer. This type of research is often carried out in town and city centres, sometimes for market research purposes. The problem here would be that the interviewer might select female respondents of a certain type (by dress, say) and so the selection of respondents is carried out in a non-random fashion.

Purposive Sampling

So far, we have touched on the general issues and the different techniques involved in drawing samples. For large-scale surveys, such techniques have been refined in order to achieve a high level of accuracy in design and in projections from the results of the work. But, as Hartmann points out, 'in much research, however, it may be neither necessary nor desirable that samples should be representative.

The object may simply be to test a particular hypothesis or to make comparisons between different groups' (1987, p. 16). He gives the example of work which compared attitudes to black people in 'high immigration' and in 'low immigration' areas. In this work, two such areas were 'identified, suitable schools selected, and quota samples drawn from each school' (1987, p. 16). He refers to this method as 'purposive sampling'.

Resource Considerations

The above brief discussion of sampling touches on the different ways in which researchers turn their attention to questions of how to arrive at a representative sample of the population under investigation. But considerations of resources often force researchers to make decisions about sample size and then ensure that the sample is drawn as accurately as possible. Moser and Kalton describe how their national survey of media habits in the 1950s progressed: ' it was agreed that the sample should be of the order of 3,000–4,000; the actual number finally decided on – 3,000 – was determined mainly by the number of interviewers available and how many interviews could be managed in the time at the survey's disposal' (1971, p. 146). Nevertheless, their sample is clearly much larger than the samples of about 1000 respondents used by Morrison and others which are discussed above. Smaller samples can often be used to provide meaningful data. Golding and Middleton used a ' stratified random probability sample' of 650 respondents in two cities for their study of 'images of welfare' (1982, p. 157). From this last example, we can see that a sample of 300 or so respondents was taken from two cities of some 500 000 residents. As with Hartmann above, the aim was to explore attitudes rather than perhaps make statistically significant projections.

In practice, as we have seen, the sample size can range from a few hundred to over 1000 respondents for a national survey of public opinion; problems usually occur if the sample size is considered to be too small. The crucial point is to attempt to achieve a degree of representativeness of the population at large by ensuring an equal weighting of categories (such as sex, age, income) so as to replicate their proportions in the population at large.

These considerations notwithstanding, the answer to the question of 'how many respondents do I need?' remains somewhat blurred. Statistical considerations can produce certain answers but, as we have also seen, other considerations often intervene. The examples of survey work given above have also offered a range of possibilities of sample sizes ranging from 650 respondents upwards. Such samples require considerable funding and may therefore be beyond the means of the unfunded researcher. In which case, samples will be considerably smaller: research students may be able to work with a sample of between 100 and 300 respondents; undergraduate and postgraduate students with samples of about 30 upwards. In spite of the small sizes of such samples, though, the procedures for ensuring elements of representativeness remain crucial, as do the general rules about questionnaire design (see section 9.5).

9.4.2 Choosing the Respondent

An equally important consideration, and it follows on from the discussion of sampling, is to identify precisely who the chosen respondent is. This, in fact, may be more of an issue where households are selected for surveys which seek to compare different media habits, for example. But who is to be interviewed? Who is the householder and how is that to be decided? One has to be clear about whose opinions are being canvassed. It could be the opinions of the main householder, roughly translated as the wife or husband in the household, or of the first adult to answer the door. The issue is consistency and relevance of the answers to the questions asked. If you are interested in why a particular family subscribes to cable, it may be more appropriate to ask the main householder rather than a child, and so on. If one is interested in family viewing behaviour, all the members of the family could be questioned either together in a group interview or individually using individually designed questionnaires (see Chapter 10).

9.5 Designing the Questionnaire

Before one begins to set out the questionnaire in a logical sequence or in its final form, it is worth spending some time working out what sort of questions need to be asked. This might sound trite but given that compromises are going to have to be made, the researcher will have to decide which questions *must* be included, which questions *have* to be included, which questions *ought* to be included, and any others which *can* be included if space permits.

Certain questions are almost standard in all questionnaires. These are the questions which seek out basic socio-demographic data such as sex, age, education, place of birth, place of work, marital status, family situation, income, media use, and the like. At times, such questions may present difficulties. Questions about personal income, for instance, may be problematic, since respondents may be reluctant to reveal their actual and precise income. One way round this is to offer respondents categories and to allow them to place themselves in the most appropriate category. Instead of simply asking for a bold figure, one can present a category such as '£16 000 to £30 000'. Which questions may be difficult to answer will obviously vary from situation to situation and the researcher must therefore be sensitive to the cultural and other factors which play a dominant part in the lives of different groups of respondents. Importantly, such questions already begin to limit the number of other questions *about the specific research area* which can be posed. They too take up space and time so the amount of either available for other questions is immediately reduced.

9.5.1 Framing Questions

In principle, the subject of questionnaire design appears straightforward. Questions are to be asked of respondents and these may, on the surface, appear unproblematic. But this is not always the case. Two specific problems can arise and both have to be confronted by the researcher:

- question wording
- question order.

Question Wording

This is the simpler problem. Questions should be worded in a clear and simple way and should be set out in such a way as to require the minimum amount of effort on the part of the respondent to answer them. It should also be remembered that the researcher should anticipate the problem of analysing the responses when designing the questionnaire. For ease of computer analysis, all questions should be of a type so that the answers can be easily and speedily converted into a numerical equivalent for computer analysis purposes (or 'coded'). Because there are many types of questions which can be asked, some attention will have to be paid to how the information is to be analysed.

Closed questions, which require simple 'Yes/No' answers or factual data, can be dealt with fairly easily. In the Figure 9.2 Question 1 offers three choices 'Yes/No/Don't know' and can be easily coded as '1/2/3' respectively. If necessary, follow-up questions can also be used to tease out more information, and again sometimes the answers can be easily coded as figures (Question 4). The purpose of asking the follow-up questions is to determine more precisely the nature of the work undertaken and the respondent's place within the hierarchy of work. Without the follow-up questions, the answer 'engineer', for instance, to question 2 would really be quite meaningless. Similar examples can be found in relation to, say, television-viewing or newspaper-reading. Asking respondents which papers they read tells us little about which parts of the newspaper they read. This may, or may not, be significant to the research, but awareness of such pitfalls is one way of ensuring that glaring gaps do not appear in the research.

Open-ended questions, as we shall see, need to be dealt with differently, since they are written in such a way as to give the respondent the opportunity to raise several points. They require a great deal more work

1. Are you currently in full-time work?

   Yes　　　　No **(Go to Question 5)**　　　　Don't know/No answer

2. What is your full-time occupation?

   \- -

3. Can you tell me what sort of things you do?

   \- -
   \- -
   \- -

4. How many people are you responsible for at work?

   \- -

5. If 'No', you are unemployed, retired, house-wife/husband, other?

   \- -
   \- -
   \- -

Figure 9.2　Questionnaire design: Example 2

and the answers need to be analysed prior to coding in order to find out whether there are common elements between them. If there are, then similar responses can be grouped together and given an identical code. Unfortunately, in carrying out such a grouping of responses, slight variations and differences are ironed out altogether.

Question Order

This problem is more difficult to overcome, though here again awareness of it can lead to a better questionnaire and, arguably, better research. Where questions are placed within a questionnaire is as vital a consideration as the wording of those questions. On the one hand, one must avoid the sorts of questions which narrow response choices. No researcher should ask questions which do not allow for proper answers or which direct the respondent in some unintentional (or intentional) way. Such is the problem with the famous 'when did you stop beating your husband/wife?' question: it cannot be answered without convicting the respondent!

At a different level, bad wording and bad placing of questions can be equally disastrous. We can see this in Morrison's study of public attitudes towards the BBC. In comparing his work with the work of others on the same topic, Morrison found discrepancies between the surveys of public opinion which he put down to 'the differential placement' of questions. His point is critical and can best be illustrated by referring to his explanation. If, according to Morrison, one simply asked respondents whether they would like to see adverts on the BBC as a way of reducing the licence fee, then it is highly likely that respondents will answer the question in the affirmative. Self-interest in paying less for the BBC would be a major consideration and respondents are more likely to consider it a relevant factor in answering the question.

If, on the other hand, that same question is preceded by a series of questions which alert the respondent to the consequences of the BBC taking advertising, then the likelihood that simple self-interest will play a significant part in determining the answer is reduced. In this way, where the question is placed both in a numerical sense but also in a contextual way, can impact on the meaning of the question and on the results. Morrison found that though 54 per cent of his sample 'approved of the BBC taking advertisements if it meant reducing the licence fee' only 29 per cent of these respondents – or 14 per cent of the total sample – said 'they would still accept them if it meant less choice of programmes' (1986, p. 3). This contrasted with other research which found 66 per cent and 67 per cent 'approving adverts on BBC TV' (ibid, p. 11).

This example shows how the nature of the questionnaire itself can have an impact on the results produced. In a simple sense, both sets of results are reflecting fairly accurately the respondents' answers but *they are only reflecting answers to the questions asked.* A careful researcher needs, therefore, to be vigilant and alert to the limitations of questionnaires, particularly if the questions are not contextualized in any way.

Pre-testing

One useful way of overcoming some of these potential difficulties is to pre-test or 'pilot' the questionnaire. Briefly, pre-testing the questionnaire involves trying it out on a small number of people in order to see that it works as intended. This is an opportunity to assess the clarity of the questions; to check that respondents understand the questions and answer the questions asked; and to ensure that the interview flows in an efficient and purposeful manner. Pre-testing can iron out many of the potential difficulties which the researcher, who is bound up intimately with the subject, cannot always anticipate.

Using Prior Research

Another way of ensuring that the questions 'make sense' is to build the questionnaire around some other, and prior, research. Both Tunstall and Hess, for instance, spent a considerable time interviewing journalists before they embarked on their field-work. Tunstall interviewed 186 journalists at length prior to designing and sending out his mailed questionnaire. The interviews were an essential part of the process leading up to the design of the questionnaire. For his part, Hess interviewed 150 reporters and these interviews preceded the next stage of the project, the survey.

Spending time thinking about questions, and the sequence of the questions, ensures that, at the end of the day, a better questionnaire is produced: better in the sense of ease of use and of economy; better also in the sense of providing meaningful information collected in a proper way. Once this stage has been completed, once the questions have been selected, there are a number of things which need to be done to ensure that the operationalisation of the questionnaire is carried out with a minimum of fuss and with a maximum of effectiveness. Many of these things can best be described as simple and common-sense arrangements and procedures.

9.5.2 Putting the Questionnaire into its Final Form

Introducing the Researcher

Perhaps the first action in the long process of putting the questionnaire into its final form, is to try to contact all would-be respondents by letter, forewarning them of someone calling round to interview them about the research. As discussed above, this does have many advantages and acts as an introduction for the interviewer. Another simple procedure is to include on the front page of the questionnaire, a short paragraph or two to introduce the researcher and the research (see Appendix 9.1 for an example). This paragraph can be read out to the respondent (or, if it is a self-completion questionnaire, can be read by the respondent) and its function is to introduce the researcher – that is, you are *not* selling double-glazing – and the research in such a way as to authenticate it or to grant it some legitimate/bona fide purpose. Some form of identification may also be of help to the interviewer.

Using Case Numbers

The other items to include as a matter of course on the front page of the questionnaire are space for the name and address of the respondent and a unique case number for each questionnaire. Since the information is likely to be processed in some way, it will become necessary at some point during the research to be able to identify individual respondents, hence the unique case number. This unique case number can have another use if self-completion questionnaires are going to be used. Let us say that 100 questionnaires are to be posted to households in North London. If the questionnaires do not have a unique case number, it will not be possible to track which have gone to which address nor, more importantly, to identify which questionnaires have been returned completed and which questionnaires have not. It would then be impossible to send out reminders or a second batch of questionnaires to non-respondents, because they cannot be identified.

Ordering the Questions

What comes after the front page of the questionnaire will necessarily vary from one questionnaire to another, depending on the subject matter to be investigated (and the questions to be asked). However, it is best to start with a set of straightforward and easy questions. This will put the respondent (and the interviewer) at ease and will be less threatening than a full-scale assault on the respondent's value system. Further questions can then be used to get at the information one requires.

A useful practice which can be adopted at this stage – or at the stage where the questions have been selected and set out in some sort of order – is for the researcher to attempt to justify to himself or herself each question and its place in the questionnaire and to outline in brief what sort of information that question will provide and how it links up with the research tasks. If, while doing this sort of double-checking, it becomes clear that a particular question is of little use or that it will not provide relevant information, then it should be rejected and it can then be replaced by a more appropriate one.

The questions then need to be placed in their proper sequence, and the whole questionnaire set out in such a way as to ease its completion. This requires related questions following one another and a certain amount of routing or directional devices to guide the interviewer and/or respondent. It also requires the inclusion of simple and clearly set out instructions on how to complete the questionnaire! The example in Figure 9.3 illustrates these simple points as they would arise in a self-completion questionnaire.

In this case, there would have been no point asking question 3, and all subsequent questions about television use, of someone who did not have a television set. Directing the interviewer from question 1 to question 7 overcomes the embarrassment of asking irrelevant questions, and speeds things up considerably. A useful device to make life even easier for the interviewer is to place question 7, and those subsequent questions which will be asked of this respondent, on different coloured paper. Indeed, different coloured paper can be used to segment the questionnaire, so making it even easier to navigate one's way through it. (It is also worth noting from this example that there is a space included for 'Don't knows/No answer'. Often respondents do not answer questions or genuinely do not know the answer to questions, so this alternative must always be provided as a matter of course.)

1. How many television sets do you have in your household?
   Please circle the correct answer

1	2	3	More than 3	None	Don't know/ No answer

   If the answer is 'None' or 'Don't know', **please go to question 7 on the green sheet.**

2. Do you have a video recorder in the house?

Yes	No	Don't know/No answer

3. How many hours *a day* do you spend watching television?
   _____ hours

Figure 9.3 Questionnaire design: Example 3

Asking Open-ended Questions

Not all questions need be in simple 'Yes/No' formats. It may, for instance, be desirable to find out some information which cannot be easily compressed into a box or a number *at the interviewing stage*. To ask such open-ended questions in a questionnaire, one has to set the question down followed by an appropriate space for the response to be written. The format for a self-completion questionnaire is shown in Figure 9.4, where respondents are encouraged to write down as many answers as they wish. Such a question will invariably elicit some sort of response. It could be 'because of the choice of channels', 'I wanted to watch local television', 'I like sport' and/or a multitude of other answers. (All these answers could be taken down verbatim.) Once the survey has been completed, it will then become possible to code and analyse all the responses (see below for analysis).

Asking Complex Questions

Unlike the simple questions asking for views, some questions are fairly complex in their construction, in that they may give respondents a choice between varying opinions. One such question can take the form shown in Figure 9.5. Apart from being a mouthful, these choices are not easy to remember, especially when a respondent is then bombarded by a list of statements (some of which may be contradictory, so as to provide a check that the respondent is not giving responses off-the-cuff). One way of overcoming the need for repetition is to provide the respondent with a simple card which lists the five choices. In which case, the preamble to the question can be followed by:

> Please let me know which of the views on this card reflect your opinion . . .

Varying the Questions

These different questions can all be incorporated into the same questionnaire. Questions can be varied to:

- provide a change of rhythm;
- elicit different types of responses to different types of questions; and
- tease out inconsistencies in responses.

For example, by offering alternatives which are obviously contradictory, one can work out if the respondent has simply responded off-the-cuff without thinking about the answers or whether some thought has gone into it. Similarly, if all the boxes in the same column are ticked, then it is clear that either the respondent has not bothered to

4. Why did you decide to subscribe to cable television? *Please write down as many answers as you want.*

Figure 9.4 Questionnaire design: Example 4

5. I am going to read out to you some things which have been said about satellite television. Can you tell me whether you 'strongly agree with the statement', 'agree with the statement', 'neither agree nor disagree', 'disagree with the statement' or 'strongly disagree with the statement'.

Figure 9.5 Questionnaire design: Example 5

think about the answers or has simply given answers so as to conclude the interview speedily.

The End of the Questionnaire

What mix of questions a researcher will adopt depends very much on the area of research and the sort of information to be collected. But, at the end of these questions, it is vital to include the *must* questions identified above. One important reason for putting them at the end is to provide a sort of conclusion to the questionnaire . . . 'Now finally can I ask you a few questions about yourself . . .?'. Another reason is that some of these questions, particularly relating to income, deal with tricky information or information which respondents are not too happy to divulge. If these questions were at the beginning, the respondent might feel ill at ease at having to answer so many personal questions. By placing these questions at the end one ensures that the respondent is less likely to be hostile or to view the questions themselves as too personal – after all, the legitimacy of the research has already been established, and all the questions have already been asked.

9.6 Designing for Analysis

If structuring the questionnaire is intended to be a means of collecting information easily, are there procedures which will make it easier to analyse the information once it has been collected?

The simplest answer is 'Yes', though the answer itself is dependent on an assumption made throughout this chapter, namely, that some form of computer analysis will be undertaken during this research exercise. The assumption is a sensible one for unless one has a mere handful of respondents, any attempt to analyse data in depth is likely to be almost impossible. Even twenty questions asked of ten respondents will generate too much information in the form of relationships, for example, between occupation, income and television-viewing, to be easily manipulated without the use of some form of computer program. So some form of computing analysis is to be recommended and there are now simple packages for the analysis of social science data – SPSS (Statistical Package for the Social Sciences) being the most common – which can be used by almost everyone with a little bit of practice.

9.6.1 Coding

But computer programs for data analysis only deal with numbers, they do not deal with statements, opinions, or long drawn out answers. This means that the researcher needs to convert the answers into individual numbers, and that each of these numbers has to be fed into the computer programme for analysis. There are, therefore, a number of steps that can be taken to expedite this process.

The first step is to include on the questionnaire, and at the right hand margin next to each question, one or more coding 'boxes' into which one can put a number. Each number will come to represent the numerical equivalent of the answer. For example, see Figure 9.6. In the case of question 1, one can code the answer '1' as 1, the answer '2' as 2, '3' as 3, 'None' as 0. The convention is to code 'Don't know/No answer' as 9. So, in that particular box we would place the figure which represents the answer.

This process of coding the answers is also designed to cope with much more complex questions, as has already been suggested. So that even a range of answers to the question about 'how many hours a day do you watch television?' can be dealt with easily. Answers to such a question may include the following: 1 hour, 3 hours, 5 hours, 1.5 hours, and so on. One can either code the answers into appropriate groupings, thus, 'up to 1 hour' can be coded as '1', 'more than 1 hour

1. How many television sets do you have in your household?
   Please circle the correct answer.

   1   2   3   more than 3   None   Don't know/No answer ☐

   If the answer is 'None' or 'Don't know', **please go to question 7 on the green sheet.**

2. Do you have a video recorder in the house?
   Please circle the correct answer.

   Yes   No   Don't know/No answer ☐

3. How many hours *a day* do you spend watching television? ☐
   ____ hours

Figure 9.6 Questionnaire design: Example 6

but less than 3' can be coded as '2', and so on, or one can simply enter the raw data into the computer program and instruct the computer to group and code the answers. The advantage of this latter method is that the raw data can always be retrieved or easily re-coded if necessary. On the other hand, if it was coded prior to being entered into the computer program, one would need to go back to the questionnaires to retrieve the raw data and then input it into the computer program.

This practice of coding can also be applied to all the answers to question 4 in Figure 9.4. Here, similar answers could be grouped together and coded as 1, 2, 3 or more. In this instance, it is best to write down all the answers and then to give them the required code. This can then be used to place the appropriate number in the appropriate box. It is vital, however, that the coding of the answers is such that it is not possible to include an answer under two different codes or that two codes (or more) refer to a similar answer. Coding, therefore, must be as clearly set out as possible to avoid any confusion over the answers given by respondents.

Coding is thus a vital part of the research and all questionnaires should have a coding sheet which parallels in every detail the questions on the questionnaire. This will enable researchers to make sure that the right codes apply to the right answers.

Each box will contain one digit only, but that digit can refer to ten different answers, for example, '1', '2', '3' . . . '9', '0'. If more than ten different answers are likely, it is possible to place two boxes, rather than one, next to a specific question. This will increase the number of available different choices from ten (that is, '0'–'9'), to one hundred (that is, '00'–'99').

9.7 Hitting the Street . . .

All the above stages of the research cannot prepare the researcher for that moment when the first question is asked, when the first door-bell is rung of the first phone-call is made, or when the first questionnaire is mailed. (Some thought ought to be paid at this point to mode of dress as well as the mode of address to be adopted by the interviewer.) Nevertheless, the stages discussed above will ensure that no major or significant unforeseen problems are likely to arise and that the interviewer/s are well prepared to meet most eventualities. Exercising care and being sensitive to the needs and wishes of the respondent is important; one should not invade privacy against the wishes of an individual and one should not be insensitive to the feelings of the respondent. Furthermore, one should be aware of the fact that respondents may be less willing to be disturbed at certain times, for instance, meal times or 'peak hour' television times, than at others. And, with luck and perseverance, the completed questionnaires will start rolling in.

9.8 Summary

Survey work involves:

- Decisions about the area of research.
- Decisions about how best to collect the information required;
- If by interview, then how many people to be interviewed? In a survey of public opinion, it may be necessary to work with a representative sample of the public or a sample which allows for comparison between certain key variables such as sex, age, class. A small-scale survey of public opinion could be carried out with, say, about 300 respondents. If, on the other hand, the research area focuses on a specific area where there are a finite number of respondents, for example, all second year Luton or Cambridge University students, or all lobby correspondents working for national newspapers, then it may be possible to attempt to obtain complete questionnaires for all the individuals concerned); and
- Depending on the above, a decision must be made about what sort of survey to conduct: face-to-face interview, mailed, phone: this decision usually depends on the availability of resources
- Designing the questionnaire
- Pre-testing or piloting the questionnaire
- Revising the questionnaire in view of the results from pre-tests or pilots
- Analysis of data

References

Gamson, W. (1992) *Talking Politics* (Cambridge University Press).

Golding, P. and S. Middleton (1982) *Images of Welfare* (Oxford: Martin Robertson).

Hartmann, P. (1987) *Media Research: Aspects of Method*, Communication and Education, unit 21, block 6: 'Communication, media and society' (Milton Keynes: Open University).
Hess, S. (1981) *The Washington Reporters* (Washington: The Brookings Institution).
Lavrakos, P. (1995) *Telephone Survey Methods* (London: Sage).
Morrison, D. E. (1986) *Invisible Citizens. British public opinion and the future of broadcasting* (London: Broadcasting Research Unit monograph/ John Libbey).
Moser, C. and G. Kalton (1993) *Survey Methods in Social Investigation*, 2nd edn (London: Dartmouth).
Peacock Committee (1986) *Report of the Committee on Financing the BBC*, chaired by Prof. A Peacock (London: HMSO) Cmnd. 9824.
Tunstall, J. (1971) *Journalists at Work. Specialist correspondents: their news organizations, news sources, and competitor colleagues* (London: Constable).
Worcester, R. (1992) 'So near . . . so far', in A. H. Wood and R. Wood, *The Times Guide to the House of Commons*, p. 289 (London: HarperCollins).

10

Media Audiences: Focus Group Interviewing

10.1 Introduction

Discovering *how* audiences make sense of media messages is not easily done through survey research. Survey research is good at providing a snapshot of audience beliefs, attitudes and behaviour – the *what* of audience–media relationships – but is much less suited for telling us about the *why* or *how* of such relationships. For examining the dynamics of what experiential knowledge and frames of interpretation audiences bring to bear in their use of media content, what role media use has in the everyday life of audiences, or how audiences use the media as a resource in their everyday lives, it is necessary to turn to more qualitative methods, which allow us to observe in a more 'natural' setting than that of the survey or the laboratory experiment how audiences relate to media (both as technologies and as content).

Participant observation is clearly one method meeting these requirements, but problems of access often rule out any extended use of this method for the study of audiences in their 'natural' home environment (Silverstone, 1991). This is not to say that participant observation in the home setting is impossible: indeed, a number of media audience studies have successfully observed media use in a family setting, including Hobson's (1982) study of audiences for a popular British soap opera, Morley's (1986) study of *Family Television* in Britain, and several studies reported in *World Families Watch Television* (Lull, 1988), including a study of video and television in the American family by Lindlof and his colleagues (Lindlof, Shatzer and Wilkinson, 1988).

Semi-structured individual interviews or semi-structured group interviews are research approaches which allow the researcher a potentially much richer and more sensitive type of data on the dynamics of audiences and their relations to media than the survey. At the same time, these approaches are comparatively cheap (if time-consuming), and they are not burdened by the resources and lengthy access negotiations often needed for participant observation.

In this chapter, we will introduce the focused group interview as a method for studying media audiences. While the individual in-depth interview and the focused group interview produce similar data in many respects, our reasons for focusing on the group interview are twofold:

(i) group interviews are more cost-efficient than individual interviews – a wider range of people can be interviewed within the same limitations of time, resources, and research money; and
(ii) groups allow the researcher to observe how audiences make sense of media *through conversation* and interaction with each other.

10.2 Brief History

The focused group interview has gained widespread popularity as a research method for studying media audiences. With the rise of 'reception studies' in media research during the 1980s, it became a key component of the arsenal of approaches deployed by communications and media researchers. The history and origins of the method, however, extend much further back in time, as well as across to many other fields of study.

In a delightful account of personal history, Robert Merton (1987), in his article on the focused interview and focus groups, traces the conception and development of the method back to the early 1940s. He refers to radio audience research at the University of Columbia with Paul Lazarsfeld at the Columbia Office of Radio Research, and to research on film audiences, notably in Merton's work on Army morale-boosting and training films for the Research Branch of the United States Army Information and Education Division. Robert Merton and Patricia Kendall's article 'The focused interview', published in 1946 (Merton and Kendall, 1946), and the book-length treatment published a decade later (Merton, Fiske and Kendall, 1956),[1] are generally reckoned to mark the birth of the method for the study of media audiences and communication processes.

Despite the early origins in the social sciences, it was in commercial marketing research rather than in sociology and related disciplines that the method became widely used in the next few decades. Not until the late 1970s and early 1980s did the approach experience a renaissance in the social sciences, bringing with it renewed examination of its methodological merit and applications (Morgan and Spanish, 1984; Morgan, 1988; Krueger, 1988; Stewart and Shamdasani, 1990; Morgan, 1993), although, interestingly, few of these more recent accounts of the method have said much about its use in media and communication research.

The renaissance, in the last fifteen to twenty years, of the focused group interview as a method for media and communication research relates to the turn away from the traditional effects paradigm, and variations thereof which include such predominantly survey-based approaches as cultivation analysis, agenda-setting, and uses and gratifications research. The turn in the media audience research of the 1980s and 1990s was away from questions about media *influence* and *effects* on audience behaviour and beliefs, and toward concerns with how audiences *interpret*, make sense of, use, interact with, and create meaning out of media content and media technologies. In the words of one prominent media scholar:

> The form which 're-conceptualization' took here involved an attempt to carry over cultural studies' alertness to discursive and symbolic processes into an analysis of the organization and forms of viewing activities rather than those of media texts themselves. 'Influence', whatever its strength and direction, had to work through meaning, and it was to the formal and social complexity of meaning-production that the new research addressed itself. Meaning was seen as *intra-textual* (requiring analysis of textual structures), *inter-textual* (requiring analysis, among other things, of genres and relations between them) but also finally and decisively *interpretative* (requiring research into the situated practice of 'receptive' understanding). (Corner, 1991, p. 270)

For many of the audience 'reception' studies of the 1980s the choice of focus group discussions, participant observation, and related ethnographic methods marked a deliberate and conscious rejection of traditional quantitative approaches. But as Schlesinger *et al.* (1992) have eloquently argued, while there are good reasons for adopting 'qualitative' approaches in the study of media audiences, there are no grounds for making the qualitative emphasis 'into an article of faith that excludes any attempt at quantification' (p. 8). Schlesinger *et al.* advocate – and in this they reflect a more general trend in the new audience research (see, for example, Schrøder, 1987; Höijer, 1990; Livingstone, 1991) – the use of quantitative methods *in combination with* qualitative approaches and techniques.

10.3 When to Use Focus Group Interviews

As in all research, the choice of method should principally reflect the purposes and objectives of the study to be carried out, although other more pragmatic factors, such as convenience, available resources, and time will often play a role in determining how to approach a particular problem.

Focus group interviews may be the single substantive mode of data-collection in a piece of research; but more frequently the approach has been used in conjunction with other, complementary, types of data-collection. In media research, it has notably been used together with questionnaires, observation (ethnography), and analyses of media content. Likewise, the use of focus groups may be appropriate at different points in the progression of a study: they may be used at a very early stage for exploratory purposes, to explore which issues and topics people are concerned about within a particular domain or field, and how they talk about these issues. Such exploratory data will help in the construction of relevant questions for a larger survey study using questionnaires. In this respect, focus group interviews are invaluable both in terms of providing pointers to relevant issues, themes, and concerns, but much more specifically and crucially, in terms of ensuring that survey questions deploy vocabularies and reference frames which resonate with those of the respondents who are to be surveyed. Alternatively, a survey study or a content analysis of media may have drawn attention to a number of topics that require further and more detailed examination through the use of focus group discussions.

Discontent with the 'passive' audience view and with the stilted view of media influence seen as the defining characteristics of traditional approaches to the study of media audiences, the new 'reception' and ethnographic audience studies of the 1980s and 1990s have been keen to employ methods of investigation which allowed for a more active and meaning-constructive role for audiences. To many of the qualitative audience studies of the 1980s and early 1990s, the choice of focus group interviews as a method of investigation has thus been governed by the desire to examine, through a more 'natural' setting and frame than that of the survey or experiment, how media audiences relate to, make sense of, use, negotiate, and interpret media content:

> The first priority was to determine whether different sections of the audience shared, modified or rejected the ways in which topics had been encoded by the broadcasters. (Morley, 1980, p. 23)

> the aim was to discover how interpretations were collectively constructed through talk and the interchange between respondents in the group situation. (Ibid., p. 33)

> Specifically, it is a study of patterns of *involvement* in an episode of the world-wide hit *Dallas*, focusing on how viewers discuss the programme in nearly natural settings. (Liebes and Katz, 1986, p. 152)

> we wished to include as a primary element of our study an investigation into how viewers made sense of, and evaluated, the programmes we chose for analysis. (Corner, Richardson and Fenton, 1990, p. 47)

While the qualitative depth sought by these studies could equally well have been obtained through in-depth individual interviews, there are at least two important reasons for choosing the focus group discussion over the individual interview as a method of investigation.

The first reason concerns the argument that the generation of meanings and interpretations of media content is 'naturally' a social activity, that is, audiences form their interpretations of media content and their opinions about such content through conversations and social interaction:

> Why groups? By choosing the method of focus-group interviews . . . we were, in effect, operationalizing the assumption that the small-group discussion following the broadcast is a key to understanding the mediating process via which a program such as this

> enters into the culture. That such discussions take place – albeit casually and sporadically – we now know from the evidence in the background questionnaires. Further confirmation comes from the discussions themselves, during which participants refer to prior conversations about the program and its characters. (Liebes and Katz, 1990, p. 28)

The second, and perhaps more pragmatic, reason for choosing focus group discussions over individual interviews, is that they offer dynamics and ways – not available in individual interviews – of eliciting, stimulating, and elaborating audience interpretations. It is precisely the group dynamics and interaction found where several people are brought together to discuss a subject, that is seen as the attraction of this mode of data-collection over individual interviews:

> The hallmark of focus groups is the explicit use of the group interaction to produce data and insights that would be less accessible without the interaction found in the group. (Morgan, 1988, p. 12)

> Focus groups impel participants to think about and stay with the subject being discussed in a way which is surely *not* natural. The analytic abilities revealed in some of these discussions is probably far beyond the level of everyday discussion of television and is probably inspired by the seriousness with which participants' opinions are solicited. Group members were asked to generalize about the themes, messages, and characters, as well as about the functions of such programs for the viewer, at levels of abstraction which are unusual in gossip. Thus, the focus group was a catalyst for the individual expression of latent opinion, for the generation of group consensus, for free-associating to life, and for analytic statements about art. But even these more formal discussions have an informal thrust; in fact, a major part of our analysis is devoted to the casual commuting in the focus groups between the story and real life, where the story serves as a basis for interpreting and evaluating life and vice versa. The group context induces the expression of such latent thoughts. Negotiation within the group then produces an awareness of others' thoughts. The result is an incremental input into the world view of the community. (Liebes and Katz, 1990, pp. 28–9)

Gamson (1992) further spells out the advantages of focus groups over individual interviews and surveys as a method for understanding how people socially construct meaning about public issues:

> 1. To talk about issues with others, people search for a common basis of discourse . . .
> 2. Focus groups, compared to survey interviews, allow us to observe the natural vocabulary with which people formulate meaning about the issues. . . .
> 3. Through challenges and alternative ways of framing an issue, participants are forced to become more consciously aware of their perspective. (Gamson, 1992, pp. 191–2)

Of course, some of the reasons *for* using focus-groups may also be used as arguments *against* this approach. Some individuals inevitably exert more influence than others in a group situation, to the extent that they may begin to dominate the discussion (although this can often be countered and minimised by a skilful moderator, see below). Group discussions also tend to work towards 'consensus' ground – dissenting views may be marginalised and disagreement among participants becomes less visible as the group pressure moves discussion toward a common frame. These are well-known processes. Both Gamson (1992) and Liebes and Katz (1990), however, argue that these processes make the group-discussion a more 'natural' form of data-generation:

> Group dynamics are such that opinion and participation are *not* equally weighted; some people have disproportionate influence. But real life is like that: opinions are not as much the property of individuals as public-opinion polling would have us think. Opinions arise out of interaction, and 'opinion leaders' have disproportionate influence. (Liebes and Katz, 1990, p. 29)

Though the idea of getting groups of people together to 'talk about media content' may sound like a productive way of generating 'rich', 'natural', 'detailed', and 'complex' data about how people interpret, accommodate, negotiate, and use media content, the reality is often less rosy. People do not 'naturally' volunteer elaborate interpretations of media content, nor do people necessarily consciously think about, let alone articulate, how they *use* media content in their daily lives:

> That television programmes are topics of conversation is obvious, but do we really elaborate our interpretations here? Relying on everyday experience it seems more realistic to suppose that we discuss television programmes very briefly and at a superficial level, as when we talk about the weather. In news viewing, for instance, Levy (1977) has shown that some viewers even use television news to provide them with items for small talk or chit-chat, accordingly not elaborations of their interpretations. (Höijer, 1990, p. 34)

Focus group discussions, in order to produce 'useful' data, require active input and structuring on the part of the convenor or moderator (see below, for more detail about this role). Indeed, the 'focus' of the discussions needs to be set very clearly, and the framework within which participants are being asked to articulate their views and comments needs be clear (although discussions would often work gradually from loose and unstructured talk toward the more specific areas of interest to the researcher).

10.4 Steps in Focus Group Research

The steps involved in conceptualising, carrying out, and analysing focus group discussions are at a general level very similar to those of survey research (see Chapter 9) or content analysis (see Chapter 5). They involve definition of the research problem, creation of the research instrument (in this case an interview guide), sampling, pilot-testing, and so on. One of the clearest expositions yet of the steps involved in focus group research is that offered by Stewart and Shamdasani (1990), see Figure 10.1.

Here we will discuss some of these steps in more detail and with reference to and illustrations from media audience research which has used focus groups.

10.4.1 Sampling and Recruitment of Groups

> Focus groups are conducted to obtain specific types of information from clearly identified sets of individuals. This means that individuals who are invited to participate in a focus group must be able and willing to provide the desired information and must be

> representative of the population of interest . . . A focus group is not just a haphazard discussion among people who happen to be available; it is a well planned research endeavor that requires the same care and attention associated with any other type of scientific research. (Stewart and Shamdasani, 1990, p. 51)

That 'individuals who are invited to participate in a focus group must be able and willing to provide the desired information and must be representative of the population of interest' may seem obvious enough, but it is important to note that, unlike surveys, the total number of participants in a focus group study is comparatively small; it is therefore essential that the sampling of groups takes careful note of any particular demographic, occupational or other dimensions, along which the researcher is expecting or hypothesising that differences will occur.

Problem Definition/Formulation of the Research Question

Identification of Sampling Frame

Identification of Moderator

Generation and Pre-Testing of Interview Guide

Recruiting the Sample

Conducting the Group

Analysis and Interpretation of Data

Writing the Report

Figure 10.1 Steps in the design and use of focus groups (Stewart and Shamdasani, 1990, p. 20).

Indeed, focus group studies in media research have rarely sought to obtain groups representative of the general population as such. Rather, they have selected groups according to specific dimensions thought to be of significance to the way in which people use and interpret media content. Additionally, audience studies using focus group methodology have often aimed to draw participants from 'naturally' existing groups or communities, which exist independently of the research:

> Our methodology was designed to explore the ways in which social interaction mediates audience understandings. Therefore, instead of working with isolated individuals, or collections of individuals drawn together simply for the purposes of the research, we elected to work with pre-existing groups – people who already lived, worked or socialized together. (Kitzinger, 1993, p. 272)

Likewise, Corner and his colleagues chose their principal participant groups from already 'pre-constituted' 'interest groups':

> We anticipated that the main political parties would have reason to be interested in this topic (even though nuclear energy is not a simple partisan issue). We accordingly obtained the participation of respondent groups from the local Labour, Conservative and SLD parties. The net was extended to groups from the local Rotary club, one from the Labour and Trade Union Resource Centre of unemployed people, a women's discussion group, a group of comprehensive school pupils, a group of medical students, some Friends of the Earth members and a set of workers at the Heysham nuclear power plant. (Corner *et al.*, 1990, pp. 48–9)

Burgess and Harrison (1993) in their research on the circulation of claims and the role of media in relation to a controversial environmental issue, complemented a general household survey with a focus-group study involving just two groups. However, each of these groups was convened not once but six times over a half-year period with a view to examining how claims developed during this period. They deliberately chose one group consisting of local people who were generally supportive of the development in question, and another group consisting of local people who were 'all paid-up members of nature conservation and environmental organizations' (p. 202), and who were, by implication, against the controversial development examined in the study.

In a study of press coverage and public understanding of the new genetics, Durant and his colleagues (Durant, Hansen and Bauer, 1996) chose a combination of types of groups. In addition to a number of 'general population' groups, they chose groups consisting of participants who, through their interest group membership or occupation/profession, had 'specialist' knowledge or concerns (moral, legal, health, and commercial) relevant to the subject under investigation.

Liebes and Katz were interested in examining why the American television serial *Dallas* was almost universally popular. More specifically, they wished to examine whether and how audience interpretations of and involvement with the serial varied depending on the cultural background of the viewers:

> Thus, we chose four widely different groups within Israeli society to compare with each other, with second-generation Americans in Los Angeles (as representatives of the audience for whom the original program was intended), and with Japanese in Japan (where the program failed). In the choice of the Israeli groups, in particular, we hoped to be able to demonstrate that the nature of involvement in the program, in spite of its universal popularity, nevertheless varies with the social and cultural background of the viewers. (Liebes and Katz, 1990, p. 21)

> All told, the sample consisted of sixty-six groups of (usually) six persons of like ethnicity, age, and education . . . for a total of some 400 participants. The analysis involved ten groups of Israeli Arabs, sixteen groups of Israelis of Moroccan origin, ten groups of recent immigrants from Russia to Israel, six groups from kibbutzim, ten groups from the Los Angeles area, and eleven groups from greater Tokyo. (Ibid., p. 24)

Like Corner *et al.* (1990), Philo (1990), in his analysis of media coverage and public beliefs relating to the British miners' strike of 1984–5 also aimed for groups which were ' "natural" in the sense that they had some existence prior to the research project' (p. 22) although at the same time 'the people did have to be selected such that they could highlight possible differences in perception caused by factors such as class and cultural background' (p. 23). Philo brought together a total of 169 people in sixteen groups, which fell into four main categories: (1) groups with a special knowledge or experience of the strike (for example, miners, police); (2) occupational groups; (3) special interest groups; and (4) residential groups.

> This selection of groups made it possible to hold constant some key variables such as regional area, while varying others such as class/cultural background. Sometimes these variables could be compared in the same group. (Philo, 1990, p. 23)

If the objectives of the research allow that participants be recruited from naturally existing groups or communities, this clearly makes the task of finding, contacting and engaging the desired types of participants a great deal easier than drawing participants completely at random. Constituencies where participants can be drawn from existing lists – provided access is granted – include for example: local, regional, or national pressure groups, consumer organisations, special interest groups, or party political organisations who can be contacted through their administrative offices or headquarters, and who may provide access to their membership lists; large employers, companies, trade associations, and trade unions, who, likewise, may allow access to directories of employees and members; public institutions, associations (for example, viewers and listeners' associations, fan clubs, parents' groups, women's associations, ethnic societies, religious societies, housing associations), and professional societies (for example, of doctors, scientists, solicitors, accountants, journalists).

Where the types of participants sought after do not belong to existing groups or communities, or cannot be drawn from pre-existing directories or membership lists, it is necessary to resort to the same kinds of sampling or recruitment methods normally used in survey research. These include contacting people in shopping centres, 'on the street', or in other public places;[2] 'advertising' for participants on public notice boards in work places, community centres, or shops – or even through advertisements in local or regional media outlets; or contacting people by post (perhaps by random sampling of names and addresses from electoral registers) or by telephone.

10.4.2 Numbers of groups and participants

How many groups? How many participants in each group? There is no single right answer to either of these two questions. The number of groups will depend on the aims of the research and on available resources. If focus groups are used merely for exploratory purposes and/or for generating ideas for a larger – perhaps survey-based – study, then as few as two, three, or four groups may be sufficient (Hedges, 1985; Morgan, 1988). Where focus groups form a central and more substantive part of the data-collection of a study, it would generally be difficult to justify fewer than six groups. As indicated by Morgan (1988), one approach is to vary 'the number of groups according to whether the additional discussions are producing new ideas' (p. 42). This strategy was followed by Livingstone and Lunt

(1993) in their study of audience interpretations of television talk show programmes: 'The number of focus groups was determined by continuing until comments and patterns began to repeat and little new material was generated' (p. 181). Livingstone and Lunt thus conducted twelve focus group discussions with a total of sixty-nine participants in groups of between four and eight people.

The single main factor (cost and resources notwithstanding) in deciding on the number of groups must be the types of comparisons across different group or population characteristics specified by the objectives of the research. Thus, if the aim is to examine how audience interpretations of a television programme vary according to social class, sex, age, or according to interest group membership, profession or occupation, or life-style, then there must be sufficient groups to represent these dimensions or populations.

> One important determinant of the number of groups is the number of different population subgroups required. The more homogeneous your groups are in terms of both background and role-based perspectives, the fewer you need . . . [I]f there are several distinct population segments in the groups that you are studying, you may want or need to run separate groups in each, e.g., groups composed entirely of men and run separately from groups composed entirely of women. Running a minimum of two groups in each distinct segment will obviously increase the total number of groups (Morgan, 1988, p. 2)

The number of groups used in the media audience studies of the 1980s and 1990s has varied considerably. Morley (1980), in his now classic study of audiences for the current affairs programme *Nationwide* interviewed twenty-nine groups (although three of these were omitted from his analysis due to faults in the tape-recording) of, mainly, between five and ten people. Morley's later study, *Family Television* (1986), involved eighteen families. Liebes and Katz's (1990) study of cultural differences in the interpretation of *Dallas* comprised sixty-six groups of, usually, six participants (three married couples) in each group. Kitzinger's (1993) study of audience understandings of AIDS involved fifty-two groups with a total of 351 participants, and group sizes generally in the region of between four and nine participants. In their study of women and television violence, Schlesinger *et al.* (1992) conducted fourteen group discussions with a total of ninety-one women (with group sizes of between five and nine participants).

Durant *et al.* (1993) conducted twelve focus group discussions with groups of between seven and nine participants.

As indicated by these examples, the number of participants in each group may vary considerably – from as few as two people to as many as twenty-five (one group in Kitzinger's 1993 study of AIDS representations and interpretations). There also, however, appears to be – in the audience studies mentioned here – a general consensus that the optimum group size for focus group discussions is in the region of between five and nine people (Morgan, 1988, recommends between six and ten people).

The cost advantage of using group discussions in preference to individual interviews clearly deteriorates with very small groups. With fewer than six participants in each group it may also be difficult to generate and maintain a dynamic and lively discussion. Conversely, larger groups, while more cost-efficient and less likely to be atypical, also have distinct disadvantages. The larger the group, the more likely is it that less vocal and less confident participants will be marginalised and will tend to 'hide' behind the more articulate members. It becomes more difficult for the moderator to keep the discussion focused, and to avoid participants speaking at the same time (Hedges, 1985).

There seems to be some consensus then, that focus groups should be no larger than ten to twelve participants (Hedges, 1985; Morgan, 1988; Krueger, 1988) and that the ideal group size is between six and ten.

10.4.3 Arranging Participation

Once the appropriate type of participants have been identified, these should be contacted and if – possibly after additional screening questions – they are indeed the type of participants looked for, they should be formally invited to participate in a group discussion. At the point of invitation, prospective participants should of course be told in general terms what the purpose of the focus group discussion is, where it will take place, with whom, and who the researchers are and what they represent.

If an incentive is offered (most people are rightly reluctant to give up what could be anything between 1 and 3 hours of their time – in some studies, a whole day [Schlesinger *et al.*, 1992]), it should also be made clear at this point what the incentive is and how and when it will be paid. Incentives can take numerous forms, although a cash payment tends to be the most widely acceptable form of incentive: Durant *et al.* (1993) in their focus group study carried out in 1993 paid each participant a flat fee of £10 plus travel expenses for interviews lasting between one and two-and-a-half hours; Schlesinger *et al.* (1992) paid participants £20 plus all expenses (including travel, lunch, and child care) for participation in a full-day session; Press (1991) paid each participant $25 for sessions lasting between two-and-a-half and three hours.

If the participants who have been approached agree to participate, it is important to send a written confirmation of their agreement to participate along with confirmation of the location, date, and time of the focus group. It is normally advisable to contact participants again immediately prior to the date of the focus group interview – say, the day before – to remind them and to give any final details about how to get to the location.[3]

10.4.4 Interview Setting or Location

The location chosen for focus group discussions will vary, depending on the purpose of the research, convenience, and practical feasibility. Liebes and Katz (1990) held their focus group discussions in people's homes – this being important both to the purposes of the research and in terms of bringing together families who knew each other. Gamson (1992) likewise stressed the need to involve people who knew each other for discussions on the 'participants' turf rather than in a bureaucratic setting' (p. 193). Consequently, Gamson's focus group discussions were held in the homes of individual participants. Durant *et al.* (1996) held the focus group discussions in the private homes of people who specialised in making their homes available, for a fee, for such purposes. This approach had the advantage that a non-threatening, non-bureaucratic setting combined with a 'homely' atmosphere in which the host served light refreshments to the participants.

In contrast, Schlesinger *et al.* (1992) held the majority of their focus group discussions in a university setting. As their subject of study included 'domestic violence toward women' and a large proportion of their focus group participants were women who had been at the receiving end of domestic violence, a domestic setting would clearly not have been appropriate for the focus group discussions, let alone conducive to 'open' and 'frank' discussion.

While a domestic setting may be a more 'natural' location than an institutional setting (for example, a university department, an office in the work-place of a professional group) for focus group discussions, the choice of setting always needs to be considered in relation to the nature of the topic or issue to be discussed, and practicality. It needs to be borne in mind that the setting – any setting – inevitably exerts a 'framing' influence on the nature of participants' responses and on the group discussion as a whole.

With the groups selected and convened we come to the core part of the process, the focus group discussion itself. There are two key components to be considered here:

- the moderator role and
- the interview guide.

10.4.5 The Moderator Role

The role of the moderator will vary depending on the subject of analysis, the type of response which is sought, and the nature of the participants. It is in the nature of focus group discussions that the role of the moderator or facilitator is essentially to 'facilitate', 'moderate', and 'stimulate' discussion among the participants, not to 'dominate', 'govern', or unduly 'lead' such discussion. In practice, however, the degree to which the moderator plays an active steering role is a sliding scale from continuous active intervention to a much less active, opaque background role. Typically, the principal roles of the moderator are to ensure that:

- the issues, topics, and foci outlined in the interview guide are covered in the course of discussion (this task includes managing the time spent on each topic),
- a reasonable balance of contributions is maintained (that is, no single individual is allowed to commandeer and dominate the group), and
- the discussion is kept on course and not allowed to drift off in directions of little or no relevance to the study.

However, these roles can be fulfilled in either more or less active ways. Gamson (1992), for example, was keen to minimise the facilitator's intervention:

> To encourage conversation rather than a facilitator-centered group interview, the facilitator was instructed to break off eye contact

> with the speaker as early as politeness allowed and to look to others rather than responding herself when someone finished a comment. (p. 17)

Other scenarios, and other types of participants (such as children), may call for a more actively steering role of the moderator.

In media and communications research it is often the researcher himself or herself who acts as the moderator for group discussions. This has the distinct advantage that the moderator is fully aware of the nature of the research and its objectives, although it also carries with it the danger that the moderator may be tempted to steer responses in the directions which best fit his or her pre-conceived expectations of the research. If the moderator is someone other than the researcher(s), it is important that he or she is appraised fully of the aims of the research, the topics or issues to be covered, the extent of active steering and probing required. These requirements should be clearly stated in the interview guide (see below).

Depending on the nature of issues or topics to be discussed and on the type of participants, it may also be desirable to specify particular socio-demographic and other characteristics of the moderator. Thus, the gender and age of the moderator will be important where groups of teenagers are brought together to discuss their sexual behaviour. There may be types of issues and group constellations where it would be desirable to match the 'race' and ethnicity of the moderator with those of the participants in the groups. Social class matching could also be important. Such specific requirements notwithstanding, the successful moderator will more generally be a person who has such difficult-to-define attributes as the ability to establish rapport with group participants, the ability to put participants at ease, the ability to stimulate discussion among participants rather than with the moderator himself or herself, and the ability to keep the discussion gently on course without imposing an overly restrictive agenda or format on the participants.

10.4.6 The Interview Guide

Though a major strength of the focus group discussion, compared with a survey questionnaire study, is precisely its openness and the flexibility it offers for participants to respond, at length, in their own 'language' and on their own terms, this characteristic should not be confused with a 'free-for-all' 'unstructured chaos'. Focus group discussions must have a 'focus'. It is the job of the moderator or facilitator to ensure that the discussion in a focus group stays focused on the subjects or issues relevant to the research, but it is the job of the researcher to draw up – on the basis of the definition of the research problem and issues or phenomena to be investigated – a guide or manual for the moderator to work from and follow.

The focus group interview guide is principally a 'menu' of the topics, issues and areas of discussion to be covered, but, in addition to simply listing these, it should also give directions as to:

- the sequence of topics/issues to be covered;
- the nature and extent of prompting and probing;
- the nature and use of visual or verbal aids, and the points during the course of a group discussion where these should be introduced.

One of the main reasons why it is important to have a clear interview guide, and to ensure that it is followed consistently through all the focus groups involved in a study, is to enable comparisons between groups. Focus groups, as we have seen above, are often constituted with a view to examine variations relating to the particular socio-demographic, experiential, professional, or other characteristics of the participants. Only if the topics or issues discussed across different groups are the same, and only if the way in which discussions progress and are conducted is consistent, is it possible to say with some confidence that whatever differences and variations occur are the product of factors and characteristics other than those of the prompting used or manner of moderator–intervention.

Focus group discussions in communication research generally follow a 'funnel-approach', that is, they progress from the general to the more specific, from non-directive questions (which allow participants to choose their own frame of reference and articulate their thoughts) toward more focused questions, requiring participants to discuss particular specific aspects of 'the problem'. In studies of media audiences, the start of a group discussion would often consist of the group viewing a television programme (or an excerpt, or an edited compilation); this is then followed by asking the participants in very general and vague terms 'what they thought about the programme' or 'what the programme was about', thus giving the participants the chance to define not only the 'frame of reference' for discussion of media content, but also, of course, the types of issues seen as important *and* the language for discussion. The mode of progression followed by Schlesinger *et al.* (1992) is typical for research in this field:

> The format for programme discussions was broadly standardised, although where necessary, due allowance was made for specific issues raised within a given group. After filling in the short questionnaire on immediate reactions, the discussion of each programme opened with a request for initial reactions and responses. Group members were invited to offer judgements on specific aspects of the programme: for example, whether they liked or disliked the programme, regarded it as 'good' or 'bad', or found it entertaining. By permitting the initial reaction to remain open, we sought to elicit the themes and issues which were most salient for group members. Initial reactions were followed by more focused discussions guided by a series of questions posed by the researcher, who acted as moderator . . . Although group members were free to raise any topic they wished, the researcher raised a standardised set of issues in each session, thus ensuring a degree of comparability across groups (p. 28)

The sequence typically followed in media audience research using focus group interviews is that of, first, exposure to selected media material (a television programme, a film, selected newspaper coverage, and so on), followed by, second, undirected general discussion, moving gradually – under the moderator's direction – toward more specific foci, issues, topics, and questions. This, however, need not be the sequence. In particular, it will not be the sequence in studies which aim in the first instance to establish how different groups of people talk and think generally about particular issues before introducing particular media content into the discussion. Press (1991), for example, aimed first to establish how working-class and middle-class women talk about morality and abortion, and second, to examine how the viewing of a television programme with an abortion storyline influenced the language and mode of discussion employed by the groups:

> The interviews began with a series of questions about the respondents' activities as a group and about their television viewing habits. Later I asked them to describe and discuss their experiences with their own decisions about unwanted pregnancies or those of their friends or relatives. . . . The respondents then viewed a 30-

> minute version of an episode of *Cagney and Lacey* dealing with abortion, from which sub-plots and commercials had been edited. After viewing the tape, the women were asked specific questions about their reactions to the positions expressed by the characters in the show. (p. 423)

Similarly, Durant *et al.* (1993) were keen to explore general public thinking and meanings regarding genetics before introducing particular media 'stimuli' into the group discussions. Thus initial discussion about genetics, stimulated only by a three-dimensional model of the DNA double helix, was followed, some way into the group discussions, by a second stimulus consisting of two newspaper articles (one negative in its coverage of genetic research, the other positive), and, later still, by a third stimulus, a controversial documentary programme dealing with advances in genetic engineering. As in the case of the study by Press (1991), a major objective of the research was to examine how far group sentiments, vocabulary, and mode of discussion were influenced by exposure to the media material. In cases such as these it is clearly essential therefore that the 'script' – that is, the sequence of discussion and introduction of stimuli – is laid out clearly in the interview guide, and strictly adhered to by the moderator.

The interview guide used by Liebes and Katz (1990) is exemplary, and may serve as a model. It details not only general introductory comments to be used and the types of questions or issues to be addressed, but, additionally, provides guidelines for the length of time allowed for each question, and the degree and wording of further probing. Figure 10.2 shows selected key excerpts from Liebes and Katz's interview guide.

As with other types of research instrument, it is always important to pilot-test the interview guide for focus group discussions by conducting one, two, or sometimes more, pilot group discussions. Pilot-testing will throw up potential problems with the type of stimuli used, with sequencing, with the framing and wording of questions, and so on.

10.4.7 Recording the Data

What are the data produced by focus group discussions? The principal data produced by focus groups are the verbal responses, statements, opinions, arguments and interactions of the participants. Additional

We are conducting research about *Dallas*. We are trying to understand why the program manages to interest people all over the world.

5 min. 1. What happened in the episode we have just been watching? 'How will you tell it tomorrow morning to someone who has not seen it?'

IT IS IMPORTANT TO SUMMARIZE AND CONTINUE PROBING UNTIL SOME FORM OF ANSWER HAS BEEN GIVEN TO THIS QUESTION.
PROBE: 'So if I understand you, the story is so and so . . .'

INVITE CORRECTIONS.

2. ASK TO RANK THE THREE MOST IMPORTANT CHARACTERS IN ORDER OF IMPORTANCE. TRY TO ACHIEVE CONSENSUS OR ESTABLISH CLEAR OPPOSING VIEWS. THEN PROCEED TO ASK ABOUT THE FIRST CHARACTER.

5 min. Who is the most important character in this episode?

- Who is she/he? What do you know about him/her? (Try to get at family and other connections.)
- What motivates the character? What does (s)he believe in?
- What things get in the way?
- Do you like him/her? (Try clarifying differences of opinion.)

3–5 min. Is *Dallas* about real people?
IF YES: What kind of people is it about?
IF NO: How are the *Dallas* people different from real people?
PROBE: Do you know any people like the *Dallas* people?

Figure 10.2 Selected key excerpts from the interview guide used by Liebes and Katz, 1990, pp. 159–60.

data may include observational accounts of facial expressions, gestures, and body language more generally, although it is not often that such observations – if recorded at all – have been used to any great extent in the audience studies of the past decade or so.

Focus group discussions should as a minimum be recorded on audio cassette tape – participants should always be made aware at the outset that the discussion will be recorded, and reassured where appropriate of the confidential and anonymous use of the material. Generally, it will be the responses of the group as such, rather than individual contributions, which is of relevance to the research, but where the research aims are such that individual contributions need to be identifiable, it is important to keep a record of who is who in the group – and on the tape-recording. A good starting point for the group discussion is therefore an introductory round where each participant is asked to briefly introduce himself or herself (name, interests) – if this is tape-recorded the researcher then has a 'voice-identification' for each participant for the remainder of the taped discussion. The 'on-tape' identification is often matched with a standard questionnaire (sex, age, occupation, newspaper reading, television viewing behaviour, special interests and/or relevant experience, and so on) filled in by each participant prior to the discussion.

Video-recording of interview discussions offers the advantage that the contributions of individual participants can be identified more easily, and gestures and body-language observed directly. Video-recording is however also considerably more complicated (equipment, lighting, camera-angles) than audio-recording, and it is potentially rather more intrusive.

The principal record of a focus group's discussion, then, normally consists of an audio-tape recording and additional observational notes jotted down by the moderator or an observer during the discussion. While it is possible to commence analysis directly from listening to the taped recording of the interview, it is more often the case – and there are strong practical and methodological reasons for this – that audio-recordings are first transcribed before starting analysis. It is easy to flick forwards and backwards through a written transcript, to put it down and come back to it, to annotate, and, indeed, to share it with colleagues, where the research is a team-effort. Far more important, however, are the analytical possibilities that open up in terms of computerised textual analysis, when the focus group discussion exists as text (a transcript) rather than as sound (an audio tape recording). And this brings us to the final step in the focused group interview: the analysis and write-up.

10.5 Analysing and Reporting Focus Group Discussions

Focus group interviews produce a large amount of textual data. Even a relatively small number of focus group interviews can result in several hundred pages of transcription. How to analyse this material? One dilemma facing the researcher is between, on the one hand, reading through the interview transcripts to select 'striking' or 'typical' quotes which illustrate, confirm, and enhance the researcher's (pre-conceived) ideas of the processes and phenomena which are being investigated, and, on the other hand, to remain open to new ideas, unanticipated responses, unexpected conflicts in the statements of participants, and so on. In the words of Höijer (1990):

> When analysing reception interviews you certainly need sensibility and intuition, but you also have to be methodical, because you cannot grasp the totality of an interview and even less the totality of a set of interviews. Whether you are generous with citations or not, you will be influenced by your hypothesis and expectations as well as the very natural phenomenon that some individuals' statements will have a greater impact on you than others. (p. 40)

Schlesinger *et al.* (1992) likewise caution against the subjective selections of quotes sometimes seen in presentations of qualitative data:

> Qualitative results arising from interpretative methods, such as participant observation, in-depth interviews and group discussions, present researchers with a series of dilemmas regarding analysis and presentation. Various strategies, such as case studies and the presentation of verbatim accounts, are often employed. These have the benefit of 'fleshing out' and illustrating the significant themes and patterns identified by the researcher(s). Often, however, it is difficult for readers to understand *how* certain materials are chosen over others and *why* certain quotes take precedence over those which never appear. In this study we have attempted a systematic approach to the development of significant themes and illustrative quotes arising from group interviews. (p. 31)

Focus group discussions will almost inevitably generate some topics, frames, references, and argumentative angles which are new and unanticipated, but it is also of course in the nature of such discussions that they are *focused* around the topics and phenomena determined by the researcher. One task for the analysis, then, is to examine, categorise, and analyse the types of responses generated in relation to the 'headings' and specific 'foci' determined by the research framework and set out in the interview guide. The need to do this in a systematic fashion was emphasised above.

The way to commence the analysis task is to start by developing a scheme for categorising and labelling the responses, statements, arguments, and exchanges recorded in the interview transcripts. The 'categories' may be the 'headings' used in the interview guide, or, more often, they will be a modified version of these combined with any additional categories which may have presented themselves, unexpectedly, in the course of the group discussions. As in content analysis (see Chapter 5), a pre-requisite for developing good categories is to 'soak oneself in the material', that is, to read through the interview transcripts several times to become familiar with the spread of arguments, topics, and issues covered. Additional observational notes taken during the interviews may also contribute to the development of analytical categories.[4]

> Once the fieldwork was completed, members of the research team discussed preliminary interpretations of results and developed a set of general categories for grouping and analysing the recorded transcripts . . . Using the Macintosh-based 'Hypersoft' qualitative data analysis package, quotes were grouped into these categories. For example, two of the main categories were 'Victims' and 'Perpetrators'. Under these headings we grouped all comments about these two categories and, using a further refinement, the interpretations of causes, motives and justifications were also classified. (Schlesinger *et al.*, 1992, p. 31).

The categories which are used for classifying the contents of interview transcripts will of course vary entirely depending on the foci, purposes, and objectives of the research. Additionally, it will often be necessary systematically to classify and analyse the contents of interview transcripts along both different *types* and different *levels* of categories. Thus, one coding sweep through the material may be concerned with coding statements and arguments in terms of the principal frames (Gamson, 1992), themes and sub-themes (see Höijer, 1990, and Durant *et al.*, 1993). A second coding sweep, at a more detailed level, may be concerned with classifying 'causes, motives, and justifications' (Schlesinger *et al.*, 1992), anchors, metaphors, and positive or negative evaluations (Durant *et al.*, 1993) and so on.

The coding and analysis of interview transcripts is now (in sharp contrast to the situation only some fifteen to twenty years ago) most powerfully done with the help of microcomputers and a range of software available for the coding, analysis, and retrieval of qualitative data, such as the open-ended, unstructured text produced by focus group discussions. The software programs available for this type of analysis range widely: from basic index and retrieval programs which enable you to go directly to any word or string of words in the entire body of interview transcripts, to examine specified words in their immediate context, to list the entire vocabulary (in alphabetical order, or in order of word-frequency) of the group interview transcripts; to more complex and elaborate programs which enable you to attach 'codes', 'tags', 'labels' to words, sentences, arguments, statements – any string of text – and to perform quantitative analyses of the coded units, as well as analyses of 'networks' of arguments and 'associations' between related types of statements, subjects, contributor characteristics, and so on. A more detailed discussion of ways of managing and analysing the data generated by qualitative methods such as focus group discussions and participant observation is given in chapter 11.

Reporting the results of focus group interviews is, like all data analysis, an act of synthesising, summarising, and the reduction of an unstructured mass of textual data to its 'essentials', key trends, and representative examples. Though it is tempting – with the 'rich' qualitative textual data produced by focus group interviews – to quote comprehensively from the transcripts, to, as it were, 'let the data speak for itself', this approach to reporting does not achieve the task of summarising, let alone 'analysing' the material. Verbatim quotes to illustrate key points, modes of discussion, vocabularies, frames and so on should indeed be used in the reporting of results – not to do this would negate one of the major reasons for using focus group discussions: to capture the way in which participants 'naturally' talk about, make sense of, reason about, and generate meaning in relation to specified issues, topics, and phenomena – but these should be limited to 'representative' illustrations. Any quantitative coding which has been done on the transcripts is helpful when reporting the results both in terms of finding and selecting (this is where computer text-retrieval programmes come into their own) representative verbatim quotes relating to particular dimensions of analysis, and in terms of justifying that the quotes presented in the report are indeed representative of some larger body or trend in the data.

Reporting the results of focus group interviews is also an act of relating the textual data to the 'research problem, or objective' as it was articulated before commencing the research (and before the decision that 'focus group methodology' would be the most appropriate method for studying the research problem) and to the wider theoretical framework of the study. Faced with the large and rich body of textual data generated by focus group discussions, it may often seem difficult to decide which aspects to report on and which to leave out. Essentially, the analysis and reporting should proceed along the lines of the 'headings' outlined in the interview guide – these were drawn up in relation to the problems, objectives, issues, and hypotheses articulated as part of the theoretical framework for the study and the 'statement of the research problem'. Additional 'headings' (that is, concepts, issues, frames, phenomena) may, and most often do, present themselves in the process of reading through the material and 'soaking oneself' in the textual data – these 'headings' and their associated results are added to the write-up.

The report of focus group research – again like the report on any other kind of empirical research – should not simply present the reader with results or findings, but must also enable the reader to understand the process of the research – what was done, how it was done, with what subjects it was done, where, and by whom it was done. It is particularly important to remember to include in the report a full account of:

- who the participants were (and what they represent);
- how they were recruited;
- where and by whom they were interviewed;
- the nature and format of the group discussions;
- the use of stimuli;
- the nature of probing; and the ways in which interviews were recorded and analysed.

Much of this information should be presented in a 'design, sample, and methods' chapter, sandwiched between introductory chapters (outlining the research problem, theoretical framework, and reviews of related research) *and* the presentation of results and findings. In order to maintain a reasonable 'flow' and in order not to burden the reader unnecessarily with technical detail, it may well, however, be preferable to relegate some of the more detailed methodological descriptions and accounts to an appendix. Most of the media audience studies referred to in this chapter offer exemplary models in terms of detailed accounts of their methodology, but perhaps one of the clearest and most concise expositions of methodology is that offered by Schlesinger and his colleagues in their study of *Women Viewing Violence* (1992).

10.6 Summary

- Focus group interviewing generates a potentially much richer and more sensitive type of data on the dynamics of audiences and their relations to media than the survey.
- Focus group interviewing has become central in media audience research of the 1980s and early 1990s, as such research has turned away from questions about media *influence* and *effects* on audience behaviour and beliefs toward concerns with how audiences *interpret*, make sense of, use, interact with, and create meaning out of media content and media technologies.
- Focus group interviews may be the single substantive mode of data-collection in a piece of research; but more frequently the approach has been used in conjunction with other, complementary, types of data-collection. In media research, it has notably been used together with questionnaires, observation (ethnography), and analyses of media content.
- Unlike individual interviews, focus group interviews more closely approximate the 'naturally' social activity of generating meanings and interpretations in relation to media use and content. Through group dynamics they also offer ways – not available in the individual interview – of eliciting, stimulating, and elaborating audience interpretations.
- It is rarely the case that people will 'naturally' volunteer elaborate interpretations of media content. Focus group discussions therefore require active input and structuring on the part of the moderator. Indeed, the 'focus' of the discussions needs to be clear, although the structuring and focusing will often progress from the loose and open-ended to the more disciplined during the course of a focus group interview.
- The steps in focus group interviewing can be summarised as follows (from Stewart and Shamdasani, 1990): (1) problem definition/formulation of the research question; (2) identification of sampling frame; (3) identification of moderator; (4) generation and pre-testing of interview guide; (5) recruiting the sample; (6) conducting

the group; (7) analysis and interpretation of data; (8) writing the report.

- The sampling and constitution of focus groups is important, particularly where comparisons between groups are envisaged and where group answers and arguments will be related to 'independent variables' such as demographic and other characteristics. A case is often made for selecting groups from 'naturally existing' constituencies – for example, pressure groups, political organisations, professional associations, religious communities.
- The number of groups in a study will depend on the aims of the research and on available resources. If used for exploratory purposes, as little as two, three, or four groups may suffice. If this method constitutes a more substantive part of a study, it would be difficult to justify fewer than six groups. Several audience studies of the 1980s and 1990s have used between twelve and twenty groups.
- There is a general consensus that focus groups should be no larger than ten to twelve participants, and that the ideal group size is between six and ten.
- The choice of a location or setting for focus group interviews is important. The setting inevitably exerts a 'framing' influence on the nature of participants' responses and on the group discussion as a whole. The choice of setting needs to be considered in relation to the nature of the topic or issue to be discussed and, of course, in relation to practical feasibility.
- The role of the moderator will vary depending on the subject of analysis, the type of response which is sought, and the nature of the participants. It is in the nature of focus group discussions that the role of the moderator is to 'facilitate', 'moderate', and 'stimulate' discussion among the participants, but there is considerable flexibility as to how forcefully this is done. The role of the moderator must be clearly defined in the interview guide.
- The focus group interview guide is principally a 'menu' of the topics, issues or areas of discussion to be covered, but, in addition to simply listing these, it should also give directions as to: (1) the sequence of topics/issues to be covered; (2) the nature and extent of prompting and probing; (3) the nature and use of visual or verbal aids, and the points during the course of a group discussion where these should be introduced.
- The sequence typically (although there is nothing sacrosanct about this) followed in media audience research using focus group interviews is that of, (1) exposure to selected media material (a television

programme, a film, selected newspaper coverage, and so on), followed by, (2) un-directed general discussion, moving gradually – under the moderator's direction – toward more specific foci, issues, topics, and questions.

- While focus group discussions will almost inevitably generate some topics, frames, references, and argumentative angles which are new and unanticipated, it is also in the nature of such discussions that they are *focused* around the topics and phenomena determined by the researcher. One task for the analysis then is to examine, categorise, and analyse the types of responses generated in relation to the 'headings' and specific 'foci' determined by the research framework and set out in the interview guide. We emphasise that this needs to be done in a systematic fashion.

Notes

1. The original 1956 book had long since been out of print, even when Merton wrote his historical article in 1987. A second edition was finally published in 1990 (Merton, Lowenthal and Kendall, 1990).
2. Gamson (1992): 'We chose public sites where a recruitment table for the project was not out of place, and where it was possible to carry on a conversation and establish some rapport with potential recruits. This led us to focus on neighborhood and community events of various sorts – festivals, picnics, fairs, and flea markets, for example. We also posted notices of the research, with a phone number to contact us at various neighborhood and work sites. We avoided recruiting at any event or any site associated with a political cause or tendency, since we were eager to avoid any kind of political atypicality' (p. 16).
3. A variation on the mode of recruitment is the two-stage recruitment approach where suitable participants are first identified and contacted by the researcher, and it is then left to each of these contact-participants to bring together a group (friends, colleagues, family). Gamson (1992) used this approach, as did Liebes and Katz (1990), who contacted individual couples, who in turn invited other couples to form focus groups.
4. Indeed, the analytical categories may derive from the reading of, not only the interview transcripts, but a much broader set of documents, publications, and media, see, for example, Gamson (1992).

References

Burgess, J. and C.M. Harrison (1993) 'The circulation of claims in the cultural politics of environmental change', in A. Hansen (ed.) *The Mass Media and Environmental Issues*, pp. 198–221 (Leicester University Press).

Corner, J., K. Richardson and N. Fenton (1990) *Nuclear reactions: form and response in public issue television* (London: John Libbey).
Durant, J., A. Hansen and M. Bauer (1996) 'Public understanding of the new genetics', in M. Marteau and J. Richards (eds) *The troubled helix* pp. 235–48. (Cambridge University Press).
Durant, J., A. Hansen, M. Bauer and A. Gosling (1993) *The Human Genome Project and the British Public: A Report to the European Commission* (London: The Science Museum).
Gamson, W. A. (1992) *Talking Politics* (New York: Cambridge University Press).
Hedges, A. (1985) 'Group interviewing' in R. Walker (ed.) *Applied qualitative research*, pp. 71–91 (Aldershot: Gower).
Hobson, D. (1982) *Crossroads: The drama of a soap opera* (London: Methuen).
Höijer, B. (1990) 'Studying viewers' reception of television programmes: theoretical and methodological considerations', *European Journal of Communication*, **5**(1), 29–56.
Kitzinger, J. (1993) 'Understanding AIDS: Researching audience perceptions of Acquired Immune Deficiency Syndrome', in J. Eldridge (ed.) *Getting the message: news, truth and power*, pp. 271–304 (London: Routledge).
Krueger, R. A. (1988) *Focus groups: a practical guide for applied research* (London: Sage).
Liebes, T. and E. Katz (1986) 'Patterns of involvement in television fiction: a comparative analysis' *European Journal of Communication*, **1**(2), 151–71.
Liebes, T., and E. Katz (1990) *The export of meaning: Cross-cultural readings of 'Dallas'* (New York: Oxford University Press).
Lindlof, T. R., M. J. Shatzer and D. Wilkinson (1988) 'Accommodation of Video and Television in the American Family', in J. Lull (ed.) *World families watch television*, pp. 158–92 (London: Sage).
Livingstone, S., and P. Lunt (1993) *Talk on Television: Audience Participation and Public Debate* (London: Routledge).
Livingstone, S. M. (1991) 'Audience reception: The role of the viewer in retelling romantic drama', in J. Curran and M. Gurevitch (eds), *Mass media and society*, pp. 285–306 (London: Edward Arnold).
Lull, J. (1988) *World families watch television* (London: Sage).
Merton, R. K. (1987) 'The focussed interview and focus groups: continuities and discontinuities', *Public Opinion Quarterly*, **51**(4), 550–66.
Merton, R. K., M. Fiske and P. L. Kendall (1956) *The focused interview: a manual of problems and procedures* (Glencoe, Ill.: The Free Press).
Merton, R. K. and P. L. Kendall (1946) 'The focused interview', *American Journal of Sociology*, **51**, 541–57.
Merton, R. K., M. F. Lowenthal and P. L. Kendall (1990) *The focused interview: a manual of problems and procedures*, 2nd edn (New York: Collier Macmillan).
Morgan, D. L. (1988) *Focus groups as qualitative research* (Newbury Park, Calif.: Sage).
Morgan, D. L. (ed.) (1993) *Successful focus groups: advancing the state of the art* (Newbury Park, Calif.: Sage).

Morgan, D.L. and M.T. Spanish (1984) 'Focus groups: a new tool for qualitative research' *Qualitative Sociology*, **7**, 253–70.
Morley, D. (1980) *The 'Nationwide' Audience* (London: British Film Institute).
Morley, D. (1986) Family television (London: Comedia).
Philo, G. (1990) *Seeing and believing: the influence of television* (London: Routledge).
Press, A.L. (1991) 'Working-class women in a middle-class world: the impact of television on modes of reasoning about abortion', *Critical Studies in Mass Communication*, **8**(4), 421–41.
Schlesinger, P., R.E. Dobash, R.P. Dobash and C.K. Weaver (1992) *Women viewing violence* (London: BFI).
Schrøder, K.C. (1987) 'Convergence of antagonistic traditions? The case of audience research', *European Journal of Communication*, **2**(1), 7–31.
Silverstone, R. (1991) 'From audiences to consumers: The household and the consumption of communication and information technologies', *European Journal of Communication*, **6**(2), 135–54.
Stewart, D.W. and P.N. Shamdasani (1990) *Focus groups: theory and practice* (Newbury Park, Calif.: Sage).

11

Computer-Assisted Handling and Analysis of Data

11.1 Introduction

Most kinds or types of mass communication research – like social science research more generally – tend to produce large volumes of data. This is so, pretty much regardless of the method or approach adopted, and regardless of whether the research and data are principally qualitative or principally quantitative. While it is clearly possible to plan a research project, conduct research and collect data, and analyse data and write up a report of a study with 'pen and paper', few would contemplate doing all of these tasks without the use of a computer, whether for simple word-processing tasks or for more complex quantitative or qualitative analysis of data.

The revolution which has taken place in the last two decades in information technology, and more particularly in the ready availability of computers, has brought the power of computer-assisted data management and handling out of the daunting laboratories of university mainframe computers and on to the researcher's desk (or into his or her knapsack). The last ten to fifteen years have also seen a welcome erosion of the traditional notion that computers were for natural scientists or number-crunching empiricists in the social sciences, but had little, beyond the use as glorified typewriters, to offer the qualitative social scientist, let alone researchers in the humanities.

During the early 1980s scholars with an interest in textual analysis (including linguists, historians, literary scholars, medievalists, theologians) began to recognise the potential of computers for the storing and analysis of texts; anthropologists and ethnographers similarly began to discover the advantages of computers – over the more traditional methods of pen and paper, the card-index, scribbled notes

– for the management, organisation, and – subsequently – analysis of observational data. A special double-issue of *Qualitative Sociology* published in 1984 (Conrad and Reinharz, 1984) summarised many of the advances being made in the use of computers for linguists, qualitative sociologists, and so on. The late 1980s and first half of the 1990s have seen a steady proliferation, not only of computer programs for qualitative analysis (see Weitzman and Miles, 1995, for the most comprehensive and accessible overview/review yet of computer software for qualitative data analysis), but of introductions to and discussions of the use of computers in qualitative analysis.[1]

In parallel with the rise of computer applications for qualitative research, the more traditional quantitative applications of computing technology in social science research became ever more readily available and, more significantly, became increasingly user-friendly. By the mid-1980s, statistical analysis of social science data was no longer confined to large mainframe computers, but had become available (albeit mostly in a very costly form) for desk-top PCs. By the early 1990s, the traditionally large and complex programs for statistical data analysis in the social sciences had begun to take full advantage of more intuitive, menu and windows-driven user-interfaces, on-line help and tutorial systems, and multiple facilities for representing results in visually attractive and comprehensible forms. No longer does the mass communication researcher, who wishes to subject his or her data to some statistical analysis, need to know and remember a large battery of esoteric computer commands or complex program syntaxes.

In this chapter, we wish to introduce:

(1) the analysis of quantitative data using SPSS; and
(2) the computer-assisted management and analysis of 'qualitative' data.

The chapter outlines the steps involved in preparing quantitative data – whether from a survey or a content analysis – for computer-analysis, and it discusses the use of SPSS for the statistical examination of data. The chapter further discusses the organisation, management, and analysis of 'qualitative' textual data, be they in the form of participant observation field-notes, interview transcripts, or electronic newspaper text. While seeking to avoid the detailed description of individual computer programs for these purposes, we introduce readers to the significant gains of flexibility, efficiency, and reliability which computer-assisted handling of qualitative data offers over more traditional 'manual' or card-index based methods, and we outline some of the types of analysis which can productively be used in research on qualitative 'textual' data.

11.2 The Analysis of Quantitative Data Using SPSS

As indicated above, computer tools, programs, or software for analysing social science data have progressed in leaps and bounds in the last few decades, and become increasingly accessible and user-friendly. The social scientist or mass communication researcher of today, who wishes to organise, manage, and analyse his or her data by computer can choose from a wide range of powerful or less-powerful computer programs ranging from databases and spreadsheets with some (again, more or less powerful) statistical calculation facilities to statistical programs or packages designed specifically for the full range of statistical analysis used in not just social science research but in natural science and medical research.

Here, we wish to introduce the reader to the very basics of a computer program originally invented some thirty years ago with, as its name suggests, a specific view to helping in the analysis of social science data, namely SPSS – Statistical Package for the Social Sciences. SPSS is widely available at universities and social science research centres. It is available for both mainframe computing systems, and, more importantly in today's computing environment, for PCs and Macintosh computers or networks. Like all computer programs, SPSS is undergoing continuous development and adaptation to new computer environments and operating systems. When SPSS was first designed in the 1960s, data was 'stored' in the form of punch cards – so called because 'values' were indicated by holes punched on index-type cards – and users had to know a large array of general computing commands as well as commands and syntax specific to SPSS. All in all, a very different scenario from today's user interface where most, if not all, data entry and analysis can be done by choosing from and clicking on windows and menu-buttons on a computer screen.

Our objective in the first section of this chapter is to introduce the reader to:

(1) how to transfer data from a content analysis coding schedule or a survey questionnaire to an SPSS computer data file; and

(2) how to do relatively simple, but useful, types of analysis with SPSS.

Our introduction to SPSS will refer specifically to version 6.1 of SPSS for the Macintosh computer, but, while reference here is specifically to the Macintosh computing environment, it is worth emphasising that most of what we will be introducing here applies equally to SPSS 6.1 for Windows in a PC environment.

11.2.1 Three Types of Variables: Continuous, Categorical, and String

Content analyses, surveys, and potentially other kinds of approaches use research instruments such as content analysis schedules and questionnaires on which answers are circled, ticked, or recorded in the form of numbers or codes. The main reasons for using numbers or codes are:

- speed (it is quicker to write the code-number '1' than to write 'female' in the questionnaire-category which asks for the 'sex' of the respondent); and
- the need to standardise the way in which answers are recorded so that they can be subjected to quantitative analysis.

There are two different kinds of numeric codes used for the kinds of variables that you will find on a survey questionnaire or a content analysis coding schedule:

(1) *Answers that are recorded in terms of 'real numbers'*, where the number recorded on the questionnaire means just that – a person's age might be recorded as '28', meaning that the person is 28 years of age, or a respondent's height might be recorded as '165', meaning that the respondent is 165 centimetres tall. Variables which consist of real numbers are often referred to as *continuous* variables.

(2) *Answers that are recorded in terms of arbitrary or nominal 'codes'*, where the code or number refers to particular dimensions of a variable – for the variable 'sex', the code '1' might be used to mean 'female' and the code '2' to indicate that the respondent is 'male', or for the variable 'newspaper' on a content

analysis schedule, the code '1' might be used to indicate the '*Daily Telegraph*', '2' for the '*Times*', '3' for the '*Independent*' and so on. These are just arbitrary codes of convenience – we could equally well have used the codes '1' for 'male' and '2' for 'female', or the codes '6' for 'male' and '8' for 'female'. Being merely arbitrary codes of convenience, these codes have none of the numeric properties associated with real numbers. In other words, although possible to do, it would not make sense to calculate the 'difference' between 'male' and 'female' respondents in the survey by subtracting '1' from '2', nor would it make sense to perform any other arithmetical calculations such as finding the average of '2's and '1's (males and females). Variables which consist of a limited set of codes or categories are often referred to as *categorical* variables.

In addition to the two types of numerically coded data described above, a content coding schedule or a survey questionnaire may contain non-coded *textual* information. For a content analysis of newspapers, it would often be desirable to write down the headlines of individual articles in full on the schedule; survey questionnaires will often have open-ended questions, where respondents are invited to write their answers or comments in their own words. While such textual information may in turn be subjected to some kind of categorisation or numeric coding in preparation for subsequent quantitative analysis by computer, it is perfectly possible (and increasingly advisable due to the advances in computerised analysis of qualitative textual data – see Section 11.2) to enter full textual information into computer programs designed for quantitative analysis. In contrast to the 'numeric' variables described above, textual information is known in computer terminology as '*string*' variables – that is, they consist of strings of letters or characters.

11.2.2 From Coding Sheets or Questionnaires to the Computer

In order to use a computer for quantitative analysis of the kind of data generated by a content analysis schedule or a survey questionnaire, it is necessary first to transfer the data from the schedules or questionnaires into the computer. This means transferring the data from the schedules or questionnaires into a document – a 'file' – stored on the computer. This can be done in a number of ways,[2] but probably the simplest and most basic way of doing this is to type the data/codes/numbers from the completed questionnaires or content coding schedules into an SPSS data file. The procedure for doing this will now be explained. As an example, we shall use the content analysis schedule described in Chapter 5 (see Figure 5.1) and the associated data generated by that study (Hansen, 1993).

Open SPSS and Create and Name a New Data File

Before we can do anything with SPSS, we need to 'launch' or open the SPSS program. We find the SPSS application icon (Figure 11.1) on our Macintosh computer and launch the program by double-clicking on the icon.

SPSS opens, by default, with an empty data-entry window (Figure 11.2). The data-entry window is divided into rows and columns, and is of course empty because we have not yet typed in any data. It also has not got a specific name, but simply says 'untitled data'; the first thing to do is to name the data set that we are about to create. However, SPSS will not let us name an empty file. In order to be able to name the file that we are about to create, we therefore, for now, put a 'dummy' value – say '1' – in the first cell, the top left cell, of the data-entry window. Having done this, we can now name the file as follows: we pull down the **File** menu from the menu bar at the top of the screen and choose the **Save As** option. This brings up a dialogue box on the screen, into which we type a name indicating the nature of our data; in our example, which uses the data from a content analysis of British newspaper coverage of the environmental pressure group Greenpeace, we shall use the name 'Greenpeace Newspaper Data' for our data-set. When this has been done, we click the **Save** button of the dialogue box, which returns us to the data-entry window.

Figure 11.1 The SPSS application icon

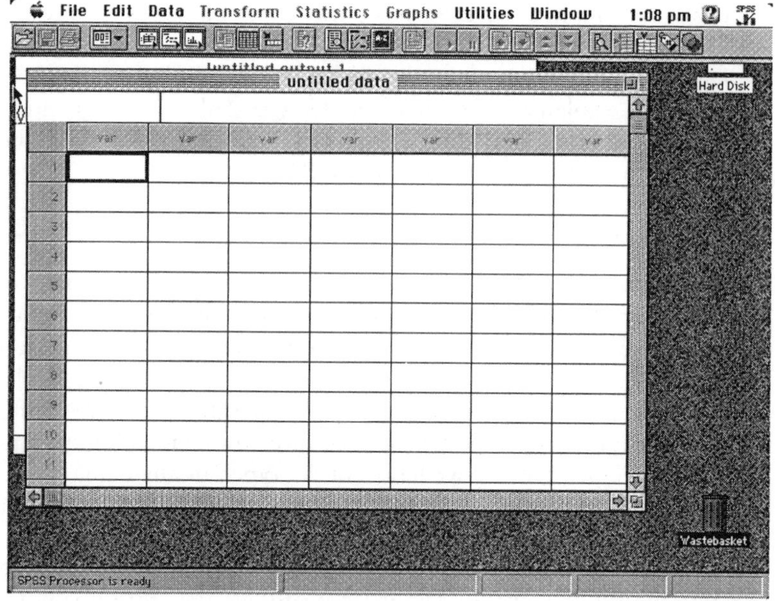

Figure 11.2 The SPSS data-entry window

Case, Variable, Values

Each row in the window represents a *case* – in the content analysis which we shall use as an example here, a 'case' is an individual newspaper article. For each newspaper article in the analysis we have completed a single content coding schedule (see Figure 5.1). In a survey, a 'case' would normally be the individual respondent or person interviewed, although there are other possibilities, for example 'a household'.

Each column in the data-entry window represents a *variable* – a variable is an individual dimension or characteristic analysed, such as 'date', 'which newspaper the article appeared in', 'the number of words in the article', 'the manner in which Greenpeace was referred to' and so on. In a survey, a 'variable' would be such dimensions as 'the age of the respondent', 'annual income of the respondent', 'newspapers read by the respondent', or 'weekly amount of television viewing'.

Each variable in a content analysis or survey can take on a number of *values* – thus, in our content analysis example, the value '3' for the 'newspaper variable' indicates that the article appeared in the *Independent*, the value '403' in the wordcount variable indicates that the length of the article was 403 words, and so on. It is these values that are typed into each cell of the data-entry window: each cell then represents a *single value* of a *variable* for a *case*.

Defining Variables and Entering Data

Before we can start thinking about doing any actual analysis of our data we need to type the data-values into the data-entry window *and* we need to define each variable. In other words, we need to tell SPSS that the value '3' for the newspaper variable means the '*Independent*', the value '4' for the 'how quoted' variable means 'referred to indirectly', and so on.

To start entering our data for the first case of our content analysis, we click in the first cell (top left-hand cell) of the data-entry window. We now pull down the **Data** menu in the menu bar at the top of the screen, and choose **Define Variable**. The Define Variable dialogue box (Figure 11.3) appears on the screen. The first variable on our coding schedule is the newspaper variable, indicating in which newspaper the article analysed appeared. In the 'variable name' box, we delete the default name 'VAR00001' and instead type in the name 'newspapr' – yes, it is spelt incorrectly; the reason for this is that SPSS will

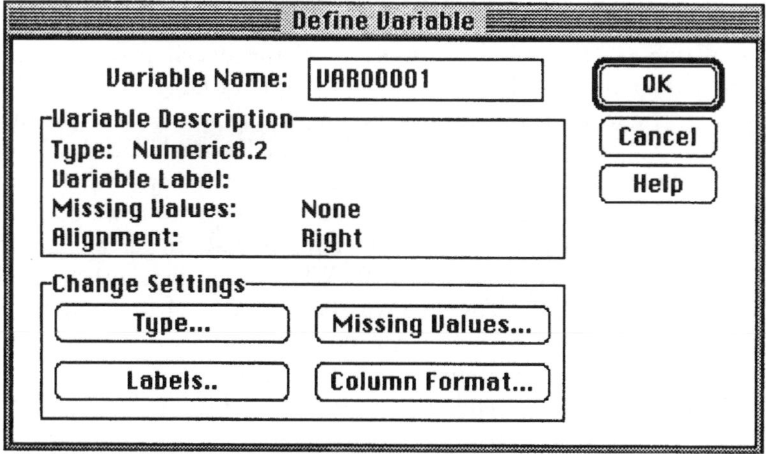

Figure 11.3 The Define Variable dialogue box

only accept variable names of up to a maximum of eight characters. There are also a few other rules applying to variable names: they must begin with a letter (not a number); they must not end with a period; and each variable name must be unique (the same name cannot be used for two different variables in a data set).

In the lower part of the Define Variable dialog box, there is a rectangle with four buttons: 'Type . . .', 'Labels . . .', 'Missing Values . . .', and 'Column Format'. We click on the 'Type . . .' button to bring up the 'Define Variable Type:' dialogue box shown in Figure 11.4.

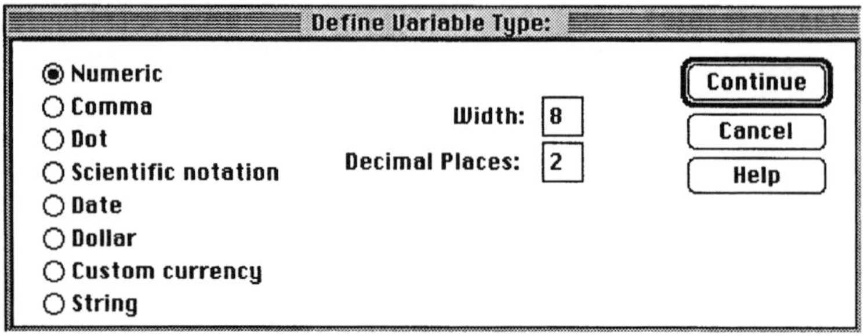

Define Variable Type:

Numeric
Comma
Dot
Scientific notation
Date
Dollar
Custom currency
String

Width: 8
Decimal Places: 2

Continue
Cancel
Help

Figure 11.4 The Define Variable Type dialogue box

The category 'Numeric' is ticked by default. As our variable 'newspapr' is coded using numbers, we leave 'Numeric' ticked. In the box labelled 'Width' we can specify the width of the column for this variable – that is, the number of characters allowed for this variable; our codes (values) for the 'newspapr' variable only run into two-digit figures, so we can change the default of '8' to '2' in the Width box. Then we move to the box labelled 'Decimal Places', which has a default value of '2' decimal places. Our 'newspapr' variable is coded using only whole numbers ('1', '2', '3' up to '10'); we do not, then, need any decimal places, and therefore replace the default '2' in the Decimal Places box with a zero '0'. When this is done, we click on the 'Continue' button. This takes us back to the 'Define Variable' dialogue box, where we now click on the 'Labels . . . ' button to obtain the 'Define Labels:' dialogue box (Figure 11.5).

In the box saying 'variable label:' we can type in the full name of the variable – spelt correctly – 'newspaper'. The variable label is optional, and for this particular variable is not really necessary, as the 8-letter variable name itself indicates perfectly clearly what the

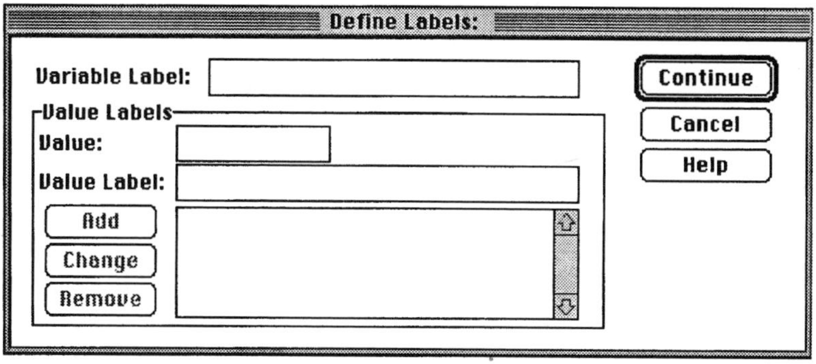

Figure 11.5 The Define Labels dialogue box

variable refers to. A data-set would often, however, include variables, the meaning of which would not easily be expressed within the confines of an 8-letter name and in such instances it is useful to be able to provide a longer 'label'. Take, for example, the variable of the content schedule which asks 'how is Greenpeace quoted or referred to?' As a variable name for this we could choose, say, 'grnpquot', but what this refers to would not however be immediately clear, and it would therefore be helpful to add also the fuller label: 'how is Greenpeace quoted or referred to?'.

We then move to the Value Labels rectangle of this dialogue box. Like variable labels, value labels are optional – in other words, it is perfectly possible to run SPSS analyses of data without specifying value labels for a coded variable such as 'newspapr'. Not specifying value labels, however, makes reading the tables produced by SPSS rather cumbersome, as we would have to remember what each value refers to. For example, for the 'newspapr' variable we would have to remember that the value '1' meant the '*Daily Telegraph*', '2' '*The Times*', and so on. If we define the labels in this dialogue box, these will be listed in any subsequent analysis output, thus freeing us from having to memorise the meaning of these codes.

On our content analysis coding sheet, the 'newspapr' variable can take one of ten different values: we now need to list in the dialogue box what each of these values mean. We type the first value '1' in the 'value:' box, and then type in the meaning of this value, 'Daily Telegraph', in the 'Value Label' box. We then click on the 'add' button and the value and label will move into the rectangular box with the scroll bar on the right hand side. Next we type in '2' in the value box and 'Times' in the label box, click on add, then '3' and so on, until we have entered all ten values for the 'newspapr' variable. We click on 'Continue' to get back to the 'Define Variable' dialogue box.

There are two further buttons which allow us to define 'Missing Values' for the particular variable, and to define the 'Column Format' (width, left or right alignment or centring of the data entered in each cell). For this particular variable 'newspapr' we need not, however, make any changes to either 'Missing Values' or 'Column Format', so we click on 'OK', which takes us back to the data-entry form (Figure 11.2). Here, we can now type in the appropriate value as it appears on the coding schedule for our first case or newspaper article (say, '4' – meaning the *Guardian*). When first typing in the value, this appears in the line above the cell area of the data-entry table. The value is automatically transferred to the currently active cell when we move on to the next cell.

We can now move on to define the second variable on our coding schedule, namely the 'date' variable (date–month–year). We click in the top cell of the second column, pull down the **Data** menu in the menu bar at the top of the screen, and choose **Define Variable**. The 'Define Variable' dialogue box (Figure 11.3) appears again on the screen, and we are ready to repeat the definition tasks described above for the previous variable. However, the 'date' variable is different from the previous variable, which consisted of nominal values; thus, in the 'Define Type' dialogue box we need to tick the 'date' option rather than 'numeric', and so on. When we have carried out the relevant definitions for this variable, we return to the data-entry table and now type in the date as it is recorded on the coding schedule for our first newspaper article (say, '21.04.91' – indicating 21 April 1991).

We then move on to define the third variable, the newspaper headline. This variable again is different from the two previous ones in that it consists of actual words, text, rather than numbers: we need to define this variable type then as a 'string' variable. It is also necessary to define the column width for this variable such that there will be sufficient space to accomodate the full length of headlines; newspaper headlines of course vary considerably in length, but a column width setting of say 240 characters should be sufficient to accomodate most headlines.

Following the same procedure as outlined above for the first variable 'newspapr', we continue to define each of the remaining variables from the content coding schedule, and for each variable, to enter the relevant data for our first case in the appropriate cells. When this is accomplished, we can then proceed to enter the data from the second case, the third case, the fourth case, and so on, starting a new row of data for each new case. As we have already defined the variables – the columns of the data-entry table – for the first case, entering the subsequent cases in the data-entry table is simply a matter of typing the information or data for each variable into the appropriate cells – in other words, once the variables have been defined for the first case (the top row), they have been defined for all subsequent cases.

For this introduction, we have entered a total of only thirty-seven cases, fifteen from the newspaper *Today* and twenty-two from the *Guardian*, into the data file 'Greenpeace Newspaper Data'. Figure 11.6 shows part of the completed data file.

11.2.3 Analysing Data with SPSS

With the variables defined and some cases of data transferred from our content analysis coding schedules into the SPSS data file we have called 'Greenpeace Newspaper Data', we are ready to start carrying out some analysis. Here we wish to introduce four basic types of analyses which are useful for describing and summarising the results of the data collected.

Greenpeace Newspaper Data

1 :newspapr 4

	newspapr	date	headline	reporter	arlength	artype	grpfocus
1	4	16.04.91	Oil slick danger t	PAUL BROWN in Geno	482	1	3
2	4	15.04.91	Britain keeps up f	PAUL BROWN	681	1	2
3	4	12.04.91	Toxic Londonderry	OWEN BOWCOTT	502	2	2
4	4	12.04.91	Agony and ivory -	IAIN GUEST	1787	2	3
5	4	10.04.91	Water proof case -	DAVID UTTING	1309	1	3
6	4	06.04.91	Acid rain damage g	PAUL BROWN, Enviro	535	1	3
7	10	15.04.91	Mediterranean oil	BRUCE JOHNSTON, Ro	493	1	3
8	10	29.03.91	Curse of mad car d	BARBARA LEWIS	411	2	2
9	10	26.04.91	How can you help p		113	2	3
10	10	26.04.91	Stop this slaughte		370	1	2
11	10	21.04.91	Polluters will pay	CATHY GUNN in the	548	2	3
12	10	05.10.91	Antarctic freeze (		65	1	2
13	10	12.09.91	Green raid bursts		94	1	1
14	10	29.07.91	Traffic damages ch	NICKI POPE	181	1	1

Figure 11.6 Part of the data file 'Greenpeace Newspaper Data'

Thus the first thing one would often want to do when first starting on analysis of one's survey data or content analysis data is to get a general 'feel' for what the data show – a general 'feel' for the distribution of different variables in the data-set: that is, how many men and how many women were there in the survey? What was their average age (and the minimum and maximum ages of respondents)? What percentage of women read the *Daily Telegraph*? What percentage of men did? Or, in a content analysis, how many articles from each newspaper? What differences in the average length of articles across different newspapers? Was the prime minister quoted more often in the *Daily Mail* than in the *Daily Mirror*? and so on.

Frequencies and Descriptives

We can begin to get a good picture of the distribution of individual variables with two types of SPSS analysis: one for analysing the *frequencies* of individual values in a variable, and the other for a *descriptive* summary of the values of a variable in terms of calculating the average (also known as the mean value) of the values of a variable and showing its minimum and maximum values. Let us start by examining the distribution (frequency) of newspapers and the distribution (frequency) of 'how Greenpeace was quoted or referred to' in our sample of data.

With the data window shown in Figure 11.6 open, we pull down the **Statistics** menu, and choose **Summarize** and **Frequencies**; in the Frequencies dialogue box (Figure 11.7), we select the variable 'newspapr' and the variable 'grnpquot': we click on the variable 'newspapr' (to highlight it) which appears in the left-hand rectangle, then we click on the arrow button between the two rectangles to transfer the variable to the rectangular box on the right; we then do the same with the variable 'grnpquot'. Now we click on the 'OK' button at the top right-hand corner of the dialogue box.

Once we have clicked 'OK' in the Frequencies dialogue box, SPSS proceeds to calculate the frequencies for the two variables we have specified. The results of this calculation appear in a new window called '!Untitled Output 1' (see Figure 11.8). In the output window, SPSS shows a table for each of the two variables used in this analysis.

The two variables analysed with the frequencies command are both categorical variables; that is, they consist of arbitrary code-numbers indicating a limited set of unique characteristics or values. As

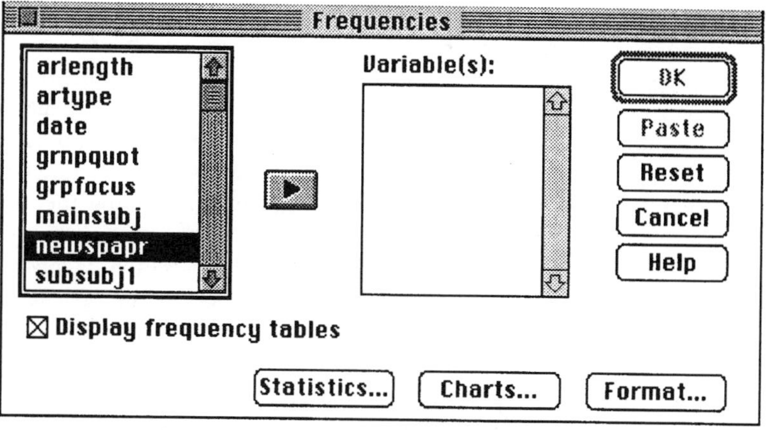

Figure 11.7 The Frequencies dialogue box

!untitled output 1

NEWSPAPR newspaper

Value Label	Value	Frequency	Percent	Valid Percent	Cum Percent
Guardian	4	22	59.5	59.5	59.5
Today	10	15	40.5	40.5	100.0
	Total	37	100.0	100.0	

Valid cases 37 Missing cases 0

Figure 11.8 SPSS Output window showing a Frequencies table for the variable 'newspapr'

indicated on p. 292, it would not make much sense to carry out arithmetic calculations on these types of numbers which are simply numeric *codes*, but have none of the properties of 'real' numbers. In other words, it would not make sense to try to calculate the average of the '4's and '10's which signify the *Guardian* and *Today* in our analysis, nor would it make sense to say that we could find the difference between the *Guardian* and *Today* by subtracting the '4's from the '10's.

One variable in the data example used here which is not a categorical variable, but consists of 'real' numbers is the 'arlength' (length of article) variable, which records the number of words in each article. For this variable it *does* make sense to calculate the average length of articles in the sample, just as it would be perfectly sensible to say that the difference between a *Guardian* article which is 400 words long and a *Today* article which is 300 words long is exactly 100 words.

Let us now describe and summarise the information we have obtained by recording the number of words (the 'length of article' variable) in each article coded in our study. Although we could do this using the frequencies command in SPSS, as we did above for the 'newspapr' and 'grnpquot' variables, this would produce a very long, and not particularly helpful or 'summarising' table showing basically the number and percentage of cases which were, say, 100 words long, the number and percentage of cases which were 101 words long, the number and percentage of cases which were 102 words long, and so on; in other words, a table showing a row of information for each value (number of words) of the 'arlength' variable. For a much more succinct summary of this variable, we need the **descriptives** procedure in SPSS.

We pull down the **Statistics** menu, and choose **Summarize** and **Descriptives**; in the Descriptives dialogue box (Figure 11.9), we click on the variable 'arlength' in the left rectangle, then click on the arrow button between the two rectangles to transfer the variable to the rectangular box on the right. We then click on the 'OK' button at the top right corner of the dialogue box.

Once we have clicked 'OK' in the Descriptives dialogue box, SPSS proceeds to calculate the mean or average for the 'arlength' variable. The result of this calculation appears in the SPSS output window called '!Untitled Output 1' (see Figure 11.10). The Descriptives table for 'arlength' shows the mean (average) length of articles in this data-set, as well as the standard deviation, the minimum, the maximum and the number of cases (37) in this data-set.

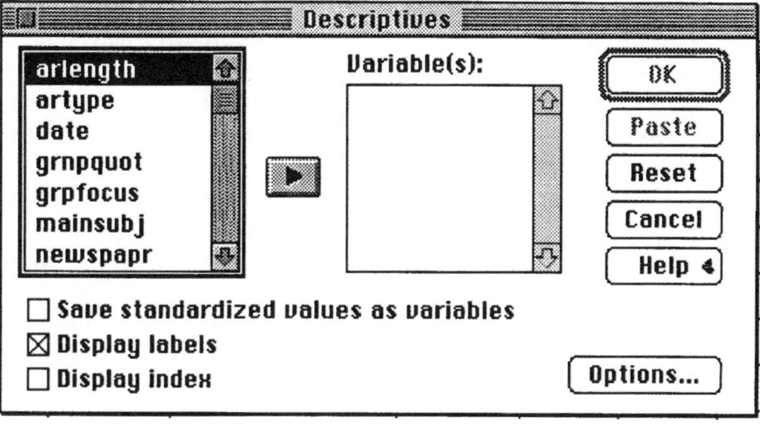

Figure 11.9 The Descriptives dialogue box

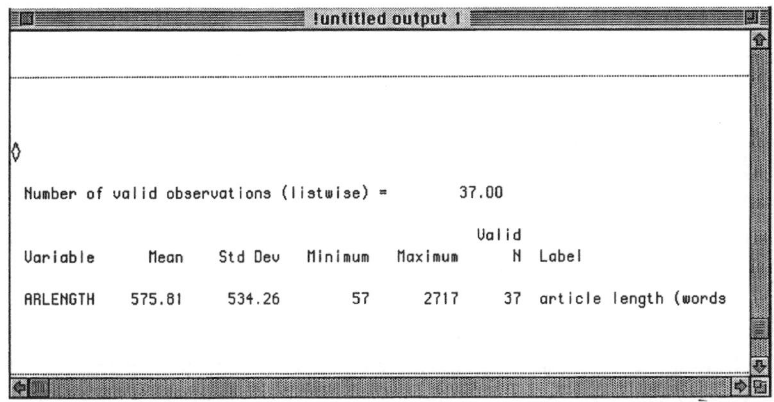

Figure 11.10 SPSS Output window showing a Descriptives table for the variable 'arlength'

Crosstabs and Means

So far, we have used two SPSS commands, frequencies and descriptives, for describing and summarising individual variables. But what if we wanted to compare the way Greenpeace is quoted or referred to across different newspapers, or to compare the length of articles across different newspapers? We might have a hunch, for example, that a higher proportion of *Guardian* articles than of *Today* articles quote Greenpeace directly; or we may wish to confirm with figures what we already know from our general familiarity with the different formats of broadsheet newspapers (for example, the *Guardian*) and tabloid newspapers (for example, *Today*), that the *Guardian* articles are on average considerably more 'wordy' than *Today* articles.

Let us examine first how Greenpeace is quoted or referred to in the two newspapers in our present data set. For this we need to compare two variables: the 'newspapr' variable and the 'grnpquot' variable. Both these variables, as we have seen, are categorical variables. To compare them we need a procedure called 'Crosstabs', which provides a cross-tabulation of the two variables.

Again, we pull down the **Statistics** menu; from this, we choose **Summarize** and **Crosstabs**; in the Crosstabs dialogue box (Figure 11.11), we click on the variable 'grnpquot' in the left rectangle, then click on the topmost of the three arrow buttons to transfer the variable to the Row(s) box. We then select the 'newspapr' variable at the left rectangle and click on the second arrow button down to transfer this to the Column(s) box on the right (NB it does not matter

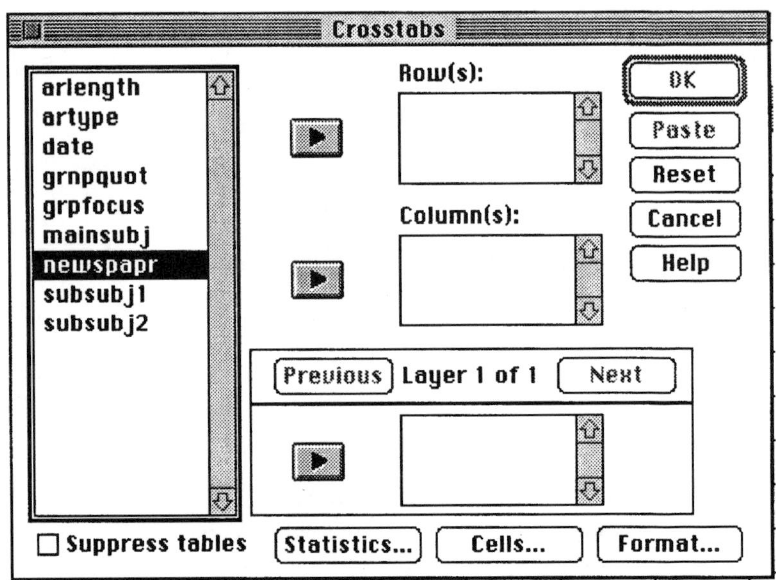

Figure 11.11 The Crosstabs dialogue box

whether we put 'grnpquot' as the row variable and 'newspapr' as the column variable, or vice versa – the contents of the cells of the resulting table will be the same whichever way round we choose).

Before we move on to carry out this crosstabulation of 'grnpquot' with 'newspapr', we need to specify what information we would like in the cells of the resulting table. We thus click on the 'Cells' button at the bottom part of the dialogue box. This brings up the 'Crosstabs: Cell Display' dialogue box (Figure 11.12): here we tick 'Row' and 'Column' in the Percentages box at the bottom left corner; then click 'Continue' to get back to the main Crosstabs dialogue box. Here we click the 'OK' button.

Once we have clicked 'OK' in the Crosstabs dialogue box, SPSS proceeds to produce a table comparing 'grnpquot' across 'newspapr'. The table appears in the SPSS output window called '!Untitled Output 1' (see Figure 11.13). The table shows, in the first column, the number and row and column percentages of *Guardian* articles in which Greenpeace was quoted directly (top cell), quoted indirectly (second cell down), or referred to but not quoted (bottom cell). The second column shows the equivalent information for *Today*.

Let us finally compare the length of articles across the two newspapers in our example data-set. This involves comparing a categorical variable 'newspapr' and a continuous variable 'arlength' consisting of

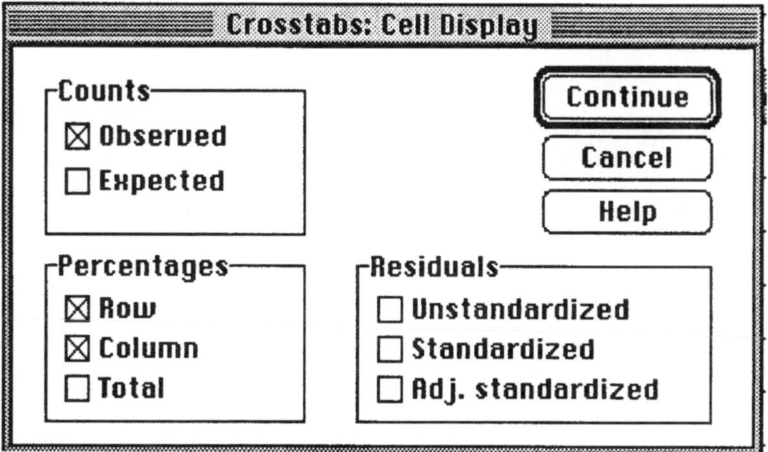

Figure 11.12 The Crosstabs Cell Display dialogue box

!untitled output 1

GRNPQUOT how greenpeace quoted/referred to? by NEWSPAPR newspaper

GRNPQUOT	Count / Row Pct / Col Pct	NEWSPAPR Guardian 4	Today 10	Row Total
1 quoted directly		5 / 62.5 / 22.7	3 / 37.5 / 20.0	8 / 21.6
2 quoted indirectl		14 / 63.6 / 63.6	8 / 36.4 / 53.3	22 / 59.5
3 referred to but		3 / 42.9 / 13.6	4 / 57.1 / 26.7	7 / 18.9
	Column Total	22 / 59.5	15 / 40.5	37 / 100.0

Page 1 of 1

Number of Missing Observations: 0

Figure 11.13 SPSS Output window showing a Crosstabs table for the variables 'grnpquot' and 'newspapr'

'real' numbers. As one of the variables consists of real continuous numbers, we need an analytical procedure which will calculate the average article length in each of the two newspapers. In SPSS, this procedure is called 'Means'. The Means command calculates the average (the 'mean') for each of the values or categories of a categorical variable.

We pull down the **Statistics** menu, and choose **Compare Means** and from the submenu, we choose **Means**; in the Means dialogue box (Figure 11.14), we click on the variable 'arlength' in the left rectangle, then click on the top arrow button to transfer the variable to the Dependent List box. We then select the 'newspapr' variable at the left rectangle and click on the bottom arrow button to transfer this to the Independent List box on the right. We then click the 'OK' button.

Having clicked 'OK' in the Means dialogue box, SPSS proceeds to produce a table of 'arlength' across 'newspapr' – the average number of words in articles in the *Guardian* and *Today* respectively. The table appears in the SPSS output window called '!Untitled Output 1' (see Figure 11.15).

We have introduced the basics of four fundamental analytical procedures in SPSS: frequencies and descriptives for analysing individual variables; crosstabs and means for comparing two (or more) variables. As the reader will have noticed from the dialogue boxes reproduced here, each of these procedures have numerous further

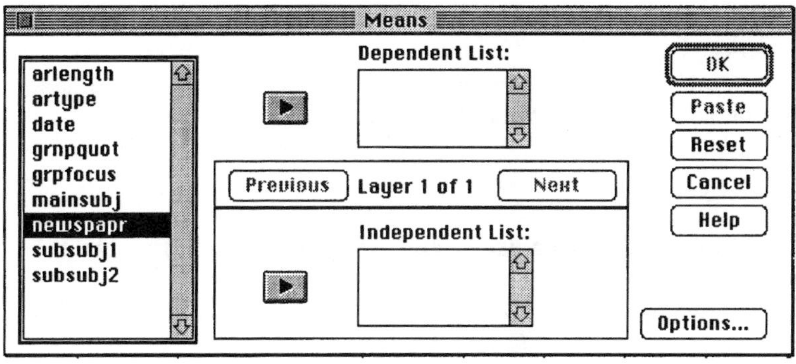

Figure 11.14 The Means dialogue box

!untitled output 1

- - Description of Subpopulations - -

Summaries of ARLENGTH article length (words)
By levels of NEWSPAPR newspaper

Variable	Value	Label	Mean	Std Dev	Cases
For Entire Population			575.8108	534.2604	37
NEWSPAPR	4	Guardian	788.0455	595.0949	22
NEWSPAPR	10	Today	264.5333	167.8374	15

Total Cases = 37

Figure 11.15 SPSS Output window showing a Means table: the average length of articles in each newspaper

options for enhancing the type of analysis and the form of output they deliver (for example, in the Crosstabs procedure we requested row and column percentages for each cell of the resulting table). For further exploration of these and other more sophisticated types of analysis, we refer the reader to the SPSS program itself – experiment with it, and use the online help functions as well as the online tutorials which come with the program. And we refer the reader to the SPSS manuals and user guides, which, as the software itself develops, have, fortunately, tended to become easier to understand for the uninitiated and perhaps not-so-statistically-minded mass communication researcher. For the PC Windows-user we also recommend two very clear and helpful introductions to statistical analysis with SPSS: Babbie and Halley, 1995, and Kinnear and Gray, 1994.

11.3 Handling, Organising, and Analysing Qualitative Data

Qualitative data in mass communication research come in a number of different shapes and forms. We can use a 'negative' definition and refer to as 'qualitative' data any data which are not: numerically coded, quantified, or consist of numbers. Qualitative data may be: focus group interview transcripts; protocols; observational notes scribbled down during participant observation and ethnographic research; notes scribbled down during interviews with research subjects; the text of newspaper articles, transcripts of television or radio programmes.

Of course qualitative data need not necessarily be 'text', but could be, for example, photographs taken to document a particular phenomenon, or a video-camera recording of television-viewers watching television or of the members of a focus group discussion interacting with each other. While computer programs for handling and analysing visual or audial data are already available, or are being developed, this area is – in contrast to the computer-assisted handling and analysis of 'textual' qualitative data – still in its infancy. In this section we wish to provide a brief introduction to ways in which computers can help and enhance the management and analysis of 'textual' qualitative data.

The computer-assisted management, organisation, and analysis of textual qualitative data can be broken down into three distinct steps:

(1) entering text/documents into a computer;
(2) organising and preparing text for analysis; and
(3) analysing text.

11.3.1 Entering Text or Documents into a Computer

As with the analysis of quantitative data, the first step before any computer-assisted analysis can commence is to transfer the textual data from whatever form they exist in into a computer. If the data are in the form of handwritten notes, memos, or answers to open-ended questions on a questionnaire, they will normally need to be *typed* into a computer file.[4] If the data are in the form of audio-recordings – such as the tape-recording of a focus-group interview – it is necessary to transcribe these, which can and should of course be done straight on to a computer.[5] If the data exist in the form of printed text – for example, newspaper text, policy documents, annual reports, historical documents, and so on – these can be scanned into a computer using the increasingly accurate and reliable optical scanners that are now widely available (alternatively, but rather more laboriously, printed documents can, of course, be typed into a computer).

If the textual data to be researched already exist in electronic form, the task of transferring these to files on a computer is much easier. When it comes to electronically available text, the mass communication researcher is increasingly in a privileged position. Newspaper text is becoming ever more widely available in electronic form, and broadcast media 'text' is following not far behind. There are now principally three forms in which newspaper and broadcast text is available in electronic form:

- on compact discs (CD-ROM),
- from commercial on-line databases, and
- from the Internet sites of newspapers and media corporations.

The last two can be accessed from mainframe computer networks, or from desktop microcomputers with the help of a modem and a telephone line, while compact discs are available for purchase and play-back on the CD-ROM drive of one's computer, or alternatively, may be available for access at a (university) library.

Depending on the electronic medium, the task of obtaining and transferring selected electronic text on to one's computer is a matter of 'capturing text on-screen' (for example, if accessing a commercial on-line database), copying text from CD-ROM to files on a computer disk, or 'capturing' or 'down-loading' text from the Internet. While the modes of retrieving and transferring electronic text differ depending on the source and medium used, these are normally fairly self-explanatory within each type.

There is, however, one important word of caution for the mass communication researcher who wishes to make use of electronically available media text for research purposes: it is essential to be fully aware of the potential limitations and 'pre-selected' nature of sources of electronic media text. Thus, CD-ROM versions and commercial 'full-text' databases of newspapers may contain only certain sections of the newspapers (they normally include only selected photographs, and do not include advertising material, stock-listings, television and radio listings, cartoons, weather-forecasts and so on). Likewise, the 'archive' material which (some) newspapers give access to on their Internet sites tends to be highly selective – in other words, one could not hope to retrieve reliably, for example, all articles which had mentioned, say, 'Nuclear energy' in the past year. For a more detailed discussion of the problems and pitfalls relating to accessing, searching, and retrieving news-text from electronic databases and media, see Hansen, 1995. For more detail about media online services and availability of news-text, see Withey and Hugget, 1991.

11.3.2 Storing and Organising Text for Analysis

Textual data are stored and organised in the form of individual computer 'files', which – following a filing-cabinet analogy – are located within 'folders', which may, in turn, be organised hierarchically – that is, a top folder or master folder with a tree-structure of sub-folders and folders within sub-folders. Though there are indeed other ways of storing textual data, for example, in a proprietary database, we advocate that qualitative textual data be stored in simple text files. Text files are simple and easy to create, and, more importantly, and in contrast to most proprietary databases, there are no immediate restrictions on size. This is important, as qualitative textual data tend to come in greatly varying unit-sizes, ranging from a one-line research memo to a 1400–word newspaper feature article, or a 12 000-word focus-group interview transcript. Furthermore, and as we shall see below, the indexing, organising, cross-referencing, and retrieval facilities which would traditionally have been the main argument for storing data in a proprietary database program are now available via programs geared to indexing and managing 'free-text' documents.

If accepting, then, that textual data is best stored in the form of straightforward text-files (such as so-called ASCII-files or files created with any one of the numerous wordprocessor programs available), then storing the data becomes essentially a question of which 'unit' of text should make up the individual file, and a question of what would be the most sensible hierarchy of files and folders. 'Units' of text may of course be 'given' – an individual interview, an individual open-ended question, a newspaper article, a research memo, a day's participant observation notes, and so on.

There is no single best way of organising individual units hierarchically into folders (groups of files) and subfolders; it all depends on 'what will work best' for the researcher in terms of keeping track of the data or information, and in terms of achieving the analytical goals which he or she has set for the research. Thus, files may be divided into folders on the basis of 'kind' – that is, for a participant observation study in a newsroom, daily write-ups of observational notes may be in one folder, formal interviews with news professionals in another folder, policy documents extracted from the news organisation in a third, research memos and emerging ideas in a fourth, and so on. Alternatively, folders may be organised on a chronological basis: a new folder for each day; or it may be that some combination of 'kind' and 'chronology' classification will work best.

For a study of newspaper text, a useful folder set-up would normally consist of a folder for each newspaper, with subfolders arranged chronologically – separate folders for each month or year or whatever timespan is appropriate for the study in question. This set-up immediately facilitates comparisons between different newspapers and comparisons of changes over time in the nature of coverage (for example, changes in the vocabulary and terminology used for characterising certain phenomena). Textual data from a survey or from focus-group interviews could sensibly be grouped in folders according to the main controlling or independent variables used in the study (for example sex, social status, age, occupation, geographical location, education).

11.3.3 Qualitative Data Analysis

The analysis of qualitative data is very much a matter of discovering what occurs where, in which context, discussed in which terms, using which vocabulary or terminologies, and it is a matter of discovering relationships and differences. A large part of the task facing the qualitative researcher, then, is one of 'keeping track' of what came from where in the body of data, what was related to what, which terms were used by whom, which ideas arose in relation to what observations, and so on. While such tasks can clearly be – and indeed were until not so long ago – performed manually with the help of pen and paper, marker and highlighter pens in different colours, scissors and glue for cutting and pasting, index cards, and so on, computers offer much faster, more reliable, and more powerful ways of managing, manipulating, and searching large bodies of textual data:

> It [the computer] can with enormous speed perform technical tasks that previously had to be done painstakingly by hand. While the difference may appear trivial in terms of scholarship, the gain can be measured not only in savings of time, but in increased accuracy, and the potential for greater thoroughness can actually result in considerable investigative advantages. (Tesch, 1991, p. 25)

However, Renata Tesch also rightly cautions against the misguided belief that computers will somehow do not just the more mechanical tasks, but also the analysis:

> The thinking, judging, deciding, interpreting, etc., are still done by the researcher. The computer does not make conceptual decisions, such as which words or themes are important to focus on, or which analytical step to take next. These intellectual tasks are still left entirely to the researcher . . . Thus all the computer does is follow instructions regarding words, phrases or text segments previously designated by the researcher as analysis units. (Tesch, 1991, pp. 25–6)

The types of software or computer programs available for managing, manipulating, searching, coding, and analysing qualitative textual data are many and varied. Furthermore, they are – like computer technology itself – in continuous development. Our modest objective here is to introduce two principal categories of computer programs for the management and analysis of qualitative data, and to give a brief indication of what they can do and how they can be useful for the researcher embarking on analysis of textual data.

The first category consists of programs for indexing and searching text, for retrieving segments of text, and for examining word-use or vocabulary. The second category consists of programs for coding text, examining relationships between (coded) segments of text, and for building theory.

Text Indexing and Retrieval

Identifying occurrence, location, and context As a starting point for analysis of qualitative textual data, it is necessary to be able to identify the occurrence and location of specific words, terms, references and mentions across the different and multiple documents or files which make up the body of data. In much the same way as the index at the back of this book provides a shortcut for the reader who wishes to look up a particular concept or issue, computer indexing programs enable the researcher to go straight to the particular places in the body of data where a certain word or reference is used. Rather than flicking or browsing through what could easily be hundreds of pages of interview transcripts to find, say all the times that interviewees had mentioned a particular soap-opera character, this type of computer program enables the researcher either to jump from one occurrence of the character's name to the next, or alternatively to 'call up' a list of all occurrences of the character's name, complete with identifiers showing the location (folder name, file name, page number) of each occurrence.[6]

Often it will not be sufficient simply to identify the location of specific words or terms – one would want to see these 'in context' in order to determine the meaning and use of a specified term or word. Instead of just listing the locations of the specified word, these programs can provide lists showing the specified word in its immediate contexts – known as a 'key-word-in-context' list, or KWIC for short. By default, a key-word-in-context list may show a line of text for each occurrence of the specified word – that is, the specified search word in the middle of the line with perhaps eight to twelve words of context on either side.

Alternatively, the researcher can specify how many words of context he or she wants for each occurrence, and whether these should be on both sides, or only on the left or the right side, of the specified search word. Further refinements to keyword searching include:

- the specification of synonyms (for example, find all occurrences of 'car' or 'automobile' or 'vehicle');
- the use of 'wildcards', that is find any word that begins (or ends) with a specified string of letters regardless of what the ending (or

beginning) letters are (for example, 'scient*' would find all occurrences of 'scientist', 'scientists', 'scientific', 'scientifically', 'scientology' and so on); and

- the use of boolean operators ('and', 'or', 'not') with or without proximity conditions – for example, find all occurrences of the words 'nuclear' or 'atomic' within ten words of 'weapons' or 'arms', but not within ten words of 'energy'.

Examining vocabulary and word-frequency Almost regardless of the nature of textual data (newspaper articles, interview transcripts, policy documents), a useful starting point for the qualitative researcher is to examine the vocabulary used for discussing, talking about, writing about the topics, themes, and issues concerned. What words, terms, slang expressions and so on are used? What differences exist in the vocabulary used by some respondents or media compared with that of other types of respondents or media? What are the most frequently used words, and, perhaps equally revealing, which words or terms are used very infrequently (or not at all, as the case may be)? Which new terms or concepts are added over time? Computer programs of this kind (often referred to principally as concordance programs: for example, The Oxford Concordance Program [OCP] and Concorder) can – albeit with varying degrees of refinement – provide vocabulary lists detailing each individual word used in a body of text. These lists can be ordered by frequency of occurrence or alphabetically (in ascending or descending order), and some of the programs further allow you to define an exclusion list – that is, a list of commonly used words (such as are, is, was, were, have, has, had, I, you, he, she, it, we, they) not to be counted or listed.

Examining co-occurrence and associated words Perhaps one of the most powerful and productive uses of programs in this category is for examining the co-occurrence of words, for examining which words are associated with or tend to occur in the context of which terms. Co-occurrence and word-association provide important clues and pointers to the 'framing', 'thinking behind', the perspective, or the ideology of a text. For example, it clearly makes a difference whether, say, 'alcoholism' or 'drug-abuse' are discussed in terms of 'treatment', 'health', 'victims', 'patients', 'social skills', or, alternatively, in terms of 'deviance', 'crime', 'law-enforcement', 'punishment'. Similarly, the analysis of co-occurrence may help reveal not just the general ways in which key actors are described – their characteristics and attributes – but also the legitimacy and authority with which they are, differentially, invested by the text:

some sources and actors for example may be quoted as 'saying', 'testifying', 'stating', 'declaring', 'arguing', 'explaining', while others may be quoted as 'alleging', 'asserting', 'speculating', 'claiming' – two sets of associated words which invest the quoted actors or sources with different degrees of authority or legitimacy.

Text Coding, Relationships, and Model-Building

The second category of computer programs is those designed for electronic coding or tagging of text segments, for examining relationships between coded segments of text, and, on the basis of such relationships, for building and graphically representing models of relationships in texts. A 'segment' can be a word, a sentence, a paragraph – in fact, almost any length of text. In the same way as programs in category one, described above, enable the retrieval of all occurrences (with location identifiers) of a word or group of words, programs in this category allow the researcher to retrieve and list all segments of text with a specified code. Examples of programs which are designed for these purposes include the programs *NUDIST* (*N*on-numerical *U*nstructured *D*ata *I*ndexing *S*earching and *T*heory-building) and *Atlas/ti*.

Thus, the researcher analysing a series of interviews with specialist journalists, may have coded all references to or mentions of source agenda-setting – situations where the agenda for news coverage is set by sources rather than by media professionals – and would be able to retrieve these and compare what different journalists say about this aspect. The point is that the concept of source agenda-setting may be talked about and referred to in many different ways, indirectly and directly, and indeed in ways that do not deploy either the word 'source' or the word 'agenda-setting'. Unlike the word-based searches of programs in the previous category, coding or tagging thus is not dependent on the particular vocabulary or words used in the textual data.

Some programs in this category have facilities for exporting the codes attached to segments of text to statistical analysis programs such as SPSS, so that further quantitative analysis can be carried out.

Once the textual data have been coded, it would often be desirable to go further than simply examining and comparing text under each of the codes used, and to start exploring whether and how different topics, themes, and categories are related to each other. Do those interviewees who talk about source agenda-setting for example also tend to emphasise strong editorial intervention into the work of the specialist correspondent? Do references to concept X always co-occur with references to concept Y? Is the presence of concept Y conditional upon concept X? and so on. Thus, these text analysis programs not only facilitate complex coding of textual segments and fast and flexible retrieval of coded segments – itself a major advantage over traditional paper or index-card approaches to working with qualitative data – but, more importantly, they enable the examination and modelling of complex relationships, links, co-occurrences, and perspectives in qualitative textual data.

11.4 Summary

- Though computer analysis of data used to be associated almost exclusively with quantitative, statistical analysis of numerical data, the last two decades have seen major advances in the development of computer-based tools for the management and analysis of qualitative data.
- Whether dealing with quantitative or qualitative (textual) data, computer-assisted analysis involves three major steps or areas of consideration: (1) the transfer of 'raw' data from their original form or medium (such as coding schedules, questionnaires, hand-written notes, printed text) to the computer medium; (2) the organisation of data (in data files, text files, folders, and so on) on the computer medium; (3) analysis of data, using appropriate computer applications or programs.
- SPSS is a powerful and flexible program for the statistical analysis social science data, including communications research data. Coded data from, for example, content analysis coding schedules or survey questionnaires are entered into an SPSS data file, where each column represents a variable (such as sex, age, occupation) and each row represents a case (such as a survey respondent, a newspaper article). 'Data' may take the form of one or more of three principal types of variables: categorical variables, continuous variables, and 'string' variables (such as words, text).
- The choice of analytical procedures in SPSS will depend in large measure on the types of variables to be analysed, as well as, of course, on the aims of the research. We have introduced four fundamental analytical procedures in SPSS: two for examining the distribution of individual variables in a data-set (Frequencies and

Descriptives); and two for examining relationships between two or more variables (Crosstabs and Means).

- When dealing with qualitative textual data, careful consideration should be given to the question of how best to organise the data in terms of files and folders (including master-folders and hierarchies of sub-folders). We advocate that textual data be entered as free-form text documents (as opposed to data-base formats with prespecified fields).
- We see computer programs for the management and analysis of qualitative textual data as falling into two major groups: (1) programs for the indexing, searching, and retrieval of text (search-and-retrieve programs); and (2) programs for the coding and code-based analysis of text (qualitative text analysis programs).
- Search-and-retrieve programs enable the researcher to examine and analyse key-words, vocabulary, word-frequencies, key-words-in-context, co-occurrences and words associated with specified key-words. These programs allow the researcher to move quickly and reliably to relevant occurrences and references in a potentially very large body of texts, and to retrieve identified relevant occurrences or segments of text, for further analysis and comparison, or for inclusion as 'examples' in research reports.
- Qualitative text analysis programs facilitate coding and analysis of coded text. The researcher attaches (electronic) codes, 'tags', labels to segments of text (such as words, a sentence, a paragraph which refer to or express the idea, phenomenon, concept, theme, issue, or topic denoted by the particular code). Coded segments can then be retrieved and examined, and further analysis can be carried out to establish how different coded segments interact and relate to each other.

11.5 Principal Computer Programs Mentioned

Atlas/ti

Muhr, T. (1995). Atlas/ti (Version 1.1) code-based theory builder, text-analysis (Berlin: Scientific Software Development).

Concorder

Rand, D. M. (1995). *Concorder version 2.0.1 (computer program).* Montréal: Centre de Recherches Mathématiques, Université de Montréal (address: C.P. 6128, succursale A, Montréal, Québec H3C 3J7, Canada). A concordance program for Macintosh computers.

A free demonstration version is available from the Internet site: http://www.crm.umontreal.ca/~rand/Concorder-Demo.html

NUD•IST
Qualitative Solutions and Research Pty Ltd. (1995). *QSR NUDIST 3.0 (computer program)* (London: Scolari/Sage, 6 Bonhill Street, London EC2A 4PU, UK).

Oxford Concordance Program (*OCP*)
Hockey, S. and J. Martin (1988b). *Oxford Concordance Program version 2 [computer program]* (Oxford University Computing Service, 13 Banbury Road, Oxford OX2 6NN, UK). Concordance program for mainframe computers. The program is also available for IBM/compatibles as *Micro-OCP*:
Oxford University Computing Service (1990), *Micro-OCP (computer program)* (Oxford University Press).

Sonar Professional
Virginia Systems, Inc. (1991) *Sonar version 9.0 (Computer Program)* (Midlothian, Va: Virginia Systems Software Services, Inc., 5509 West Bay Court, Midlothian, VA 23112, USA). Sonar Professional is a text-retrieval and analysis program available for both PC and Macintosh computers.

SPSS
Statistical Package for the Social Sciences (SPSS):
SPSS Inc., 444 N Michigan Avenue, Chicago, Ill. 60611, USA
SPSS is a comprehensive system for statistical data analysis, available for PC and Macintosh computers, and for most mainframe computers.

Notes

1. See, for example: Pfaffenberger, 1988; Tesch, 1990; Fielding and Lee, 1991; Lee, 1995; Kelle, 1995.
2. Ways of transferring data to a computer include: manual typing of data, optical scanning of coded questionnaires or content coding schedules, or, with the increasing availability of handheld computers, coding straight into electronic copies of questionnaires or coding schedules.
3. If SPSS and the appropriate data-window are not open, we start by first launching or opening SPSS by double-clicking on the SPSS icon (as described at the beginning of this section); when SPSS is up and running, and the SPSS menu bar is showing across the top of the screen, pull down the **File** menu, choose **Open**, and select the name of the data file from the dialogue box which appears on screen.

4. There are however now relatively powerful optical character-recognition scanners available, so in some cases it may be possible to 'scan' hand-written text directly into the computer.
5. Again, it is worth noting that progress is being made in terms of computer-software which can 'translate' spoken words, audio-text, into written text, so eventually it will be possible to automate the process of converting audio-taped interviews and other material into written text, thus doing away with the timeconsuming and laborious process of transcription.
6. There are many programs which will do some or all of the indexing, search, and retrieval functions mentioned here, but one of the most powerful and easy-to-use is *Sonar Professional* by Virginia Systems Inc. For a comprehensive review of programs in this category, see Weitzman and Miles, 1995.

References

Babbie, E. and F. Halley (1995) *Adventures in social research: data analysis using SPSS for Windows* (Thousand Oaks, Calif.: Pine Forge Press).

Conrad, P. and S. Reinharz (1984) 'Computers and qualitative data', *Qualitative Sociology*, **7**(1–2) Special Issue.

Fielding, N. G. and R. M. Lee (eds) (1991) *Using computers in qualitative research* (London: Sage).

Hansen, A. (1993) 'Greenpeace and press coverage of environmental issues', in A. Hansen (ed.), *The Mass Media and Environmental Issues*, pp. 150–78(Leicester: Leicester University Press).

Hansen, A. (1995) 'Using information technology to analyze newspaper content', in R. M. Lee (ed.) *Information technology for the social scientist*, pp. 147–68 (London: UCL Press).

Kelle, U. (ed.) (1995) *Computer-aided qualitative data analysis* (London: Sage).

Kinnear, P. R. and C. D. Gray (1994) *SPSS for Windows made simple* (Hove: Lawrence Erlbaum Associates).

Lee, R. M. (ed.) (1995) *Information technology for the social scientist* (London: UCL Press).

Pfaffenberger, B. (1988) *Microcomputer applications in qualitative research* (London: Sage).

Tesch, R. (1990) *Qualitative research: analysis types and software tools* (New York: Falmer Press).

Tesch, R. (1991) 'Software for qualitative researchers: analysis needs and program capabilities', in N. G. Fielding and R. M. Lee (eds) *Using computers in qualitative research*, pp. 16–37 (London: Sage).

Weitzman, E. A. and M. B. Miles (1995) *Computer programs for qualitative data analysis* (London: Sage).

Withey, R. and E. Hugget (1991) 'Fleet Street's second revolution: online technology in information gathering for newspapers', in S. Eagle (ed.) *Information sources for the press and broadcast media*, pp. 134–56 (London: Bowker-Saur).

Appendix: Sources and Resources in Mass Communication Research

Sources of information and resources in mass communication research come in many different shapes and forms – some of them relatively unique to mass communication research, but most of them similar, at least in kind, to those required by the social science researcher more generally. Our aim in this appendix is to *indicate* some of the key directories, sources of factual information, and some of the main resources available to the communication researcher. We stress that this is not, nor was it intended to be, a comprehensive guide – it is intended merely to provide some 'starting points', of interest, principally perhaps, to the novice researcher in the field. We also acknowledge a certain British bias – and more generally a bias toward English language sources – in what we list below.

We divide the sources and resources into three major areas – depending largely on the format and medium (print versus electronic) of the information offered:

(1) print-based directories and sources available in major well-stocked (university) libraries;
(2) electronic databases, also available to a greater or lesser extent through major (university) libraries;
(3) the Internet, accessible through institutional (universities) or organisational accounts, or from personal computers connected via a modem to an internet service provider such as Compuserve.

Library Print-Based Reference Sources

Guides and Bibliographies

Blum, E. and F. G. Wilhoit (1990) *Mass media bibliography: an annotated guide to books and journals for research and reference* (Urbana: University of Illinois Press).

Covers communications, book publishing, broadcasting, film, journals, newspapers, advertising, indexing and abstracting periodicals

Eagle, S. (ed.) (1991) *Information sources for the press and broadcast media* (London: Bowker-Saur).
Informative contributions explaining how press and broadcast journalists and researchers use information from various sources, and how the media organise their library and information departments

Macdonald, B. (1993) *Broadcasting in the UK – A guide to information sources* (London: Mansell).
Statistics on licence-holders, licensees, cable and satellite channels and local radio stations in the UK

Peak, S. (ed.) (1995) *The media guide* (London: Fourth Estate).
One of the most comprehensive guides to sources and resources concerning local, regional, and national media in Britain; newspapers, magazines, television, radio; circulation and audience statistics, and ownership information; contact addresses of media organisations, media bodies and associations, companies, pressure groups and interest groups; news agencies, libraries, and archives; list of annual directories, reports, and handbooks; education, training and degree courses in communication and media.

Bibliographic Sources: Books

Books in print (New Providence, N.J.: Bowker).
Annual volume. Comprehensive index by subject or by author or by title to books in print. Also available on microfiche. See also OCLC FirstSearch in the next section of this appendix

London bibliography of the social sciences. (1990) vol. 47, 24th supplement (London: Mansell).
Extensive bibliography of some 600 000 books, pamphlets, and official publications in the social sciences

Bibliographic Sources: Periodical Articles

(a) Social Sciences – generally

British humanities index (London: Library Association).
Published quarterly; annual cumulations. Subject and Author index to some 350 British periodicals in the humanities and social sciences. Leading national newspapers are also indexed.

Current Contents: Social and Behavioral Sciences (Philadelphia: Institute for Scientific Information).
Published weekly. Reproduces tables of contents of about 700 journals in the social sciences and related fields. No cumulative indexes.

PAIS International in Print (New York: Public Affairs Information Service).
Published monthly with quarterly and annual cumulations. Comprehensive subject index to books, articles and government documents published in English and other European languages

Social Sciences Citation Index (SSCI) (Philadelphia: Institute for Scientific Information).
More than 4700 journals are indexed; indexing based on citations, thus providing excellent linking and cross-referencing. See also BIDS and OCLC FirstSearch described in the next section.
Social sciences index (New York: H. W. Wilson).
Subject and author index to over 350 journals. Citations to book reviews are also included.

(b) Communications

Communication Abstracts (London: Sage) Published quarterly.
Comprehensive index and abstracts of communication-related articles, reports, and books – providing coverage in the areas of general communication, mass communication, advertising and marketing, and broadcasting. Subject and author indexes.
Market research abstracts (London: Market Research Society).
Published twice yearly: covers over thirty journals in advertising, market-research statistics, psychology and marketing. Author and subject indexes; full abstracts

(c) Sociology

International bibliography of sociology (London: Tavistock).
Published annually. Comprehensive author and subject index to articles in sociology journals
Sociological abstracts (San Diego, Calif.: Sociological Abstracts, Inc.).
Some 5000 informative abstracts per year of works and periodical articles from a wide range of journals. Author and subject indexes

Reference Books

(a) Dictionaries and Encyclopedias

Barnouw, E. (ed.) (1989) *International encyclopedia of communications* vols. 1–4 (New York: Oxford University Press).
Griffiths, D. (ed.) (1992) *The encyclopedia of the British press, 1422–1992* (Basingstoke: Macmillan).
International Encyclopedia of the Social Sciences (New York: Macmillan and Free Press) 18 vols; supplements.
Kuper, A. and J. Kuper (eds) (1996) *The social science encyclopedia*, 2nd edn (London: Routledge).
Kurian, G. T. (ed.) (1982) *World press encyclopedia* (London: Mansell).
Demographics and media statistics e.g. circulation, numbers of sets and channels available, advertising expenditure for 250 countries.
Watson, J. and A. Hill (1993) *A dictionary of communication and media studies*, (3rd edn) (London: Arnold).

(b) *Yearbooks, Periodicals, Handbooks and Directories: Media and Related Statistics*

Advertising Association (1996) *Advertising statistics yearbook* (Henley-on-Thames: NTC Publications for The Advertising Association).
Advertising expenditure in: print, broadcast media, cinema, direct mail; Statistics on advertising agencies.

Annual abstract of statistics (London: HMSO).
Annual publication: United Kingdom TV licences, number of telephone calls made, sales of UK manufactured radio, TV and video equipment, records and tapes, cinema admissions and takings.

Benn's media 144th edn (Tunbridge Wells: Benn Business Information Services). vol. 1: United Kingdom; vol. 2: Europe; vol. 3: World.
Annual publication listing national and local newspapers, periodicals and free magazines, broadcasting agencies, and media organisations. Newspaper and periodical titles, price, circulation, advertising rates, content, readership.

BFI Film and Television Handbook (1996) (London: British Film Institute).
Film, cinema, broadcasting statistics; organisations, contacts, addresses.

Culley, S. A. (ed.) (1996) *The blue book of British broadcasting: a handbook for professional bodies and students of broadcasting*, 22nd edn (London: Tellex Monitors).
Annual publication, listing the programmes and key administrative and production personnel in the BBC, Independent Television Companies, the Independent Television Committee (ITC), Channel Four, and local radio; alphabetical indexes to personnel and classified index of programmes.

Cultural Trends: incorporating facts about the arts (London: Policy Studies Institute).
Quarterly publication: each issue focuses on a special topic; covers cinema, film, broadcasting, home video, books, libraries and music (such as purchase of recorded music); demographic breakdown of audiences and consumers.

Drost, H. (ed.) (1991) *World news media directory: a comprehensive reference guide* (Harlow: Longman Current Affairs).
International press guide: Newspaper circulation, ownership figures, numbers of radio and tv sets and channels.

EBU Review (European Broadcasting Union).
Quarterly publication: various broadcasting statistics including, for example: licence figures, country of origin of programmes, exchange of news between countries.

Euromedia Research Group, The (1991) *The media in Western Europe: the Euromedia handbook* (London: Sage).
Demographics, ownership, audience profiles, circulation, financing, channels available; covers seventeen European countries.

European Audiovisual Observatory (1994) *Cinema, television, video, and new media in Europe: statistical yearbook – 1994–95* (Strasbourg: Council of Europe).
Cinema, TV, and new media in Europe; household equipment: TV, VCR, CDI etc.; media groups: ranking and turnover; film: numbers of seats,

theatres, films produced, attendances; software sales; TV: audience profiles, breakdown of channels available, programme types, revenue and ad spend for each European country.

Keesing's record of world events (London: Longman).
Continues Keesing's contemporary archives; digest of newspapers; well-indexed source of reference (Now available electronically on FT-Profile, see the next section).

Press Council, *The press and the people: annual report of the Press Council* (London: The Press Council).
Annual publication; statistics on publishing houses, ownership and circulation figures.

Screen Digest (London: Video Index).
Monthly publication: statistics on advertising, cinema, cable, satellite, TV, multi-media and video.

Social Trends (London: HMSO).
United Kingdom nationwide expenditure on books, TV, video, newspapers, communications; audience profiles: TV , radio; magazines and newspapers: circulation and profiles; numbers of public libraries; cinema: audience profiles, screens available.

Spectrum (London: Independent Television Commission).
Quarterly publication: United Kingdom viewing figures, back page statistics feature, such as cable ownership figures.

United Nations (1995) *World media handbook: selected country profiles* 50th anniversary issue edn (New York: United Nations).
International demographics, print and electronic media figures, telecommunications figures.

Willing's press guide: a guide to the press of the United Kingdom and to the principal publications of Europe, the Americas, Australasia, the Far East and the Middle East, 122nd edn (East Grinstead: Reed Information Services).
Annual publication on newspapers: price, circulation and audience figures, proprietors, advertising rates, content.

World radio and TV handbook (London: Billboard Ltd).
Annual publication.

(c) UK and international statistics directories

Fleming, M. C. and J. G. Nellis (1994) *International statistics sources: subject guide to sources of international comparative statistics* (London: Routledge). Statistics guide.

O'Brien, J. W. and S. R. Wasserman (eds) *Statistics sources: a subject guide to data on industrial, business, social, educational, financial, and other topics for the United States and internationally* (Detroit: Gale Research Company).

Purdie, E. (ed.) (1996) *Great Britain Office for National Statistics: Guide to official statistics* (London: HMSO).
Directory of official sources of statistics.

United Nations (1982) *Directory of International Statistics (vol. 1)* (New York: United Nations).

Key to official data sources (for example, UNESCO) on libraries, newspapers, broadcasting, film and cinema

UNESCO *Statistical yearbook* (Paris: UNESCO).

Books: numbers published; newspapers: circulation; film: numbers produced, cinema attendance; libraries: availability, members, attendance; TV: programme breakdown, numbers of licences and receivers.

Databases

Electronically-based databases are a field of continuous and rapid flux and development. The distinguishing lines between electronic databases and information available via the Internet are also increasingly difficult to spot – see the next section about the Internet. Here we list some of the main databases for mass communication researchers.

News, Newspapers, Magazines Online

FT-Profile, owned by the Financial Times Group, is a full-text database which contains the full text of articles from a large variety of newspapers, magazines, business and specialist data, and research reports. For the mass communications researcher, its full-text archives of newspapers, news agencies, government press releases, and magazines are particularly useful. The full-text of articles from all the national British broadsheet – and several tabloid – daily and Sunday newspapers can be searched and retrieved with sophisticated keyword-searching. Several British regional newspapers are also included. FT-Profile also holds many international newspapers and news sources, including *Asahi News Service* (Japan), *TASS* (Russia), *Associated Press*, *Reuter News*, the *Washington Post*, *The Economist*, the *Ottawa Citizen*, the *Moscow Times*, the *Irish Times*, *La Stampa*, BBC Summary of World Broadcasts, and so on. Key media and communications related magazines held on FT-Profile include: *Campaign* (news and comment on the advertising industry), *Media Week* (news, information, statistics on media industry, advertising volume, circulation and viewing figures). Other useful files for the mass communication researcher include *Keesing's Record of World Events* (reviews the world's press and information services to produce reports on all major economic and political events worldwide), and, for the UK-orientated researcher, *Hermes* (the complete text of press releases from the major British government departments).

A few of the newspapers on FT-Profile can be searched as far back as the early-to-mid 1980s, but most of the newspaper archives date back only to the late-1980s/early 1990s. FT-Profile can be accessed – by registered users or subscribers – via a desktop computer and modem; for the unfunded mass communication researcher, limited access may be possible via a University Library subscription. Other databases providing similar – or more comprehensive – data include TEXTLINE (in Britain) and NEXIS (in the USA).

CD-ROM News

The British broadsheet newspapers are available on compact discs, published on a quarterly basis and available, in most cases, from 1990 and onwards. Search and retrieve facilities tend to be less sophisticated than on the online databases such as FT-Profile, but for the researcher who wishes to 'work' extensively with the text of one or two newspapers, compact discs offer a much cheaper alternative to online databases.

Communications and Social Sciences Databases

Less than a decade ago, the mass communications researcher searching for published literature in a specific field or on a specific topic faced the rather laborious and time-consuming task of trawling through printed abstracts and citation-indexes, such as *Communications Abstracts*, *Sociological Abstracts*, *The Social Sciences Citation Index* (SSCI), *Current Contents*, *PAIS International*, and so on. In today's computer-assisted electronic environment, the task of searching systematically for references, literature, research publications has, thankfully, become much easier. Most of the abstracts and indexes to research in mass communications and the social sciences more generally are now available on compact disc – while expensive for individual subscription researchers will often have access to these through their institutional library.

Moreover, researchers will increasingly have access – via their institutional library – to online services which offer powerful search and retrieval facilities across a broad and ever-expanding set of indexes, abstracts, catalogues. Two such services are BIDS and First-Search.

BIDS

The Bath ISI Data Service, owned by the Institute for Scientific Information Inc., USA, provides access to three multidisciplinary Citation Indexes (Science Citation Index (SCI), Social Science Citation Index (SSCI), and Arts & Humanities Citation Index (A&HCI)) containing details of articles drawn from over 7000 journals worldwide. Searches can be performed for all years from 1980 onwards. The BIDS service can – provided the researcher has access via an institutional subscription – be searched from a library computing terminal or from a networked desktop computer. It offers sophisticated and fast searching facilities: relevant articles can be searched for on the basis of 'words in title', 'words in keyword indexing', 'author name', 'journal title', and so on, using boolean operators (and, or, not). The resulting references can be displayed on the computer screen and/or retrieved. Relevant references can be retrieved or downloaded in a format which enables the researcher to import them straight into his/her personal bibliographic database (bibliographic databases available for both PC and Macintosh users include *EndNote* and *ProCite*), thus eliminating entirely the tiresome task of manually typing references into one's computer.

FirstSearch

FirstSearch, owned by the Online Computer Library Center (OCLC) Inc., USA, provides access to an even wider range of databases, publications and documents. Like BIDS, FirstSearch provides indexes to articles from journals (over 14 000 journal titles). Unlike BIDS, which focuses on articles in journals, FirstSearch gives access to WorldCat – a major database for books – as well as a range of other special focus databases, such as ERIC (database for education), FactSearch (facts and statistics), and GPO (US Government Publications).

The Internet

The Internet – a vast global network connecting networks of computers from educational institutions, government agencies, business, industry, and so on – is rapidly becoming an important resource and research tool for the mass communication researcher.

There are principally three ways in which the Internet serves as a resource for the mass communication researcher:

(1) electronic mail communication with other researchers, colleagues, sources, friends, and so on;
(2) Usenet Newsgroups or discussion groups; and
(3) a vast database of information of all kinds and in a wide variety of formats from text to video.

Here, we wish to indicate briefly how the Internet can be used as a vast database of information and resources for the mass communication researcher, as well as to point the reader in the direction of some key 'sites' accessible via the Internet (electronic mail and usenet newsgroups are equally important, but are now probably so familiar to mass communication researchers that they require no further introduction).

The World Wide Web (WWW) is now the key service (other services include: e-mail, ftp, Gopher) on the Internet for information, education, and entertainment of all kinds (ranging from individuals maintaining 'pages' detailing their personal biographical details, interests, hobbies to organisations and institutions offering information and services).

In order to access *World Wide Web* pages or sites it is necessary to use a browser such as Netscape Navigator, Microsoft Internet Explorer, or Spry Mosaic. These enable the user to access Web pages or sites by either typing in unique addresses (also known as URLs – Uniform Resource Locators), or by clicking on highlighted links, for example highlighted links listed as the results of a search (see next paragraph).

Searching for relevant information and relevant sites on the World Wide Web ('the web') is very similar to searching for references in a library catalogue, directory, or electronic database. The main difference is that to search the World Wide Web it is necessary to use a *search tool* service. Examples of currently popular search tool services are *Lycos*, *Yahoo*, *AltaVista*, and *Webcrawler*. These and other search tool services enable the user to type in search words or combinations of search words (or strings of text), and, with varying degrees of sophistication, they facilitate the use of boolean (and, or, not) conditions, wildcards, and related search definitions. Some of the search tool services also categorise sites along categories such as 'Education', 'News', 'Reference', 'Social Science', 'Arts', 'Government', 'Health', 'Entertainment', and so on. A good starting point for a search may thus be to examine one or more of these categories, and to follow sub-paths within individual categories toward ever more specific subject categories. Thus, using the Yahoo search tool, one might want to start with the 'Social Science' category, then on to the 'Communications' sub-category, then, perhaps, on to the 'Media Literacy' sub-category, and from there on to specific sites listed.

It is important to be aware that search tools such as Yahoo, Lycos, AltaVista, and WebCrawler will rarely, if ever, find exactly the same sites in response to a query, nor can they ever give a complete listing of what is available on the web, as the web itself changes faster than any database can be updated. It is thus a good idea to use two or more of these search tool services rather than confining searches to just one.

Searches result (provided of course that any matching references are found) in a listing of highlighted site names, each with additional details such as the exact internet address and usually a brief description of what the site contains. A relevant site is then accessed by clicking on the highlighted site name or address (alternatively, by typing the listed address into the appropriate box in the browser software). Once a relevant site has been accessed, this will normally contain further subsections or files (as well as links to other relevant sites) which are highlighted and again accessed by clicking on the highlighted text/links. Text, images, video, and sound can be 'downloaded' or 'copied' directly to the computer from which one is accessing web sites.

The World Wide Web is constantly changing and evolving. New sites and sources are added continuously, and others disappear or are replaced. As with the other sources and resources listed earlier in this appendix, we could not hope to offer a comprehensive list of web sites relevant to the mass communication researcher. The search tools available on the Internet are the key to finding relevant information and sites. Below, we do, however, offer *examples* of the kinds of sites which will be of interest to mass communication researchers.

Communication Institute for Online Scholarship (CIOS)
address: **http://www.cios.org/**

The Communication Institute for Online Scholarship is a US not-for-profit organization supporting the use of computer technologies in the service of communication scholarship and education. Services provided include: electronic conferences for areas of study in communication; electronic white pages for finding individuals in the communications field by name or interest; bibliographic indexes to the professional literature in communication; tables of contents for current communication serials; events calendar (calendar of international conferences, submission deadlines, meetings, and so on); links to other organisations in the communications fields, such as the Speech Communication Association (SCA) and the International Association for Mass Communication Research (IAMCR).

Internet Movie Database
address: **http://www.imdb.com/**

Describes itself as 'the most comprehensive free source of movie information on the internet'. It currently covers over 75 000 movies with over 1 000 000 filmography entries and is expanding continuously. It covers: filmographies for all professions in the industry; plot summaries; character names; movie ratings; year of release; running times; soundtracks; genres; production companies; reference literature; filming locations; release; and a wide variety of other details.

British Broadcasting Corporation (BBC)
address: **http://www.bbc.co.uk/**

Offers information on all aspects of BBC services, including: television, radio (national and regional), programme schedule information, education, research, the World Service, technical services, job advertisements.

Similar sites are available for other UK broadcasting companies (e.g. Channel Four television has a web site at **http://www.channel4.com/**) and broadcasting organisations elsewhere in the world: ABC television in the USA at **http://www.abctelevision.com/**; CBS television in the USA at **http://www.cbs.com/**; Canadian Broadcasting Corporation at **http://www.cbc.ca/; see also CNN below.**

The Electronic Telegraph
address: **http://www.telegraph.co.uk**

An electronic version of the *Daily Telegraph*. In addition to today's news (text and photographs/images), the site gives access to an archive of articles dating back to October 1994. The archive can be easily and quickly searched using 'natural language' keywords.

Similar sites are available for other UK newspapers (such as the *Guardian* and the *Observer* at **http://www.guardian.co.uk/** or *The*

Times and *Sunday Times* at **http://www.the-times.co.uk**) and for other newspapers worldwide: try for example the site **http://www.esperanto.se/kiosk/** which provides links to the sites of a large range of newspapers throughout the world.

CNN Interactive
address: **http://cnn.com/**

The Cable Network News site gives access to current news stories and a wide range of news and information under categories such as 'sports', 'weather', 'sci-tech', 'showbiz, 'style', 'earth', 'world'.

The Social Science Information Gateway (SOSIG)
address: **http://www.sosig.ac.uk/**

The Social Science Information Gateway (SOSIG) provides easy access to information sources over the networks. All of the resources that appear on the Gateway have been described, classified and entered into a searchable database. Links to UK-based and worldwide social science sites and resources.

UK Government Information (CCTA)
Address: **http://www.open.gov.uk**

Provides searchable index to UK government departments, press releases, and publications. Access to full text of news releases and many documents and publications.

Index

Note: 'n.' after a page reference indicates the number of a note on that page.